The Origins of the Restoration Movement:

An Intellectual History

Richard M. Tristano

For Barbara

GRC A-81/P-470
December, 1988

The cover depicts Thomas Campbell composing the Declaration and Address. It is a reproduction of a stained glass medallion in the Thomas W. Philips Memorial, The Disciples of Christ Historical Society, Nashville, Tennessee. (Courtesy of the Disciples of Christ Historical Society.)

Published by the Glenmary Research Center
750 Piedmont Ave. N.E.
Atlanta, Ga. 30308

ISBN: 0-914422-17-0

Table of Contents

91039

Acknowledgments

It is a pleasure to thank all of the people who helped me complete this work. Chronologically, at least, first thanks is due to Rev. Bernard Quinn. It was Father Quinn who, as former director of the Glenmary Research Center, suggested the Churches of Christ as a topic of study. I am certain that this study is not quite what he had in mind originally; still I hope he finds that his direction has resulted in something useful. To Rev. Lou McNeil, present director of the Glenmary Research Center, I owe many thanks. First of all, it was he who informed me of the intellectual connection between Alexander Campbell and Catholic neo-Thomism, and he was a constant guide through the difficulties presented by the philosophy of John Locke and others. Most of all, I thank him for his confidence in me and for his almost inexhaustible patience in letting me cultivate some new ground at the Research Center.

The staff at the Glenmary Research Center helped in innumerable ways. David Dybiec, Antonette Willingham, and Phillip Brown assisted me often in the preparation of this manuscript. I thank Joseph Flowers, Jr. for preparing computer compilations of church membership statistics which I used in this study. I am especially grateful to Mary May, whom I shall call editor, but who in fact performed many other duties as well in guiding this study to publication.

I gratefully acknowledge the kindness of Dr. Channing R. Jeschke, Librarian of the Pitts Theology Library, Candler School of Theology, Emory University. He has graciously opened up to me the vast resources at his disposal. Without them, this research would have been impossible. Dr. Robert Hooper and Dr. William Collins of David Lipscomb University gave generously of their time, not only reading the manuscript but also sharing their expertise with me.

Dr. Mac Lynn, also of David Lipscomb University, has been an invaluable resource who saved me from many errors. His three-page summary of the Restoration Movement was a constant reminder that brevity and clarity are just as important as evidence and detail. Of course, neither he nor anyone else mentioned here is responsible for my errors or for my opinions.

-RMT

Introduction

This is the third in a series of studies on Southern religion. The first focused on the two predominant white religious groups in the South: Southern Baptists and United Methodists. The second study was confined to black evangelical religion. Both of these studies were historical in nature and concentrated on examining the origins and basic beliefs of each group. The general purpose of this series is to foster a better understanding of Southern religion by studying some of its components.

In truth, this third study is more dissimilar than similar to its predecessors. Part of the reason for this is rooted in the Restoration Movement itself. First of all, the movement is not exclusively "Southern"; it was established and grew on the frontier, from Pennsylvania to Tennessee. More important, it was not "Southern" in a cultural sense. This can be best demonstrated by the fact that unlike Baptists, Methodists, and Presbyterians, the Restoration Movement did not split into Northern and Southern wings before the Civil War. The reasons for this lack of identification with the Southern world view are complex. In essence, the Restoration Movement was a critique of American religion in general and of Southern religion in particular. The movement rejected both the denominationalism of American religion, and the emphasis on the emotive and on personal "experience" which was characteristic of nineteenth-century Southern religion.

Before continuing, it is really necessary to give a brief overview of the Restoration Movement which spawned three very different contemporary groups. The first is the Christian Church (Disciples of Christ), the most liberal of the three groups. Each of the three Restoration groups developed, in large part, out of the issue of extracongregational societies. The general trend over the last half of the nineteenth century was to create various boards and agencies to supervise specific tasks. By the turn of the century the need for a general convention was broadly recognized, and in 1917 the International Convention of Disciples of Christ was established. In the 1960's further discussion was underway for a major restructuring of the fellowship's organization, leading to the adoption of "A Provisional Design for the Christian Church" in 1968. The result was a form of church government which was democratic but which many also perceived as being fully "denominational."

In this church there are three levels of church polity: general, regional, and congregational, each managing its own property, finances, and programs. A general assembly meets biennially, elects officers, and has a general office located in Indianapolis.

Thoroughly ecumenical, the Disciples became charter members of the Federal Council of Churches when it was organized in 1908, and in 1950 they were among the original members of the National Council of Churches. They have been active in the World Council of Churches since its founding in 1948.

The Disciples took with them the greater share of the Restoration Movement's historic institutions of higher education. Bethany College in West Virginia (founded by Alexander Campbell) and Transylvania College in Lexington, Kentucky are the two oldest colleges in the movement. Butler University, Drake University and Eureka College are among the better known Disciples' colleges and universities. Texas Christian University in Fort Worth, Texas is the largest and best known educational institution associated with the Restoration Movement.

The Christian Churches and Churches of Christ is the middle group within the Restoration Movement. This group gradually split from the Disciples over many years. The origin of this fissure can be traced back to the late nineteenth and early twentieth centuries. While these developments are part of the intellectual history of the Restoration Movement they do not relate to its intellectual origins. Briefly, then, the Restoration Movement was affected by the general growth in influence of American religious liberalism and the disputes revolving around Darwinism and biblical infallibility issues which were a part of the times. Open communion and cooperation with non-Disciple Christians in organizations such as the National Council of Churches was also a source of controversy.

While these issues were discussed for decades, it was not until 1927 that the first move towards separation became concrete. In that year the conservative Disciples acknowledged that they were outvoted at the Convention and so formed one of their own, the North American Christian Convention. While still designating themselves as Disciples of Christ, in reality they constituted a separate group. The reorganization of the Disciples of Christ in 1968 precipitated a formal break. In 1971 they requested the *Yearbook of American Churches* to list them as a separate religious body.

The Christian Churches and Churches of Christ consider themselves to be a non-denominational fellowship. There is no general organization. The North American Christian Convention is headquartered in Cincinnati and meets annually. It is not considered an official agency but rather a gathering of interested individuals for consultation and fellowship. There is also a National Missionary Convention, founded in 1947 with headquarters in Copeland, Kansas. The two most influential periodicals are the *Christian Standard* and the *Restoration Herald,* both published in Cincinnati. There is also a *Directory of Ministry* which is the principal means of identifying member congregations. Milligan College in eastern Tennessee is a liberal arts college, but most higher educational institutions associated with the centrist group are Bible colleges. Johnson Bible College in Kimberlin Heights, Tennessee is one of the oldest of these institutions, while Cincinnati Bible Seminary (1923), which also has a graduate school, would be one of the largest of the newer schools.

The Churches of Christ constitute the most conservative wing of the Restoration Movement. The issues which prompted this group to split from the main body of Disciples were the organization of a missionary society and the use of instrumental music during church services. There were also sectional and social factors which help explain the rift and account for its largely Southern character.

The Churches of Christ are organized along strictly congregational lines. Each congregation is autonomous. There is no general organization, not even a convention of "messengers." In the absence of organization there is a plethora of periodicals which in a literal sense function as the primary means of communication among this avowedly non-denominational body of Christians. There are over one hundred periodicals published by members of the Churches of Christ. Among the most influential are the *Gospel Advocate,* published in Nashville, Tennessee, the *Firm Foundation* (Austin, Texas); and *Restoration Quarterly* (Abilene, Texas). There are seventeen colleges and universities associated with the Churches of Christ, including David Lipscomb University, Nashville, Tennessee; Abilene Christian University (Abilene, Texas); and Pepperdine University in Malibu, California.

I have identified two motives within the Restoration Movement, a "truth motive" and a "unity motive." The truth motive is contained in the idea that Christian truth can be found in the teaching and practices of the New Testament alone. This is a radical interpretation of *sola scriptura,* which seeks to eliminate as the basis of communion "opinions" contained in creeds, the proclamation of church councils and other ecclesiastical institutions, and theological disputation. The Restoration Movement in a very literal sense has sought to *restore* the faith and practice of primitive Christianity. The uniqueness of the Restoration Movement lies in the attempt to utilize the truth motive of primitive Christianity as a means of uniting all Christians. Confident that the New Testament is clear and precise about the essentials of Christian belief and practice, it would serve as the means of eliminating disagreement among the "sects." Explicit is a highly developed sense of the unity of the Church of Christ and a rejection of the idea that the Church could be divided legitimately into a variety of believing bodies which determined their own corpus of belief, practice, and polity. The Restoration Movement began as an explicit rejection of denominationalism.

The three Restoration religious bodies have divided largely over their respective attitudes toward the two motives. In other words, the liberal Disciples have in large part sacrificed the truth motive for the unity motive. They would openly admit to being a denomination and have concentrated on reducing barriers between Christian bodies. James DeForest Murch, who was associated with the centrist Restoration group, speaks of the "Great Apostasy in world Protestantism," by which he means the growth and influence of religious liberalism. He also speaks of the "Great Controversy" of which he writes:

> In 1911 [Charles Clayton] Morrison ran a series of articles advocating the reception of the unimmersed into the churches, thus creating the major issue of the Great Controversy - 'open membership.' This and other liberal views he espoused were arrived at in his own thinking because of the liberal premises he had accepted.[1]

These "liberal premises," according to Murch, amounted to the substitution of the gospel of Christ with "another gospel." In other words, reducing barriers through open communion was tantamount to ignoring the teaching of the New Testament, regarding the proper immersion of repentant believers in baptism. From the conservative perspective, the truth motive was lost to a false kind of Christian unity, false because it violated the teaching of Jesus Christ.

Similarly, the Churches of Christ have emphasized the truth motive. They have been scrupulous in adhering to the teaching of the New Testament as they see it. For example, they practice only *a cappella* singing because the New Testament does not specifically mention that instruments were used in church services during apostolic times. There has been a tendency, especially before more recent times, toward exclusivism which has severely limited contacts between the Churches of Christ and other Christian bodies. One could say that in this case the unity motive has been greatly de-emphasized if not lost.

On a congregational level it is nearly impossible to tell the three groups apart. Individual churches call themselves "Churches of Christ" (e.g. Brookvalley Church of Christ) and "Christian" (e.g. First Christian Church) regardless of their affiliation with any of the three religious bodies. Obviously though, profound differences lie beneath the similarities of name.

A brief statistical profile may help the reader to understand the numerical importance of the Restoration Movement and the geographical strengths and weaknesses of each of the three Restoration groups. According to the study *Churches and Church Membership in the United States 1980* the number of total adherents are as follows: The Christian Church (Disciples of Christ), 1,212,977; the Christian Churches and Churches of Christ, 1,127,925; and the Churches of Christ, 1,600,177. The three groups are roughly comparable in size, though the Churches of Christ is the largest. This illustrates a remarkable rate of growth in the conservative group in the twentieth century, although it seems that growth has slowed in recent decades. In 1906, when the Churches of Christ requested the United States Religious Census to list them as a separate entity, they numbered 159,658 members, perhaps ten or fifteen percent of the Disciples' total. In 1971 the Disciples' membership was cut almost in half by the creation of the centrist nondenominational fellowship. Combined, the three Restoration religious bodies constitute the largest native religious group in the United States.

Based on the one hundred counties in the United States with the largest number of adherents, the following configuration emerges:

Christian Church (Disciples of Christ). Of the 100 counties with the largest number of Disciples of Christ adherents, 10 are in Texas, followed by Illinois and North Carolina (each with 9); Illinois (8); Missouri (7); Kansas and Ohio (each with 6); California, Kentucky, and Virginia (each with 5).

The observation that the Disciples are mostly a northern group is belied by numerical strength in Texas, North Carolina, Kentucky, and Virginia. The Texas statistics, however, are somewhat deceiving. While there are large numbers of Disciples in the larger cities such as Dallas, Fort Worth, and Houston, it should also be pointed out that adherents of the Churches of Christ outnumber Disciples in Texas by a margin of nearly three to one. The strength in North Carolina and Virginia is more authentic. These two states are exceptions to the sectional pattern.[3] Kentucky, which represents the old heartland of the Restoration Movement, is nearly evenly divided between the three Restoration bodies. It is interesting that the only eastern county (outside the South) is Kings County, New York. Brooklyn (i.e. Kings County) ranks nineteenth on the list, with adherents totaling 6,066. It is quite clear that the Restoration Movement was a frontier phenomenon which occurred almost exclusively west of the Appalachians.

Christian Churches and Churches of Christ (hereafter Christian Churches). The fact that the division between this centrist group and the more liberal Disciples was largely ideological is demonstrated by the fact that the two groups thrive in basically the same parts of the country. Indiana has a remarkable total of twenty-four of the largest one hundred counties of Christian Churches adherents. In fact, the Disciples and Christian Churches share Marion County (Indianapolis) Indiana as the county with the largest number of adherents for each group. In Marion County, the Disciples number 22,874 and the Christian Church numbers 22,709 adherents. Ohio is second (18), and Illinois third (15); Kentucky and Virginia each have five counties; California, Oklahoma, and Pennsylvania each have four of the counties with the largest number of adherents.

The Christian Churches show a high degree of compact strength in the contiguous states of Indiana, Ohio, and Illinois. Kentucky, and Virginia and (western) Pennsylvania, reflect the old heartland of the movement associated with Barton Stone and the Campbells respectively. Hamilton County (Cincinnati), Ohio is the county with the third largest number of adherents of the Christian Churches in the United States. Cincinnati has long been a major Restoration stronghold, the site of frequent meetings and debates in the early nineteenth century. It is a particular source of strength for the Christian Churches, where they have an important Bible school and publish their most important periodicals. Fulton County, Georgia ranks ninth and DeKalb County, Georgia ranks twelfth. Both counties are located in metro Atlanta and their appearance so high on the list may reflect migration patterns to large metropolitan areas outside the traditional geographical strongholds of the movement.

The Churches of Christ. This, the most conservative group, demonstrates numerical strength in rather different parts of the country: 1. Texas has 23 of the one hundred counties with the largest number of adherents; 2. Tennessee (18); 3. California (11); 4. Alabama (10); 5. Arkansas and Florida (6); 7. Kentucky (4); 8. Michigan, Missouri, Ohio, and Oklahoma, each with three of the one hundred counties.

The list illustrates the truism that Churches of Christ strength is concentrated in Tennessee and Texas. California figures prominently in all three Restoration groups; Los Angeles County, for example, appears in the top ten of all three lists. Undoubtedly this represents migratory patterns to California which apparently were especially significant in geographical areas of Churches of Christ strength. Northern, particularly northwestern Alabama is an area of Churches of Christ numerical strength which is often overlooked. Lauderdale County, whose principal city is Florence, Alabama, is the county with the ninth largest number of adherents, 13,620. Kentucky and Ohio are the original heartland of the movement while Arkansas, Missouri, and Oklahoma represent traditional areas of settlement linked to nineteenth-century migration patterns. The patterns in Florida are less clear. The counties which show up are widely distributed throughout the state: Duval County (Jacksonville) in the north; Polk, Pinellas, and Hillsborough in the Tampa-St. Petersburg-Lakeland area of central Florida; and Dade (Miami) and Broward (Fort Lauderdale) in the south. Perhaps the best explanation is the most general one, out-migration to the Sunbelt and the very fast growth in Florida's population. The origin of the prominence of Wayne, Oakland, and Genesee Counties in Michigan is clearer. This certainly is linked to the migration of Southern workers drawn to the automobile plants in Detroit and nearby areas.

This project was originally intended to focus specifically on the Churches of Christ because they are the Restoration group with the largest presence in the South. However, since primary interest is on intellectual history, this narrow focus had to be largely abandoned. This is a study of the intellectual origins of the Restoration Movement, which concentrates on the early nineteenth century and on the philosophical antecedents of the eighteenth century. This period of time antedates the actual division in the movement, so it would be anachronistic to refer to any one of the three modern religious bodies.

I have decided, therefore, to speak of the "Restoration Movement" for several reasons. First of all it seems to be a term which while not universally preferred is at least acceptable to all three Restoration bodies; it is the closest thing to a neutral term one is likely to find. Secondly, it does seem to be the term most preferred by the conservative elements and so it best preserves the project's original interest in that tradition. Finally, and most practically, it avoids the very confusing terminology of "Disciples," "Christians", and "Reformers." The meaning of each tends to vary over time and often changes with the ideology of the user. I have on occasion felt compelled to use all of these terms; I hope I have done so prudently. Hopefully the usage will be clear in their specific contexts. Above all, I have tried to avoid the use of the term "Disciple." This was the term preferred by Alexander Campbell and many writers use it to refer to the movement as a whole. I have not followed this practice because I am least concerned with the more northern and liberal Disciples of Christ denomination and did not want to lead the reader into associating the subject at hand with that modern religious body. Although the study does deal with a nineteenth-century unitary movement and despite the fact that I have tried to maintain a certain objectivity in my writing and a catholicity in the choice of my sources, I have also attempted to maintain some sensitivity to the issues that concerned the conservatives most, especially in the last two chapters. Again, this is in keeping with the original intent of the study, to examine a facet of Southern religion. In this context the conservatives predominate.

This is not a history of the Restoration Movement. Rather, the scope of this study is a history of the ideas which distinguish the movement as unique in American religious history. More specifically, it is a history of the *origin* of the ideas which constitute the Restoration Movement as an intellectual phenomenon. I have tried to eliminate all but the most crucial biographical facts. The reader may find Barton Stone, the Campbells, and Walter Scott moving from place to place for no apparent reason. I realize, with regret, that these men, and others, have been turned into abstractions. This was not my goal, but was rather dictated by the need to keep the study as brief as possible and closely focused on intellectual matters.

The movement was influenced by many factors: the Reformation, the philosophy of John Locke, the Enlightenment, and the American frontier, to name the most prominent. I have tried to explain how all of these affected the Restoration Movement, but I would like the reader to understand that this is not a history of any of these sources of influence. For example, I make no pretense of offering a complete or nuanced analysis of the thought of John Locke even though I do spend considerable space discussing his philosophy.

The reasons that I chose not to write a general history of the Restoration Movement are threefold. First and most practical, there are several works that already provide a distinguished general history. The history by Garrison and DeGroot, which has been updated by McAllister and Tucker, offers the Disciples' point of view.[4] Murch writes from the perspective of the Christian Church and Churches of Christ, and Earl West, a member of the Churches of Christ, has completed a multi-volume history of the movement.

The general reader should be aware that the preponderance of studies have been written by Disciples. They have established a Disciples of Christ Historical Society and have nurtured many studies of high scholarly quality. The interested reader must search libraries diligently to find information written by more conservative writers. I have tried not to be unduly influenced by the more liberal Restoration tradition. The reader must decide how well I have succeeded. One of the techniques I have used to foster objectivity is to rely heavily on the *Memoirs of Alexander Campbell* by Robert Richardson. First published in 1868-70 in two volumes, it is an authoritative account of the life and thought of Alexander Campbell and the Restoration Movement as a whole. Though long (over 1,200 pages) and discursive, it is less ideologically charged than more modern studies. Moreover, the serious researcher cannot help but notice that many facts and anecdotes which appear over and over again in modern works are ultimately derived from Richardson's account. It seemed best, therefore, to go back to this widely used source.

I have relied as much as possible on primary sources. I have attempted, therefore, to analyze important sources such as *The Last Will and Testament of the Springfield Presbytery*, the *Declaration and Address*, and the *Sermon on the Law*. (Just one note on a technical matter: I have made an effort to allow the persons I have studied to express themselves in their own words by quoting them directly. In these quotes, I have preserved the original spelling and punctuation even when it is contrary to modern usage.)

On occasion I have used a contrary device. When discussing issues which have produced much controversy such as the missionary society, I have quoted directly from historians associated with each of the factions and identified them as such. This was an attempt to allow those within the Restoration Movement to define the debate and to devise the vocabulary with which they define their respective positions.

It must be admitted that the whole idea of writing an intellectual history reflects leftist predilections. I am not referring to my own personal philosophy but rather to the very noticeable fact that conservatives do not generally spend much time discussing the intellectual origins of the movement. The works by Murch and Earl West are typical examples of this tendency. It is quite possible that I have written an intellectual history of an anti-intellectual movement, or at least of a movement with certain tendencies toward anti-intellectualism. These tendencies are manifest in a lack of historicity, an ambivalence toward philosophy, and a hostility toward education in fields other than "Bible-knowledge."

The second reason I chose to write a history of the intellectual origins of the Restoration Movement is that it seemed to be one of the less explored facets of a relatively rich historiography. As stated, many historians fail to give anything but the most cursory treatment to the history of Restoration ideas. One exception is W.E. Garrison's *Alexander Campbell's Theology* published in 1900. I must admit that this volume was revelatory for me.

Garrison had impeccable liberal credentials. His father, of course, was J.H. Garrison, the long-time editor of the *Christian Evangelist,* who Earl West decribes as one of the most influential "prophets of liberalism." W.E. Garrison was himself a distinguished historian. He received a doctorate from the University of Chicago. In fact, *Campbell's Theology* was in origin his doctoral dissertation. Significantly, I think, Garrison begins his work with an introduction entitled, "The Historical Method." Here is what he says in the very first paragraph:

> He who undertakes to estimate the intellectual achievements of the nineteenth century and to generalize upon the history of thought in this period, cannot fail to admit that the most fruitful and far-reaching general conception which this age has brought into prominence is the idea of development. Based upon a metaphysics which finds the essence of reality to consist, not in the changeless identity of an unknowable "substance" in which all attributes inhere, but in the process by which functions are fulfilled, forms developed and new adaptations made to changing conditions, it quickly passed beyond the limits of speculative philosophy and found application in the fields of science, history, theology, and every study which seeks a knowledge of nature, man or God. If the very essence of reality lies in development, growth and adaptation, then knowledge of any portion of reality is to be sought in the study of its process of developement; i.e., in its history. In its most general application, therefore, the idea of development gives rise to what may be called the *historical method* of studying all phenomena.[5]

To conservatives of the time in which Garrison was writing, liberalism was the great enemy and history was one of the tools used to undermine the authenticity and credibility of the Gospel. As Garrison suggests, the historical method can be used as a means of introducing the notion of development. In a metaphysics of development, the primitive church, for example, can become not the one, true and perfect order of things, but rather an example of how the church adapted itself to the particular environment of the first century and the Roman Empire. In other words it ceases to be normative and becomes instead merely a particular and transitory manifestation of church.

As a historian I tend to see history as a means of enhancing human understanding. I am not unaware, however, that history has been manipulated by even the well-intentioned. I must admit that the conservatives within the Restoration Movement have correctly identified the threat which the historical method proposes. The question that they raise is one of continuing relevance for all Christian communions: What is the relationship between the immutable truth of the Gospel and the mutability of the historical human experience? The particular problem which the conservative Restoration Movement has confronted itself with has its origins in a very ahistorical concept of church. This is a major weakness in the movement's intellectual edifice.

All this brings me to the third, and in a sense the most important reason for writing an intellectual history, namely that we can learn the most about American, and in particular Southern, religion by better understanding the intellectual bases for one of the largest religious bodies in the South. This is a plea less to understand the Churches of Christ as they actually exist, in, say, middle Tennessee, than an invitation to meditate on the values and ideas which were articulated on the American frontier in the early nineteenth century. I am suggesting that we can learn more from the ideals expressed by the founding fathers of American Restorationism than from the failures of those ideals as they came into contact with the reality of a hostile world. It is obvious that those ideals addressed and still address certain needs. Much can be learned by trying to understand what these needs were and continue to be.

It is so common as to have become a veritable tradition among Restoration writers (even "scholarly" ones) to identify themselves as members of particular wings of the movement. This practice has its origin in the fracturing of the Restoration Movement and in the tendency to speak only to an audience which consists of members of one's own faction. I accept this practice as an invitation to express my evaluation of the Restoration Movement to my own readers.

As a Catholic, an outsider, I was at first perplexed by the Restoration Movement. I remember being thoroughly confused about the three Restoration groups, especially because their names are so similar. I wondered what connection there was between the Churches of Christ and the United Church of Christ. (There isn't any, or at least hardly any.) Once I began to learn about the beliefs associated with the movement, I became confused again. This time I was perplexed by what seemed to me to be some very Catholic ideas. I refer here to two ideas in particular: reservations over denominationalism and baptism for the remission of sins. When Alexander Campbell wrote about baptism for the remission of sins he referred to "actual" as well as "formal" forgiveness in baptism.[6] He quite consciously spoke of a "third way" between what he saw as the extremism of both Protestantism and Catholicism. While he certainly did not articulate a view which was identical to Catholic teaching, he did speak in terms that fell somewhere between the orthodox Protestant and Catholic points of view. There is a real basis for discussion here between Catholics and those within the Restoration tradition.

Because I have not been trained in theology, I feel more comfortable discussing the less formally theological idea of denominationalism. In this case I feel confident that the average person in the pew in both the Catholic and (conservative) Restoration tradition would share a more highly developed notion of the unity of church. Neither would consider "their Church" to be a denomination. This too could be a real basis of dialogue, between Catholics and those associated with the Churches of Christ. Interestingly, I suspect that conservatives in both traditions would have much in common, though they would probably reject this notion, or simply ignore it.

Beyond the commonality of belief shared by both the Churches of Christ and Catholicism, is a question which the Restoration Movement has raised, even if it has in fact failed to find a solution. I refer to the idea of denominationalism. The Restoration Movement has gone beyond the kind of unity which is embodied in Protestant ecumenism both because the Restoration concept of unity is more ancient and because Christian unity really was a central tenet of the movement. Again, this is more apparent in an abstract, intellectual sense; the reality of efforts to unify the Church, within the Restoration Movement, has been somewhat less distinctive and more typical of other Protestant groups. Nevertheless, a study of the intellectual origins of the Restoration Movement invites a reconsideration of the assumptions behind denominationalism. The Churches of Christ offer one solution for the divisions of denominationalism; Catholicism offers another. The two models share some similarities and many differences, but a comparative approach could be useful.

Alexander Campbell was not the only theologian of the nineteenth century who wrestled with the consequences of modern philosophy. As we shall see, Campbell adopted a Lockean epistemology while maintaining a strict separation between the sources of knowledge of the natural and supernatural world. Gerald A. McCool suggests that the Catholic Church was very much aware of the same epistemological problem:

> Leo XIII's prescription of neo-Thomism as the system to be used in the philosophical and theological education of the Church's priests was based on the conviction that the Thomistic metaphysics of substance and accident could preserve the necessary distinction between grace and nature which post-Kantian metaphysics had shown itself unable to preserve, and that Thomism's abstractive theory of knowledge avoided the confusion between natural and supernatural knowledge of God which post-Kantian intuitive epistemology could not avoid.[7]

If the goal of Campbell and of the Catholic Church in battling modern rationalism was the same, their concerns and solutions were different. From the Catholic perspective, the centrality of individual reason in theology first surfaced in the Protestant Reformation, but had been extended to Catholic theology through the philosophy of Descartes. Rationalism and skepticism were the inevitable result of modern philosophy's separation from the Church's authoritative communication of tradition.[8] Campbell saw the threat somewhat differently. To him rationalism threatened not the Church's authority but rather that of Scripture, which was based not on natural reason but on divine and supernatural revelation.

McCool sees a real lack of historical sense in the theology of Joseph Kleutgen (1811-1883), one of the major thinkers associated with neo-Thomism:

> Kleutgen had no real sense of historical development. Development, for Kleutgen, took the form of clarification and expansion of concepts or of deductive expansion of philosophical or theological principles. He showed no awareness of the role of cultural development or of different conceptual frameworks in the history of thought. He read the historical sources of theology carefully and intelligently but he interpreted them in terms of his own conceptual framework, which was essentially the conceptual framework of post-Reformation scholasticism.[9]

I find it interesting that both McCool and W. E. Garrison use the term "development" to discuss the influence of history on theology. This indicates, I think, a profound connection between history and theology in both modern Protestantism and Catholicism, rooted in a common experience of dealing with the problems of the modern world. Modern philosophy and, less abstractly, the French Revolution presented both nineteenth-century Protestantism and Catholicism with fundamental challenges. Ideologically, the authority of both Church and Scripture was challenged by modern rationalism. On a more practical level, the privileges of the Catholic Church and the Protestant State churches were beginning to come to an end, victims of the liberal state. Of course, it was in the United States that this new religious environment was most advanced. Both McCool and Garrison represent liberal critiques of conservative solutions to these challenges. McCool would distinguish between Catholic Church and Roman theology, and would argue that Leo XIII's "prescription of neo-Thomism" froze the Church ideologically at a time when it was increasingly necessary to adapt to ever quickening change. Similarly, Garrison criticized the conservative interpretation of the "truth motive" as insufficiently historical.

Where does this all leave us? I think it leaves us with some remarkable parallels. Both the Restoration Movement and the Catholic Church discerned a threat in modern philosophy, a philosophy which was rationalistic and thoroughly secular. Both sought, therefore, to preserve the integrity of the sacred against the secular, while both also used reason and rational methodology to achieve their ends.

What can Catholics, especially in the South, learn from the Restoration Movement? First of all they need to understand that the more conservative and Southern Churches of Christ chose to sacrifice the unity motive to the truth motive. Truth, Biblical truth, is highly prized. Secondly, the more conservative elements of the Restoration Movement have preserved from their nineteenth-century origins an aversion toward secular rationalism (while maintaining, as we shall see, a religious rationalism, distinguished by a rational approach to the Bible). Through a primitive Christianity, based on an inerrant and immutable New Testament, the conservatives have institutionalized a deep suspicion toward the secular. And they have also maintained the nineteenth-century separation between the natural and supernatural worlds. In their secular lives they are quite modern: they drive automobiles, wear twentieth-century dress and use electricity in their homes. But their spiritual lives are quite different. This does not suggest hypocrisy or a radical compartmentalization of the message of Christ. It is an attitude deeply enmeshed in the philosophical origins of the Restoration Movement, and one which is not foreign to Catholicism. The Catholic Church during the Middle Ages always maintained a separation between spiritual and secular authority, although the Church had great difficulty restraining itself from acting upon the conviction that the spiritual, while separate, was also superior to the secular. And although Catholicism is somewhat less dualistic, there has always been a strong world-rejecting tendency in the Catholic tradition. By recognizing that the Gospel truth is revered but also that it is regarded as intrinsically separate from the natural world, the reader will make significant progress in understanding a dominant trait of Southern religious culture.

Chapter One

European Origins

The Restoration Movement had to confront a difficult nineteenth-century problem: how to defend the freedom of individual conscience championed by eighteenth-century thought, and still devise a way to bring individuals together with a sense of the unity of the Church of Christ. The movement, therefore, had to contend with the implications of the Protestant Reformation, with "Protestant sectarianism" as it developed over the previous 250 years, and with the emphasis of modern philosophy on individual freedom.

The Reformation

The sixteenth-century Reformation has often been depicted as a movement which promoted individualism. Certainly the Reformers rejected many of the social and communal aspects of Catholicism, of which indulgences are but the most obvious example. Martin Luther's individualism was based on his firm conviction that every person must answer for himself to God:

> The mass is a divine promise which can help no one, be applied no one, intercede for no one, and be communicated to no one save him only who believes with a faith of his own. Who can accept or apply for another the promise of God which requires faith of each individually?[1]

The sixteenth century produced intermediate forms of individualism which were not quite modern. The *cuius regio* principle — that each prince had the right to determine the religion of his realm — was widely adopted in an attempt to end the first phase of sectarian strife in Germany. While challenging the medieval concept of the universality of Christendom, the *cuius regio* principle recognized the integrity of only one individual, the prince, who as a sort of "superindividual" determined the religion of all his subjects.

As the reform spread throughout Germany and to other parts of Europe, it became apparent that without the Catholic authority structure the reform was in danger of breaking up into thousands of individual religions. To avoid anarchy and curb excessive individualism, the dogmatism of the Reformation theologies was developed. Luther's advocacy of the individual conscience was therefore tempered by his theology, which centered on the ideas of justification by faith alone and *sola scriptura*. John Calvin's theology was even more systematic and dogmatic. This Protestant reliance on a systematic dogmatism quickly led to disagreement among the reformers. By 1527 Luther and Zwingli were engaged in a polemical duel over the interpretation of the Lord's Supper. The failure of the Marburg Colloquy in 1529 to reconcile these differences all but guaranteed the continued fissuring of the reform movement.

The emphasis on theological truth also spawned an intolerance of deviation. Luther's violent denunciation of the Peasant's Revolt in his tract, *Against the Murderous and Thieving Hordes of Peasants*, was largely motivated by his abhorrence of Thomas Muntzer's radical theology. The most famous victim of Protestant intolerance, of course, was Michael Servetus. Developing an increasingly radical theology, Servetus was led to a denial of the Trinity. Passing through Geneva he attended one of Calvin's sermons, was recognized, and turned over by the reformer to the authorities. Tried and condemned as a heretic, he was burned at the stake in 1553.

In Germany, the Peace of Augsburg in 1555 in effect legalized Lutheranism and granted security to the Lutheran princes and cities. But the idea of toleration was still foreign to the age. Not until after the end of the Thirty Years War in 1648 did the Treaty of Westphalia provide a modicum of toleration for differing religious ideas and practices in the Empire, outside of Hapsburg territories. It was not until 1688 in England and not until the eighteenth or even the nineteenth century in most of the rest of Europe that the idea of tolerating sects outside of the state churches became generally acceptable.

Religious toleration is a largely Protestant idea (although a form of Catholic toleration can be detected in Christian Humanism). It grew out of the recognition of the importance of the individual conscience and the necessity to protect the doctrinal uniformity of the sect. It was the evangelicals who emphasized the individual nature of religion and the paramount importance of a personal relationship with God. On the other hand, the state churches — Lutheran, Anglican, Reformed — were generally most concerned with promoting and defending a more rigid dogmatism. Toleration was the result of the desire of the state churches to maintain doctrinal uniformity by excluding dissenting members while recognizing the importance of the individual Christian conscience, the sincerity of dissenting bodies and their right to a more or less free existence. The consequence of a relaxed policy of toleration was the development of modern Protestant denominationalism.

The Influence of John Locke

Throughout the eighteenth century, the individuality of religious experience could be seen in mystical movements such as Pietism and Methodism, which promoted personal conversion, and the rationalistic impetus of the Enlightenment, out of which developed deism.

Since the time of Descartes the principal questions in Western philosophy were: How do we come to know what we know? What do we know? How much can we know, and What are our limitations as knowers? In this context the whole thrust of philosophy (as in religion) was on the individual and how and what the individual knows. At the forefront of this inquiry was John Locke (1632-1704), whose ideas remained immensely influential throughout the century after his death.

Locke's theory of knowledge redirected philosophy towards the study of man and influenced the politics, ethics, and philosophy of religion. Over the course of the eighteenth century the inquiry which Locke had begun into the knowing processes of man did not prove the validity of knowledge but instead led to skepticism. But this philosophical process affected all spheres of thought, especially American Protestantism. It directly gave rise to the philosophy of religion of Alexander Campbell which had a profound effect on the development of the Restoration Movement.[2] It is to Locke's philosophy of religion that we must now turn.

In his *Letter Concerning Toleration* Locke defines the church as "a voluntary society of men, joining themselves together of their own accord in order to [sic] the public worshipping of God, in such a manner as they judge acceptable to him, and effectual to the salvation of their souls." He continues:

> I say, it is a free and voluntary society. ... No man by nature is bound unto any particular church or sect, but every one joins himself voluntarily to that society in which he believes he has found that profession and worship which is truly acceptable to God. The hopes of salvation, as it was the only cause of his entrance into that communion, so it can be the only reason of his stay there. For if afterwards he discover any thing either erroneous in the doctrine, or incongruous in the worship of that society to which he has joined himself, why should it not be as free for him to go out as it was to enter?[3]

This is an "evangelical" definition of church, one to which any Congregationalist or Baptist of Locke's time could accede. Moreover, it is a church organized on a largely individualistic basis. Membership consists of like-minded individuals who voluntarily join together in communion but who are principally concerned with their own individual salvation. There is no social or ecclesial structure. The acceptability of the church to God lies within the judgment of each believer. If the individual deems anything erroneous in the church he simply leaves and joins another where he is more comfortable. This then is the recipe of modern toleration as expressed through denominationalism: a collection of independent churches each of which has a right to exist and which is recognized as a Christian body consisting of sincere believers. From these churches one may freely pick and choose.

Directly following this discussion of a definition of church, Locke dismisses the idea of apostolic succession as unscriptural. This leads him to ask what things are necessary for ecclesial communion in the "Church of Christ"? Locke responds that only such things as are expressly declared by the Holy Spirit in Scripture as necessary to salvation should be a condition of membership. He continues:

> I ask, I say whether this be not more agreeable to the church of
> Christ, than for men to impose their own inventions and inter-
> pretations upon others, as if they were of divine authority; and to
> establish by ecclesiastical laws, as absolutely necessary to the
> profession of Christianity, such things as the Holy Scriptures do
> either not mention, or at least not expressly command?[4]

As we shall see this is an opinion which closely parallels that of Alexander Campbell and which became a basic principle of the Restoration Movement.[5]

Recalling recent British history and the divergent religious directions acceded to by the clergy during the reigns of Henry VIII, Edward VI, Mary I and Elizabeth I, Locke dismisses the ability of clerics to determine articles of faith and modes of worship.[6] The mechanism which Locke substitutes for "systems of divinity" is revealed in the preface of another work, *The Reasonableness of Christianity:* "The little satisfaction and consistency that is to be found, in most of the systems of divinity I have met with, made me betake myself to the sole reading of the scriptures (to which they all appeal) for the understanding [of] the Christian Religion."[7]

Locke begins the *Reasonableness* by pointing out two extreme methods of reading Scripture. He then lays out his own method for reading the sacred text as a

...collection of writings, designed by God, for the instruction of the illiterate bulk of mankind, in the way to salvation; and therefore, generally, and in necessary points, to be understood in the plain direct meaning of the words and phrases: such as they may be supposed to have had in the mouths of the speakers, who used them according to the language of that time and country

> wherein they lived; without such learned, artificial, and forced
> senses of them, as are sought out, and put upon them, in most of
> the systems of divinity, according to the notions that each one has
> been bred up in.[8]

To understand the Christian religion one must first consult Scripture, and interpret it in the "plain and direct" meaning of the word. It is the individual believer who makes this interpretation, not the clergy or any other church authority. The question of *what* is to be believed is, according to Locke, set down plainly in the Gospel: "... it is plain, that believing on [sic] the Son is the believing that Jesus was the Messiah; giving credit to the miracles he did, and the profession he made of himself.[9] Later on Locke adds the idea that those who believe Jesus was the Messiah must also believe that he rose from the dead, and also in the necessity of repentance.[10] This interpretation of what Christians are required to believe has been labelled "minimalist," although many reject the term. Nevertheless, restricting Christian belief to what is explicitly in Scripture is an idea which would become central to the Restoration Movement.

The very idea of the "reasonableness of Christianity" brings attention to the role of reason in religion and leads to a brief consideration of Locke's theory of knowledge.

John Locke is most famous as the founder of empiricism and for his theory of knowledge. In his most substantial work, *The Essay on Human Understanding*, Locke denies that ideas are innate. Instead, he insists that ideas are derived from experience which he defines as sensation and reflection. The mind derives ideas from sensation while from reflection it becomes aware of internal operations such as thinking, willing, and desiring. Ultimately, Locke concludes that "knowledge then seems to me to be nothing but the perception of the connexion and agreement, or disagreement and repugnancy, of any of our ideas." (*Essay* 4.1.2). Although it is based upon empirical knowledge, the subjectivism of knowledge is apparent since it is the (individual) mind which perceives the agreement or disagreement of ideas which constitute knowledge.

Throughout the *Essay* Locke struggles with the subjectivity of knowledge. His world is made up of particulars and he is reluctant to discuss substance, which he believes can only be known imperfectly: "I am certain, that I have evident knowledge, that the substance of my body and soul exists, though I am as certain that I have but a very obscure and confused idea of any substance at all."[11] In the *Essay* he states:

> Whatever therefore be the secret and abstract nature of substance in general, all the ideas we have of particular distinct sorts of substances, are nothing but several combinations of simple ideas, coexisting in such, though unknown, cause of their union, as makes the whole subsist of itself. It is by such combinations of simple ideas, and nothing else, that we represent particular sorts of substances to ourselves...(2.23.6)

Since Locke rejects the doctrine of innate ideas, he is forced to explain the cause of simple ideas. Human beings are virtually incapable of experiencing substance but they can perceive various qualities of things. There are primary qualities such as extension, form, solidity, and mobility. Material things really possess these qualities. There are also secondary qualities such as color, sound, touch, taste, and smell. Perception of these (secondary) qualities vary from individual to individual. What might seem bitter and cold to one person may seem sweet and hot to another. Secondary qualities, therefore, do not really exist, they are sensations which affect the individual. The logical consequences of these assumptions were elaborated by Berkeley and Hume as will be seen below.

Considering Locke's theory of knowledge, it is not surprising that he concludes that we do not know very much.[12] Reason, for Locke, is the faculty which distinguishes man from the beast and which is a crucial tool in man's ability to know. If knowledge is the perception of the agreement or disagreement of ideas, then it is reason which helps man to know:

> For as reason perceives the necessary and indubitable connexion of all the ideas or proofs one to another, in each step of any demonstration that produces knowledge: so it likewise perceives the probable connexion of all the ideas or proofs one to another, in every step of a discourse, to which it will think assent due.[13]

Locke is insistent on placing strict boundaries between reason and faith. Locke defines reason as "... the discovery of the certainty or probability of such propositions or truths, which the mind arrives at by deduction made from such ideas, which it has got by the use of its natural faculties; viz. by sensation or reflection." He defines faith as: "... the assent to any proposition, not thus made out by the deductions of reason; but upon the credit of the proposer, as coming from God, in some extraordinary way of communication. This way of discovering truth to men we call revelation." (4.18.1)

Locke "contradistinguishes" between reason and faith, and he prefers to rely on reason unless the evidence of revelation clearly exceeds the evidence of reason and its principles. He carefully whittles down the criterion by which we ought to rely on faith, first by denying that no new simple idea can be conveyed by traditional revelation, i.e., Scripture. (4.18.3) Traditional revelation conveys ideas through words which by custom revive in our minds latent ideas but not things of which we have had no previous idea at all. Similarly, revelation cannot exceed our intuitive knowledge. Even when God immediately reveals something to us, our assurance can never be greater than our own knowledge that it is a revelation from God. Finally, faith can never convince us of anything which contradicts our knowledge.

Locke admits the existence of things which are above reason, such as the resurrection of the dead, which are purely matters of faith. (4.18.7) But he immediately asserts once again the primacy of reason: "Whatever God hath revealed is certainly true; no doubt can be made of it. This is the proper object of faith: but whether it be a divine revelation or no, reason must judge..." (4.18.10) A little later on Locke includes an even clearer statement: "Reason must be our last judge and guide in everything." (4.19.14)

Removing the guiding influence of reason from revelation creates enthusiasm.[14] Locke felt so strongly about the topic that he added a chapter, "Of Enthusiasm," in the fourth edition of the *Essay.* Immediate revelation, or enthusiasm, is a much easier way of establishing opinion than strict reasoning. It "... flatters men's laziness, ignorance, and vanity ..." rises "... from the conceits of a warmed or over-weening brain ...," frees the mind from reason and reflection, and substitutes "... the ungrounded fancies of man's own brain."(4.19.3-7) What seems to disturb Locke most is that enthusiasm is a short cut to knowledge which discards experience, reflection, and reason for the conviction that one is sure because one is sure. (4.19.9)

Since enthusiasm boasts the perception of an inner light, the question arises: is this perception a revelation from God, a fancy to do something, or the work of the devil? In other words, in divine revelation there is no need to prove truth since God cannot deceive, but how can it be known that any proposition in our mind has been infused by God? The answer, according to Locke, is reason. A truth is known "...either by its own self-evidence to natural reason, or by the rational proofs that make it out to be so." (4.19.11) Since enthusiasm is the rejection of rational proof (since there is the belief that something is revelation simply because it is strongly believed to be revelation) there is no criterion for truth.

> For if the light, which every one thinks he has in his mind, which in this case is nothing but the strength of his own persuasion, be an evidence that it is from God, contrary opinions have the same title to inspirations; and God will be not only the father of lights, but of opposite and contradictory lights, leading men contrary ways; and contradictory propositions will be divine truths, if an ungrounded strength of assurance be an evidence, that any proposition is a divine revelation. (4.19.11)

Locke's discussion of enthusiasm ultimately raises the question of the criterion of revelation and of authority since for him reason is something which is "extrinsical" to our opinions, without which we cannot discern truth from falsehood. In the context of the sort of denominationalism which Locke advocates, without, one presumes, a single source of teaching authority for all Christians, how can we know if a proposition is from God or not? Locke answers the question by referring to the Old Testament where revelations from God (what Locke calls original revelations) were proven by outward signs. He mentions, for example, Moses and the burning bush and the miracle of his rod turned into a serpent. Of course revelation need not always be accompanied by extraordinary signs. In this case we have two rules by which we can judge if the internal light of private persuasion is truly revealed by God. These are reason and Scripture: "Where reason or scripture is express for any opinion or action, we may receive it as of divine authority; but it is not the strength of our own persuasions which can by itself give it that stamp." (4.19.16) Locke seems simply to accept Scripture as a true report of original revelation. The only evidence to support the claim of divine inspiration would seem to be the claims by the writers that they faithfully reported eyewitness accounts of the events and message of Jesus. The rationality of Locke's religion lies principally in his interpretation of Scripture, his exegesis of the Bible as an historical document, and in his "reasonable" approach, one which is not forced, extravagant or extraordinary but which seeks to sustain the plain, straightforward meaning of the text.[15]

Over the course of the eighteenth century Locke's philosophy had an enormous impact in Britain, the Continent, and the United States. The philosophy of Locke was so popular both because it was innovative and especially because Locke offered such a common sense approach. When confronted with paradox or inconsistency Locke never hesitated to opt for a practical if inconsistent solution. However, some of the philosophers who followed Locke were more consistent, and consequently arrived at conclusions which Locke himself would have been reluctant to make.

George Berkeley

George Berkeley (1685-1753) was an Anglo-Irishman, the Anglican Bishop of Cloyne, who brought Locke's philosophy of knowledge to the logical conclusion of denying the existence of matter. Locke had made a distinction between primary and secondary qualities. The latter were nothing but powers to produce various sensations, they were not qualities actually possessed by an object. Berkeley applied Locke's arguments to primary qualities as well. He agreed that such secondary qualities as heat, color, and sound were subjective, but argued that such primary qualities as extension, motion, and rest were equally subjective. If motion is really in the object how comes it that the same motion can seem slow to some and fast to others? And if things have real sizes and cannot have different sizes at the same time, then why does an object look larger when we are near it than when we are farther away?

Berkeley concluded that since primary qualities cannot exist apart from secondary qualities and since the latter are subjective and relative to the perceiver, then objective material existence must be questioned. Berkeley argued that sensible objects are complex ideas and that ideas cannot exist without the mind. Material objects, therefore, exist only through being perceived. To the objection that a tree, for example, would cease to exist if no one was looking at it, Berkeley responds that God always perceives everything.

David Hume

Although Berkeley eliminated the material world, he maintained the existence of an external spiritual reality and also preserved Locke's insistence that ideas had a cause, which Berkeley attributed to God. The person who applied Locke's theory of knowledge to an even stricter logic and completed the undermining of human knowledge was David Hume (1711-1776). Born in Edinburgh, Hume was instrumental in making Scotland one of the centers of philosophical inquiry, an environment which had a direct influence on Alexander Campbell and the Restoration Movement.

Hume was the author of a philosophical skepticism which could be summed up by quoting from his *Treatise of Human Nature:*

> All probable reasoning is nothing but a species of sensation. 'Tis not solely in poetry and music, we must follow our taste and sentiment, but likewise in philosophy. When I am convinced of any principle, 'tis only an idea, which strikes more strongly upon me. When I give the preference to one set of arguments above another, I do nothing but decide from my feeling concerning the superiority of their influence. Objects have no discoverable connexion together; nor is it from any other principle but custom operating upon the imagination, that we can draw any inference from the appearance of one to the existence of another. (Book 1. Part 3. Section 8)

And a little later on "... all our reasonings concerning causes and effects are derived from nothing but custom; and that belief is more properly an act of the sensitive, than of the cogitative part of our natures".

According to Bertrand Russell, Hume's philosophy represented the bankruptcy of eighteenth-century reasonableness.[16] Beginning, like Locke, by rejecting innate ideas and proceeding with sensible and empirical inquiry, Hume ends up by concluding that nothing can be learned by experience and observation. With such a conclusion it is hardly surprising that Hume formulates an ambiguous agnosticism about the existence of God. He would have admitted that the ultimate cause of order in the universe probably bears some remote analogy to intelligence but little more.[17] But the whole of the Christian world from the Fall to the Day of Judgment he would have rejected.

Deism

Hume's philosophy was part of a long tradition of skepticism about man's ability to know complex doctrines. Catholic philosophers such as Erasmus had been able to suspend their skepticism and accept the Church's teaching, but with the revolt of the Protestant Reformation acceptance of the Church's magisterial authority became increasingly rare. By the eighteenth century the traditional role of the Church had been largely replaced by reason, a triumphant scientific method, and most devastating of all, by a skepticism which rendered religion meaningless in the minds of many philosophers.

The principal religious consequence of seventeenth and eighteenth-century rationalistic philosophy was deism. There were many varieties of deism ranging from the acceptance of most Christian tenets to an attitude which approached atheism. Generally, deism rejected revelation for a religion of pure reason. The lengthy title of a treatise published in 1696 by the English deist John Toland (1670-1722) betrays deism's rationalistic bent: *Christianity not Mysterious: Or a treatise Shewing That there is nothing in the Gospel Contrary to Reason, Nor above it: And that no Christian Doctrine can be properly call'd a Mystery.*

The historical origins of the rise of deism in the seventeenth century can be traced to the Protestant rejection of tradition and the acceptance of Scripture as man's ultimate guide to faith. This reliance on Scripture presented many problems of interpretation which seemed to defy solution. One of deism's answers to this problem was to treat Scripture as simply a type of ancient literature filled with scientific inaccuracies and cultural oddities. Scripture was largely replaced with natural religion, i.e., one which was formulated by reason and experience. This approach was buttressed by Locke's theory of knowledge.

The strongest element leading to deistic thought was the Scientific Revolution. The discoveries of Copernicus, Kepler, Galileo, and Newton annihilated Aristotelian physics. The law of gravity, for one, seemed to explain the very nature and operation of the universe. For the first time humanity was privy to God's plan of creation. Hence the sentiment expressed by Alexander Pope:

> Nature and Nature's laws lay hid in night,
> God said 'Let Newton be!' and all was light.

This new-found confidence encouraged the notion of God as divine watchmaker, creating a world machine so perfectly balanced that no further adjustment need be made. God became less and less an immediate factor in life.

Voltaire (1694-1778) was one of the most moderate and influential deists. Exiled to England from 1726 to 1729, he published his *Lettres philosophiques* in 1734. The letters popularized Locke and Newton on the continent and depicted England as a land of freedom, tolerance, and progress, all of which were notably absent, according to Voltaire, from his native France.

Voltaire's religious ideal was epitomized by the Quakers, who developed a religion of the heart. He lauded their simplicity, sincerity, pacifism, toleration, and lack of priests and ceremony. Of course Quakerism is the very essence of religious individualism, and deism valued highly the right of the individuals to think for themselves on all subjects and to communicate their thoughts to others for the general welfare. The deists also affirmed the oneness of humanity. In this regard Voltaire comments in one of his letters that people are weary of sectarian disputes which have made them indifferent to religion. He comments sardonically how the great reformers — Luther, Calvin, Zwingli — have all founded sects which have divided Europe, but that the great English philosophers and scientists such as Newton, Locke, and Samuel Clarke, rationalists who tried to develop a rational and unifying religion, have attracted almost no followers.[18]

Thomas Reid and Common Sense Philosophy

Thomas Reid (1710-1796), the founder of the Scottish philosophy of common sense, published his most important work, *An Inquiry into the Human Mind on the Principles of Common Sense*, in 1764. With Reid, we come closer to the world of Thomas and Alexander Campbell. Reid, a Presbyterian minister, was born near Aberdeen. In 1764 he was appointed professor of moral philosophy at Glasgow University, where both of the Campbells subsequently studied, succeeding Adam Smith.

Reid was a convinced Berkeleyan until he realized the consequences of that philosophy after reading Hume's *Treatise of Human Nature*. He contended that Hume's philosophy was a system of skepticism and traced its origin to what he called its theory of ideas.[19] Reid distinguished several senses of the word, "idea." In popular language idea means the act of conceiving. To have an idea of something is to conceive it. But the word has also been given a "philosophical" meaning: not the act of the mind we call thought or conception but the object of thought. This is the definition accepted by Locke, Berkeley, and Hume, which led, Reid contends, to the destruction of both matter and mind in the universe.

Reid attacks the theory of ideas in two ways. He argues that ideas in the philosophical sense of the word do not exist but are the invention of philosophers. He also appeals to common sense. Explicit is a rejection of Locke's theory that knowledge is the agreement or disagreement of ideas. Instead, Reid asserts, knowledge is a complex of image and belief. The image or conception of an internal object is accompanied by an intuitive belief or judgment, which is not just a message sent to the mind by the senses but is also an *a priori* enrichment and validation of sensory information proved by a strong and irresistible conviction of belief. In Reid's words,

> ... every operation of the senses, in its very nature, implies judgment or belief, as well as simple apprehension. Thus, when I feel the pain of the gout in my toe, I have not only a notion of pain, but a belief of its existence, and a belief of some disorder in my toe which occasions it; and this belief is not produced by compar-

ing ideas, and perceiving their agreement and disagreements; it is included in the very nature of the sensation.[20]

There is a theistic presupposition in the doctrine of common sense. According to Reid there are "original and natural judgments" which are not discovered through an examination of the five senses. They are, therefore,

> a part of that furniture which nature hath given to the human understanding. They are the inspiration of the Almighty, no less than our notions or simple apprehensions. They serve to direct us in the common affairs of life, where our reasoning faculty would leave us in the dark. They are a part of our constitution; and all the discoveries of our reason are grounded upon them. They make up what is called the common sense of mankind; and what is manifestly contrary to any of those first principles is what we call absurd.[21]

Reid maintains that there is no opposition between reason and common sense. In fact they are inseparable in their nature. He ascribes two offices or degrees to reason. The first is to judge things which are self-evident; the second to draw conclusions that are not self-evident from those that are. The first of these is the province of common sense. The distinction between the two degrees is justified both because "... in the greatest part of mankind no other degree of reason [i.e. common sense] is to be found" and also because the two degrees of reason are sufficiently different to be entitled to distinct names.

> The first is purely the gift of Heaven. And where Heaven has not given it, no education can supply the want. The second is learned by practice and rules, when the first is not wanting. A man who has common sense may be taught to reason. But if he has not that gift, no teaching will make him able either to judge of first principles or to reason from them.[22]

It is common sense which enables man to judge first principles and "... in a matter of common sense, every man is no less a competent judge, than a mathematician is in a mathematical demonstration; and there must be a great presumption that the judgment of mankind, in such a matter, is the natural issue of those faculties which God has given them." Reid's argument is that to suppose that mankind has deviated from the truth in things which are self-evident is "highly unreasonable."[23]

Reid next argues that we cannot learn of first principles through experience:[24]

Thus I think it appears, that the principle we have been considering - to wit, that, from certain signs or indications in the effect,
we may infer that there must have been intelligence, wisdom, or
other intellectual or moral qualities in the cause - is a principle
which we get neither by reasoning nor by experience; and therefore, if it be a true principle, it must be a first principle.[25]

Applying this criterion to "natural theology," Reid develops an argument
which he calls the "Argument from Final Causes," concluding that "design and
intelligence in the cause may, with certainty, be inferred from marks or signs of
it in the effect."[26] Reid cites Hume as being particularly hostile to this argument,
"But says the skeptical philosopher, you can conclude nothing from these
tokens, unless past experience has informed you that such tokens are always
joined with understanding. Alas! Sir, it is impossible I can ever have this experience."[27]

By restoring a source of knowledge which is beyond the capability of experience, Reid restores the possibility of revealed knowledge as found in the
Bible. In fact Reid restores the necessity of the existence of God, which had
been undermined by skeptical thought. "It seems, then, that the man who maintains that there is no force in the argument from final causes, must, if he will be
consistent, see no evidence of the existence of any intelligent being but himself.[28]

The Influence of Common Sense Philosophy in America and on Alexander Campbell

Theodore Bozeman has suggested a summary of the principal elements of
"Baconianism" as elaborated by the Scottish School to include:

1. A spirited enthusiasm for natural science.

2. A scrupulous empiricism, grounded upon the confident "trust in the senses" and in the reality of the outer world supplied by the Realist doctrine of
"judgment."

3. A sharp accent upon the limits of scientific method and knowledge,
directed to the inductive control of generalizations by continuous reference to
"facts." Abstract concepts not immediately forged from observed data have no
place in scientific explanation.[29]

The Scottish Common Sense Philosophy infiltrated most American universities and exercised a major influence on American thought around the turn of
the nineteenth century. The philosophy provided a rational defense of or-

thodoxy against the infidelity of the Enlightenment through a dualism which facilitated an attack on both idealism and materialism.[30] The Scottish Philosophy restored realism, that we perceive an external object itself and not just an idea of the object, and therefore the validity of induction, which the idealism of Locke, Berkeley and Hume had undermined and destroyed. Furthermore, the reassertion of trust in the senses indicated a reaction against the emphasis on pure reason which was so dominant in the philosophy of the Enlightenment. By preserving the separation between the Creator and His creation the Scottish Philosophy was able to invoke Bacon and Newton and maintain the efficacy of scientific inquiry into the natural world while at the same time preserving the transcendence of God which made revelation necessary. This is precisely the position developed by Alexander Campbell.

Alexander Campbell was deeply influenced by the Scottish Common Sense Philosphy. In fact, the entire Restoration Movement is intimately related to the Scottish philosophy. As Perry Gresham, a former president of Bethany College, has observed:

> The Christian Churches would do well to study the Scottish sources of rational philosophy which Alexander Campbell brought with him from Glasgow. There is a strong measure of Adam Smith in the political ethics of the communion. Thomas Reid exercised a substantial influence over the pioneer who set the norms whereby the congregations have developed. The reasonable approach to worship and Bible study came from the moon [sic, probably *mood*] of common sense which dominated the University of Glasgow at the turn of the century when Thomas and Alexander Campbell were students. The economic and social philosophy which underlies A. Campbell's argument against Robert Owen on the occasion of the famous debate in 1829 is an interesting blend of Scottish thought adapted to the frontier in America.[31]

In the beginning of a chapter on Alexander Campbell's views on skepticism, natural theology and socialism, Robert Richardson contrasts Campbell's liberality with the narrow course pursued by sectarian editors: "They [i.e. sectarians] had adopted certain articles of belief as unquestionably true, and did not wish to have any misgivings created in regard to them. They had begun with certainties, and very naturally felt unwilling to end with doubts. Mr. Campbell and those with him, on the other hand, had begun with doubts, in order that they might end with certainties. Conservation was the aim of the former, but progress that of the latter."[32]

Beneath the hyperbole of Richardson's judgment lies a difference rooted in historical origin. The "sectarians," originating in the sixteenth-century Refor-

mation, revolted against the authority of Rome but did not reject the basic notion of orthodoxy, of right thinking, which was embodied in dogmatic theological creeds. In Campbell's view these creeds were responsible for dividing the
Church of Christ. Campbell was a post-Enlightenment thinker who had absorbed Locke's rationalism, but also Locke's low opinion of human knowledge.
Campbell, therefore, was thoroughly familiar with deism, skepticism and other
forms of modern philosophy and he understood well the arguments against
traditional Christianity. In a series of essays arguing against the socialist,
Robert Owen, Campbell astutely analyzed the basis of modern philosophy's attack on religion:

> ... having voluntarily extinguished the light of supernatural revela-
> tion, [Owen and his followers] have now candidly and honestly
> avowed that whether there is a god at all, a spirit in man that will
> survive his mortal body, a heaven or hell, is to them unknown and
> unknowable. This is the identical conclusion to which I knew
> most certainly, by all the knowledge of philosophy which I pos-
> sess, they would be constrained to come. For, as I have frequent-
> ly said, there is no stopping-place between Deism and Atheism;
> and they are lame philosophers who, taking philosophy for their
> guide, profess to hold with Herbert, Hume, Gibbon and Paine
> that there is a God, an immortal soul, a heaven or a hell. I give
> great praise to the New Harmony philosophers for their candor
> and their honesty in frankly avowing the conclusion which all the
> lights they have authorize them to maintain. I say they are good
> philosophers. They have reasoned well.[33]

In a subsequent essay Campbell penetrates the skeptical argument even
more clearly:

> *A Problem: For the Editor of the 'Harmony Gazette' and his doubt-
> ing brethren:*
>
> You think that reason cannot originate the idea of an Eternal
> First Cause, and that no man could acquire such an idea by the
> employment of his senses and reason; and you think correctly.
> You think also that the Bible is not supernatural revelation — not
> a revelation from the Deity in any sense. These things premised,
> gentlemen, I present my problem in the form of a query again:
>
> The Christian idea of an Eternal First Cause uncaused, or of a
> God, is now in the world and has been for ages immemorial. You
> say it could not enter into the world by reason, and did not enter

by revelation. Now, as you are philosophers and historians, and have all the means of knowing, how did it come into the world?[34]

Much of Campbell's fame rested on his ability to transcend traditional argumentation and to answer the question he posed in a thoroughly rational way. Campbell would agree with Locke that the source of our knowledge of the natural world is our senses and reflection, but he would deny that we could know God through our senses.[35] He preserves a dualism akin to that of the Scottish philosophers. Nature and religion, therefore, are related but separate; they are the

...offspring of the same supreme intelligence, bear the image of one father—twin sisters of the same divine parentage. There is an intellectual and moral universe as clearly bounded as the system of material nature. Man belongs to the whole three. He is animal, intellectual, and moral being. Sense is his guide in nature, faith in religion, reason in both. The Bible contemplates man primarily in his spiritual and eternal relations. It is the history of nature so far only as is necessary to show man his origin and destiny, for it contemplates nature—the universe—only in relation to man's body, soul, and spirit.[36]

The source of our knowledge of religion is the Bible which is,

... to the intellectual and moral world of man what the sun is to the planets in our system, the fountain and source of light and life, spiritual and eternal. There is not a spiritual idea in the whole human race that is not drawn from the Bible. As soon will the philosopher find an independent sunbeam in nature, as the theologian a spiritual conception in man, independent of THE ONE BEST BOOK.[37]

Reason is not excluded from religion but Campbell disapproves of speculation. He draws a parallel with scientific induction, which had been rehabiliated from the attacks of skepticism by the Scottish Common Sense Philosophy:

Speculation in philosophy has been widely discarded from approved systems. Since the days of Bacon, our scientific men have adopted the practical and truly scientific mode — that is, they have stopped where human intellect found a bound over which it could not pass, and have been content to go no farther than material objects, analyzed, gave out their qualities and left the manner of their existence as beyond the bounds of created intellect. We plead for the same principle in the contemplation of religious truth... So religious truth is to be deduced from the revelations which the Deity has been pleased to give to man.[38]

As we have seen, Alexander Campbell was deeply influenced by the philosophy of John Locke. He accepted Locke's epistemology that all knowledge is derived from the senses and reflection. Like Locke, he also accepted revelation as the word of God, while he attempted to interpret Scripture rationally. But Campbell rejected some of the implications of Locke's philosophy, the skepticism of Hume and the deism of the Enlightenment. Influenced by Scottish Common Sense philosophy, he acknowledged the validity of induction but rejected the deistic notion that we can know God through our own senses and reason. Campbell embraced a dualism which separated the source of man's knowledge of the material world from the source of his knowledge of God. Spiritual things are known only by divine revelation. Surely revelation operates through the senses, and once the idea of the Deity is suggested to the mind, reason attests, bears witness to, and demonstrates the existence of such a Being, but the Divine Concept originates from without the human mind. Through this dualism Campbell largely accepted the methodology of eighteenth-century philosophy while rejecting the results, namely deism, which had developed.[39]

The sole source of revelation is the Bible. Revelation operates through the senses, but it opens the senses to a field which is entirely closed to natural reason.[40] Campbell shared the Enlightenment's aversion to speculation, to "metaphysics." He does not deny that Scripture can be interpreted but he is hostile to creeds, for example, because they are deductions derived from theories about the facts of revelation, human attempts to discern ideas which God chose not to reveal to us and which the human intellect could never penetrate. Again, Campbell follows Locke both in his relatively low opinion of what can be known and also in the maintenance of a rational approach to religion which rejects "enthusiasm" and embraces the plain meaning of Scripture. The Bible is a book of facts, not of opinions or theories. These facts, clearly revealed and defined, and clearly limited to the Bible alone, constitute the bases of restoration. In turn, these restored Bible facts were to be the means for uniting all the sects into the one Church of Christ.

Chapter Two

Barton Stone and the American Context

The Origins of Denominationalism and its Place in American Religion

The origins of modern denominationalism can be traced back to the emphasis on the individual nature of salvation and to the dogmatic certainty which was characteristic of the Protestant Reformation. The revolt against the medieval Church was in large part motivated by the conviction that Christ and his message had been constrained by human thought and institutions. The result was a fundamental redirection away from those medieval structures and toward a more individualistic religious context. Doctrinal differences were recognized, while at the same time most Reformers felt that uniformity was desirable within geographical jurisdictions. The result was a series of state churches which, while they preserved their evangelical nature, all constituted different facets of the one, holy, catholic church.

These developments were especially advanced in England where Protestant opinion was particularly fractured. By the end of the reign of Elizabeth I the Church of England was divided among high church Episcopalians, Independents, and Baptists. Division became acute during the English Civil War which necessitated the need for Puritan unity against the king and high church advocates such as William Laud, Archbishop of Canterbury. The result was a system which acknowledged differences of opinion regarding the outward life of the Church while maintaining a certain degree of "Protestant unity," based on shared principles, but also based on an agreement to disagree. Convinced that the Church of Christ could never be represented by a single ecclesiastical structure, it was decided that a large number of smaller subdivisions of a larger entity (the "Church") was possible. These were identified by name or "denominated" and became "denominations." Through these "denominational" structures a high level of individual freedom was possible, since believers had the right to choose in which "part" of the Church they wished to participate. Since large numbers of Puritans emphasized the autonomy of the local congregation, a fair degree of local differences were permitted to develop. The entire system was held together by a highly developed notion of toleration. It is at this point in the process that Locke's epistemology and his opinion of toleration functioned as a philosophical buttress for the "Denominational System."

Within this "denominationalizing" process, the United States has occupied a unique place because of the special conditions which prevailed in the new republic. The first amendment to the Constitution specifically prohibited the establishment of a state religion. With complete freedom to organize, denominations quickly proliferated. Secondly, the American colonies had always been a refuge for various religious groups. In this sense they were the heirs to the religious situation in England which had fostered the growth of a denominational concept of church. Even after independence, each successive wave of immigrants brought with it its own religious organization. Very quickly the United States became home to a religious diversity which existed nowhere else in the Western world.

The United States, particularly the American frontier, provided a very different context from that of Europe. Theological training and philosophical inquiry were less important factors in religious thinking than the rather freewheeling competition between theologically similar religious groups which was taking place in the growing settlements across the mountains.

Many years ago Richard Niebuhr pointed out that there were several "social sources of denominationalism." Although differences among Christian groups were always at least partly theological in nature, there were social causes of division as well. National psychology, social tradition, cultural heritage, and economic interest were all factors which influenced religious thought and helped to foster the growth of denominations.[1]

Economic factors are probably the best known causes of religious differences. Research in this direction has been so prolific that it would be impossible to offer even a brief summary. Perhaps it would suffice to say that churches of the disinherited, the poor, the uneducated, have tended to emphasize an emotional fervor, a certain simplicity, an anti-intellectualism, and sometimes a program of social reformation. On the other hand, middle-class churches have focused on a religion which was more intensely personal. For their members religion would be more a question of personal salvation than social reformation, and in some cases the middle class might equate prosperity with virtue and poverty with sin.

Nationalism, language, and culture have always been important factors in the Church and became particularly so with the establishment of Reformation national churches. In the United States the immigration patterns transformed this nationalist impulse into an ethnic factor. The immediate result was a proliferation of denominations divided by national origin.

A more critical source of denominationalism was sectionalism. Early in American history divisions emerged between North and South, and more importantly for the development of religion, between East and West. The historical heartland of the Restoration Movement was neither in the North nor in the

South but in the border states along a line running from Tennessee north to Ohio on the western side of the Appalachians.

The origins of sectionalism were complex. Certainly economics was foremost among them. The East — especially New England and the Middle Atlantic States — was dominated by merchants, manufacturers and shippers, while the West was peopled by small farmers. Politically, the division was marked by the development of political parties — Hamiltonian Federalists and Jeffersonian Republicans — and by disagreements over issues such as tariffs and war with England. Perhaps the most obvious differences were social. The eastern urban centers were more class conscious and culturally European. While New York City was founding its first symphony orchestra and hosting premiers of Rossini operas, the people moving west were concerned with clearing forests, growing food, building shelters and holding on to their scalps. It is hardly surprising then that there were religious differences as well between East and West.

The East tended to maintain a religion which was typically European, bourgeois, nationalistic, and class organized. A well-structured polity which tended to reflect the order of a class-structured society, an emphasis on an intellectual conception of the content of faith, and an ethic which promoted sober middle-class values were dominant features of Eastern religion. On the other hand, the West developed religious attitudes which emphasized the emotional character of the religious experience, little patience for the intellectual structures which formal education nourishes, a dedication to a democratic and highly congregational polity, and a tendency to blur the distinction between laity and ordained clergy. Highly individualistic, Western churches also developed an ethic which condemned the excesses of the frontier, especially drunkeness, gambling, sexual license, and profanity. In a society which was extremely isolated by conditions on the frontier, the emotional side of religion often broke out in the context of large scale camp-meetings.[2]

East-West sectional differences in the South, especially religious sectional differences, were probably less noticeable than in the North. This was true because of the general state of religion in the southern colonies. Unlike the northern colonies, so many of which had been established by religious groups for expressly religious reasons, the southern colonies were for the most part founded for profit. Furthermore, the southern colonies all became royal colonies where the Church of England was the legally established religion. By the middle of the eighteenth century, most Southerners were either members of the Church of England or not members of any church at all.[3]

The Great Awakening

The Great Awakening was a movement which fundamentally altered the course of American religious history and ultimately heightened sectional differences. A radical individualism was securely lodged in Puritan thought, particularly in the tendency to speak of the necessity of the sinner coming face to face with God. Over the course of the seventeenth century the original spirit declined. The conviction of the need for a personal religious experience was gradually compromised. The Half-Way Covenant, for example, was a device to grant church membership to the grandchildren of the original New England settlers, all of whom had had a personal experience of conversion. By the 1720's, there were signs of change, of a "Great Awakening." Among the early leaders of the movement were Jonathan Edwards (1703-58), a Congregationalist in New England and William Tennent, Sr. and his sons, especially Gilbert (1703-64), Presbyterians active in the Middle Atlantic states. Their efforts were reinforced by the Methodist Revival and in particular by the preaching tours of George Whitefield which began in 1739 and which were conducted throughout the colonies.

The tendency to speak of a "regenerate church membership" and to make "experience" the most important requirement for both laity and the ministry was powerfully propounded by the Great Awakening. These tendencies had a particularly traumatic effect on the Presbyterian Church, the most conservative of the evangelical denominations. Robert Ellis Thompson speaks of the conflict between the Great Awakening and traditional Presbyterianism:

> ...the root of all the theological peculiarities of New England theology...may be traced to the extravagant individualism which has characterized her social and intellectual life. Their short-lived 'improvements' of the Calvinistic theology were but so many attempts to bring Calvinism into harmony with a principle which found its final expression in Emerson's "supremacy of the individual conscience" over all law and all forms of institutions. In her opposition to congregational independency and her maintenance of synodical authority, the Presbyterian Church held to the principle of an organic social life in both the race and the church.[4]

The conflict between "Eastern" and "Western" religion was most dramatically fought within Presbyterianism. The Presbyterian Church may have held firm but she became deeply divided. Some of those who emerged out of this conflict were Presbyterians who came to found the "Christian Church." Ultimately they became one of two groups which were the progenitors of the Restoration Movement.

Because of the relatively backward development of religion, the Great Awakening manifested itself differently in the South, where it was much more of a missionary movement than in the North. The Presbyterian awakening was begun by Northerners such as Samuel Davies (1723-1761), whose efforts in Virginia collapsed when he left to become president of Princeton in 1759.[5]

Southern Baptist revivalism owed its origin to a New Englander, Shubal Stearns (1706-1771). Originally a Congregationalist, Stearns became a Baptist in 1751. After working as a missionary in New England, he moved to Virginia in 1754, and then to North Carolina the following year, where he established the Sandy Creek Church with his brother-in-law, Daniel Marshall, and a few followers.[6] The Methodists arrived in the South a bit later. They had been preceded by an Anglican priest Devereux Jarratt (1733-1801) who had formed a large circuit which covered parts of southern Virginia and northern North Carolina. When the Methodists began to arrive in 1772, Jarratt formed many "Christian societies" with them and cooperated with their revival efforts.[7] All of these movements, especially those of the Presbyterians and Baptists, were centered away from the seaboard in the piedmont areas of the southern states. This helps to explain why the same denominations and a similar religious expression could be found on both sides of the mountains. It also accounts for the ease with which these groups and their ideas moved quickly and easily over the Appalachians.

The Awakening in the South was short-lived. Despite a brief resurgence between the years 1785 and 1788, the last quarter of the eighteenth century saw a general decline in religious fervor in the South. The reasons for this decline were mostly secular. Certainly the Revolution disrupted life sufficiently to make a strong settled religious life very difficult. Then there were all the political distractions surrounding the establishment of a new country and a new constitution. Following the treaty with England, signed in 1783, there was a frantic rush for land in the West. Francis Asbury pondered the effects of this migration on the state of religion on the frontier:

> When I consider where they came from, where they are, and how they are, and how they are called to go farther, their being unsettled, with so many objects to take their attention, with the health and good air they enjoy; and when I reflect that not one in a hundred came here to get religion, but rather to get plenty of good land, I think it will be well if some or many do not eventually lose their souls.[8]

By the year 1800 the social sources of sectionalism were in place. It remained for another religious movement to further separate Eastern and Western religion. One of the principal features of the Great Western Revival or the second Great Awakening, was that it was thoroughly interdenominational. The ease with which Presbyterians, Baptists, and Methodists gathered together in the camp meetings betray a certain commonality of belief and a general solution to what was perceived as a general problem. That problem was a decline in religious zeal. The commonality of belief was rooted in a pietistic evangelicalism which had been introduced into the South by the Great Awakening, whether in its Presbyterian, Baptist, or Methodist form.[9] This frontier belief system rejected the Newtonian universe with its clock-maker God for a deity which was intimately involved in every aspect of earthly existence. This was a benevolent God who loved people. But God's anger could be aroused by human predisposition to sin. The decline in religious zeal was God's punishment for human sin, evidence of which abounded in lack of prayer, materialism, blasphemy, fornication, alcoholism, and general irreligion. God could and would reverse this decline if people would only repent:

> Bretheren, what can we expect, if we live in disobedience, if we backslide in heart and depart from God? Will he not chastise us with the rod of blindness and barrenness? Can we expect any thing but a declension? Is it not owing to such conduct that our congregations from year to year complain of coldness and deadness. ...The truth is, we do not cry to him with suffient fervency and zeal: we do not plead the promises with sufficient faith: we are too much at our ease: we see cause for lamentation: It will not be better with us until we alter our conduct and reform our lives.[10]

The theology of revivalism, therefore, was rooted in a pietistic evangelicalism which saw a more idealized past destroyed by surrender to the sinful nature of human beings. The solution was simple: faith, confession of sin, and repentance on an individual level. Once each individual completed this process, the community could entreat God to send the Spirit and revitalize mankind. The duty of the clergy, therefore, was to exhort the laity to repent and reform, and to lead the justified in fasting and prayer until the time of providential deliverance.

It is one of the paradoxes of American religious history that one of the great "Eastern-type" churches, the Presbyterian, played such a crucial role on the American frontier. The principal reason for this can be traced to European emigration patterns. The bulk of Presbyterians who came to the United States emigrated from Ulster beginning in 1717 and continuing in waves until the Revolution. By this time the seaboard had already been settled and the best land had already been taken. The Scotch-Irish, therefore, were at the forefront of the westward movement in search of land, and by means of this movement Presbyterianism became a frontier religion.

The first occasion for a clash between the Presbyterian heritage, with its firm ecclesiastical structure, and its appreciation of right doctrine; and its American environment had been the Great Awakening. Very quickly, the Presbyterian Church was divided between "Old Side" and "New Side". The major issues were the authority of the presbyteries to enforce discipline, and the relative merit of an educated clergy versus one that had "experienced" religion. In fact it was a duel between Calvinist theology and the pietism of the Great Awakening which emphasized the importance of an inner light over objective doctrinal truth and ecclesiastical authority. A reconciliation was reached only in 1758, a compromise asserting the jurisdiction of the presbyteries while noting that candidates for the ministry were to be examined for their experimental acquaintance with religion no less than their learning and orthodoxy. Revivalist tendencies still persisted, however, even to the point that some Presbyterians began speaking of restricting church membership to regenerated adults and of treating its baptized children, in the words of one historian, "...as outside pagans, exempt even from its discipline."[11]

James McGready

The Presbyterians were intimately involved in frontier revivalism. It was very nearly one man who brought the ideas and methods of "New Side" Presbyterianism to the frontier which became the basic ingredients of the Great Revival. James McGready (1760-1817) was born in Pennsylvania of Scotch-Irish parents but moved with them to Guilford County, North Carolina in 1778. Attracted to the ministry from his youth, he returned to Pennsylvania to study with John McMillan, a New Side Presbyterian minister. McGready was "savingly converted to God" on a Sunday morning in 1786, completed his formal education, and was licensed to preach by the Redstone Presbytery (Pennsylvania) on August 13, 1788.[12] With all of these New Side credentials intact, McGready returned to Guilford County to begin his ministerial career.

Guilford County, located in the piedmont of North Carolina, was physically not very far from the frontier, and with its scattered congregations, rampant materialism, and general irreligion it resembled those frontier communities which were to give birth to the Great Revival. It was here that McGready worked out his theology of preaching the Word. In the evangelical pietism of the South the role of the minister changed from the performance of ritual to evangelization. Because of the individualistic nature of the predominant theology, individual believers were converted in the context of local congregations. The preacher, therefore, began this process of evangelization/conversion by convincing the sinner of the horror of the unconverted state. The first step is the recognition of the deadly force of sin:

> What transformed the beloved creature man, the darling of his Maker, and the governor of the lower world, into a child of wrath, a slave to his lusts, and a drudge to the devil? It was sin, that, like a deadly plague, or malignant and mortal contagion, has filled the earth with deceit and wickedness, bloodshed and violence, misery and woe, destruction and death, and has turned an early Paradise into an emblem of hell.[13]

The second step is to convince the sinner of the consequences of sin, by proclaiming the bliss of heaven and the agony of hell; and thus break the sinner down. Barton Stone himself related the effects of McGready's preaching:

> Such earnestness, such zeal, such powerful persuasion, enforced by the joys of heaven and the miseries of hell, I had never witnessed before. My mind was chained by him, and followed him closely in his rounds of heaven, earth, and hell with feeling indescribable. His concluding remarks were addressed to the sinner to flee the wrath to come without delay. Never before had I comparatively felt the force of truth. Such was my excitement that, had I been standing, I should have probably sunk to the floor under the impression.[14]

McGready's theology was much more deeply rooted in an Augustinian view of sin and grace than most other revivalists. While not rigidly predestinarian, he thought that revivals occurred not because people freely sought out grace but rather because there was such a gulf between human sin and divine grace. In the elemental battle between the free grace of God and sinful human nature, God's grace was more powerful. The Revival, therefore, was a divine means of converting society to God.[15] The preacher plays a key role in the reception of divine grace because he

> must use every possible means to alarm and awaken Christless sinners from their security, and bring them to a sense of their danger and guilt. He must use every argument to convince them of the horrors of an unconverted state; he must tell them the worst of their case — roar the thunders of Sinai in their ears, and flash the lightenings [sic] of Jehovah's vengeance in their faces.... Let them hear or not, though the world scorn and revile us, call us low preachers and madmen, Methodists — do this we must, or we will be the worst murderers; the blood of sinners will be required at our hands, their damnation will lie at our door.[16]

Once sufficiently alarmed and awakened, the sinner must plead for God's gracious offer of mercy for "It is the will of God that the sinner should try to foresake [sic] his sins, and as a guilty, condemned criminal, fall at the footstool of sovereign mercy, crying for pardon."[17] Through the Holy Spirit, the sinner is led to saving grace, the acceptance of Jesus Christ as personal savior and a new birth. "In that awful day, when the universe, assembled, must appear before the quick and dead, the question of bretheren, will not be, were you a Presbyterian - a Seceder - a Covenanter - a Baptist - or a Methodist; but did you experience a new birth? Did you accept of Christ and his salvation as set forth in the

Gospel?"[18]   According to McGready, the new birth is the "implantation of a
living principal [sic] of grace in the soul, which before was spiritually dead."
Through regeneration the whole soul is changed and reoriented away from
Satan and towards God and holiness.[19] So terrible was the terror of hell and so
glorious the bliss of heaven, that McGready for one was hardly surprised that
the new birth was accompanied by the fainting, barking and jerking which was so
characteristic of the Great Revival.

   Given McGready's proclivity towards attacking the immorality of piedmont
society and denouncing the hypocrisy of the upper classes, it is hardly surprising
that he occasioned a strong reaction to his preaching. His church at Stoney
Creek was attacked; pews were overturned, the altar was burned and finally a
death threat, written in blood, persuaded McGready to head west.[20]

   McGready took charge of three small congregations in Logan County, Kentucky in January 1797. Kentucky was in the midst of a tremendous surge in
population from 73,677 in 1790 to 220,955 in 1800. Most of the people coming to
Kentucky and Tennessee were from Virginia, the Carolinas, or other parts of
the South. Even at this early stage, therefore, both Kentucky and Tennessee
were culturally part of the South. This may help to explain why the Great
Revival, though originating on the Western frontier, eventually became a
Southern phenomenon. For two years, despite fasting and praying, "for the conversion of sinners in Logan county," there was no revival. Then in July 1799 at
the Red River church a remarkable series of events began to unfold as the congregation became alive in spirit and zeal.[21] A month later people at a sacramental service at the Gasper River congregation were so overcome with emotion
that many fell to the floor. A similar experience overcame the Muddy River
congregation in late September.

   The Great Western Revival truly got under way the following year. In June
1800, the three congregations came together at the Red River Meetinghouse for
a communion service. The three regular Presbyterian ministers of the area —
William Hodge, John Rankin, and McGready — were joined there by the
McGee brothers. William McGee, a Presbyterian, had been a convert and pupil
of McGready in North Carolina. His brother, John, was a Methodist. The emotional enthusiasm of the Methodist McGee was crucial to the great fervor of the
meeting. For four days increasing waves of emotion swept over the meeting,
with the first manifestations of the crying and shouting which were to be typical
of the Great Revival. A second meeting was planned for the last weekend in July
at Gasper River. This was to be the first genuine camp meeting. Crowds flock-
ed in from miles around, prepared to camp out for the duration of the service.
McGready reflected on the significance of the event he had witnessed:

   the power of God seemed to shake the whole assembly. Towards
   the close of the sermon, the cries of the distressed arose almost
   as loud as his [William McGee's] voice. - After the congregation

was dismissed the solemnity increased, till the greater part of the multitude seemed engaged in the most solemn manner. No person seemed to wish to go home - hunger and sleep seemed to affect nobody - eternal things were the vast concern. Here awakening and converting work was to be found in every part of the multitude; and even some things strangely and wonderfully new to me.[22]

The revival in Logan County set off a chain reaction in other parts of Kentucky and eventually in other parts of the South. The largest and most famous of all revivals was the one held at Cane Ridge, Kentucky in August 1801. The meeting was planned by Barton W. Stone, a Presbyterian minister who had known McGready in North Carolina. Stone had been pastor of two small congregations at Concord and Cane Ridge in Bourbon County since 1798. Eager to awaken his congregations, Stone publicized the meeting for over a month. He was amazed when a few weeks later as many as twenty-five thousand people converged on his simple log meetinghouse to make American religious history.

Barton Stone

Barton Warren Stone was born in 1772 at Port Tobacco, Maryland, a descendant of the first Protestant governor of Maryland, William Stone (1648-53). Stone's mother was widowed only a few years after Barton's birth. She sold the family property and moved to Pittsylvania County, Virginia near the North Carolina border. In 1790 Stone left his home to attend the academy established by David Caldwell in Guilford County, North Carolina. Caldwell was a New Light Presbyterian, a native Pennsylvanian, who had graduated from Princeton in 1761. In 1765 he was ordained and began his ministry with two small congregations near Greensboro, North Carolina. As was traditional in those days, Caldwell had established a "log college" which functioned as the principal educational institution in the area. Intent on pursuing a career in law, Stone was rather disturbed by the religious atmosphere which permeated Caldwell's academy.

After some debate, Stone resolved to "get religion." His search came to a head when none other than James McGready came to preach at Caldwell's academy. McGready preached his fire and brimstone and the need for the new birth, which pushed Stone into a spiritual turmoil without resolution. How was one to achieve the new birth? It was a question not adequately answered for Stone by McGready. Stone's second contact with McGready was even more disastrous. Speaking on the theme "Weighed in the Balances," McGready spawned an almost inconsolable hopelessness in young Stone:

He went through all the legal works of the sinner, all the hiding
places of the hypocrite - all the resting places of the deceived -
he drew the character of the regenerated in the deepest colors,
and thundered divine anathemas against every other. Before he
closed his discourse I had lost all hope - all feeling, and had sunk
into an indescribable apathy.[23]

Stone was in turmoil until he heard the preaching of William Hodge at one
of Caldwell's churches. The topic was "God is love" and after its conclusion
Stone went out into the woods to read the Bible and pray where he felt released
from his fear and apathy:

I yielded and sunk [sic] at his feet a willing subject. I loved him -
I adored him - I praised him aloud in the silent night, in the echo-
ing grove around. I confessed to the Lord my sin and folly in
disbelieving his word so long and in following so long the devices
of men. I now saw that a poor sinner was as much authorized to
believe in Jesus at first, as at last - that *now* was the accepted time,
and day of salvation.[24]

The significance of this event lay not only in Stone's rejection of the popular
Calvinism of McGready, but also in his rejection of "the devices of men." In this
way Stone turned away from the conventional process of conversion as agoniz-
ing struggle, but he also placed himself on the path of discarding all human
devices for a simple Bible-centered religion which was to be one of the principal
hallmarks of the Restoration Movement.

Early Movements for Christian Unity

The thirteen years between Stone's decision to enter the ministry in 1791
and his final break with Presbyterianism in 1804 can be summarized by a series
of meetings and events which influenced him and propelled him towards the
founding of a new religious movement. Barton Stone was not a particularly
original thinker. He rarely expressed opinions which were not shared by a good
many other people of his time. What he did do was cull opinions from several
different sources and push forward with these ideas even if it meant abandoning
some old structures. The movement which Stone helped found took ideas
which were at the periphery of other denominations and placed them in the
mainstream of a new religious movement.

Once Stone had completed his studies, he was assigned a topic by Caldwell and asked to write a discourse on the Trinity. As a candidate for the ministry, Stone was examined by the Orange Presbytery, at that time headed by Henry Patillo. Patillo (1726-1801) had been an early advocate of the toleration of diverse ideas for the sake of Christian unity. While waiting for the next session of the Presbytery to license him to preach, Stone went off to visit his brother and taught at Succoth Academy in Washington, Georgia.

The academy had been founded by Hope Hull, one of the early leaders of Methodism in the South. Hull had been an associate of James O'Kelly, the founder of an earlier "Christian" movement. After the Revolution, when Wesley realized the necessity of separating the Methodist movement in the United States from that in England, he appointed Francis Asbury as superintendent. Within a few years Asbury had assumed the title of bishop and the authority to appoint each preacher to his circuit, without appeal. O'Kelly, with the assistance of Hull and others, was at the forefront of an attempt to curb the power of Asbury. At the first general conference in 1792 O'Kelly proposed a resolution allowing a preacher to appeal to the Conference if he felt he had been treated unjustly by the bishop. The resolution was defeated and O'Kelly and others withdrew. Hull was eventually reconciled with Asbury, but the others went on to found the Republican Methodist Church. After only a few months the group renamed itself the "Christian Church" and declared that the Bible was its only creed, that all preachers were equal, that both preachers and lay people were allowed to interpret Scripture, and that each congregation was completely independent. These "Christians" were concentrated in Virginia, North Carolina and later on the Southern frontier. Their ideas played a significant role in the development of the thought of Barton Stone, especially regarding Christian unity, and on the environment in which he worked.[25]

Another early "Christian" movement was founded by two Baptists, Elias Smith (b. 1769) and Abner Jones (b.1772) on the New England frontier. Both men came to reject orthodox Calvinism and the whole idea of an orthodox body of doctrine. In 1801 Smith organized a church at Lyndon, Vermont which he simply called a "Christian church." The program of this "Christian" body can be summarized by the remarks made by a correspondent of the *Advocate and Messenger* in 1827. "We mean to be New Testament Christians, without any sectarian name connected with it, without any sectarian creeds, articles, or confessions, or discipline to illuminate the Scriptures.... It is our design to remain free from all human laws, confederations and unscriptural combinations; and to stand fast in the liberty wherewith Christ has made us free."[26] It is doubtful that these eastern "Christians" exerted any direct influence on the Great Revival, but at a later date Barton Stone did attempt for many years to reconcile this eastern group with Alexander Campbell, an attempt which failed because of mutual distrust. In 1931 this Christian Church united with the Congregational Church. Thirty years later another merger was effected creating the United Church of Christ.

Stone and Revivalism

Barton Stone has long been associated with the Great Western Revival. No doubt this is due to his pastoring at Cane Ridge, Kentucky where the largest and most famous revival took place. As we have seen, Stone's role at Cane Ridge was largely limited to traveling to Logan County to observe McGready's work, pronouncing it good, and then advertising a similar revival to be held at Cane Ridge. Stone's attitude toward the Revival was practical; he thought that the Camp Meetings stirred up the spirit and heart religion and so were useful. But the emotional aspects of revivalism never occupied a central role in Stone's theology. This is not to deny the influence of revivalism on the thought of Stone, but it ought to be kept in mind that the Revival occupied only a few years in his life and work.

One of the principal influences of revivalism is found in Stone's rejection of the Calvinistic pattern of conversion. As William Garrett West describes it:

> Stone encouraged the pattern of conversion which broke the Cal-
> vinistic scheme developed by Presbyterians in Kentucky, a
> scheme which asserted that man must wait until God was ready
> to strike with the sword of the Spirit. Stone cried out that God
> had already struck the hour of salvation and continued to strike.
> The revival was his proof that salvation could invade men's lives
> without years of waiting.[27]

Based on his own experience Stone felt that conversion best occurred "... with a Bible in hand, a prayer in the heart, and the Confession of Faith buried in the dust of neglect."[28] Stone enhanced man's role in devising a new scheme of salvation.[29] He rejected the Calvinist idea of election, that sinners can do nothing to be saved until God instills faith and repentance in them, because he could not understand how God could grant his grace to some and withhold it from others. God offers grace to all, but men and women must take the next step.

The role of the Gospel is crucial in Stone's scheme of salvation. The sinful person is converted through the testimony of the Scriptures. The Gospel must be accepted as true. This acceptance is based both on rational grounds and through faith, "He [God] deals with man as a rational creature. The strongest motives are presented to our understandings; but they cannot move, excite, or influence us, unless we believe: in other words, they are no motives at all, without faith." The Word is not only the foundation of faith, but produces faith. The cruelty of Calvinism, according to Stone, was that it made God a tyrant who demanded that sinners believe the Scriptures but who gave the capacity to believe them only to a few.

Stone rejected this construction, asserting that God gave the Gospel to the fallen, not the perfect, and would never command fallen creatures to believe, while denying them the capacity to do so. In a frontier environment which had hardened the doctrines of total depravity and predestination to the point that the sinner could do nothing but wait for the grace of God to initiate conversion, Stone asserted that no special illumination was necessary to understand the Word of God. Sinners could believe the testimony of Scripture before the Holy Spirit operated on them.

Stone himself acknowledged some imperfection, eccentricity, even evil in the revivals, but for him the good greatly outweighed the evil. The greatest good was that the revivals were great ecumenical movements where Baptist, Methodist, and Presbyterian ministers all came to preach the Word of God. Moreover, they were spontaneous outbursts of fellowship:

> Out of the abundance of their hearts they [the people who attended the revivals] spoke often one to another on the subject of religion; controverted notions were not the themes of their conversation, but the soul-cheering doctrine of heaven, and its divine effects, as experienced by themselves and others. Here was unity indeed - not in opinions, but in spirit.[30]

Revivals were crucial to the Restoration Movement not for their methodology or emotionalism, but because they were promoters of Christian unity and it was this spirit which gave great impetus to Stone's Christian movement.

The Break With Presbyterianism

Revivalism had another important but indirect effect on the thought of Stone and the Restoration Movement. The Revival became the focal point of dispute within the Presbyterian Church. Within a few years a dispute arose between revivalist and anti-revivalist parties in which the latter prevailed. Faced with what was in effect an ultimatum to abandon either revivalism or the Presbyterian Church, revivalists such as William Hodge and James McGready chose orthodoxy and were marginalized within an institution which allowed no place for their method.[31] Others, including Stone, felt forced to sever their ties and form new religious bodies. One of the ironies of the Great Revival as a movement of Christian unity was that ultimately it spawned three distinct Presbyterian schisms: the Stoneite "Christian Church," the western expansion of the Shakers, and the Cumberland Presbyterian Church.

Stone was deeply influenced by the liberalism of North Carolina Presbyterianism, personified by Henry Patillo, who had expressed theological ideas
similar to the revivalists. Patillo emphasized the need for a new birth, he attacked denominationalism and urged the close cooperation of Christian bodies. He
held that Christians ought to be allowed to differ peaceably about doctrine
without letting their differences divide them. Stone recalled that when Patillo
had examined him on the subject of the Trinity he kept the questions very brief
and indefinite, "doubtless to prevent debate on the subject in the Presbytery,
and to maintain peace among its members."[32] But peace among the Presbyterians was not to last, and Stone found himself at the center of an
acrimonious debate. A little more than three months after the Cane Ridge
meeting, the official Presbyterian Church in the form of the Washington Presbytery reacted to the growing tide of revivalism. The Presbytery presented formal charges against Richard McNemar, a Presbyterian minister and one of the
most radical of the Kentucky revivalists. The general tenor of the charges
revolved around McNemar's Arminianism. Specifically, he was charged with
declaring that Christ had died for the salvation of the entire human race without
distinction, that a sinner has the power to believe in Christ at any time, that a sinner has as much power to act faith as to act unbelief, and that faith consisted of
believing that Christ was one's personal savior.[33] This amounted to nothing less
than the rejection of the doctrine of election, the importance of confessions, and
the traditional excruciating conversion experience. It was also a rejection of
traditional Presbyterianism, and the Church recognized it as such.

No action was taken against McNemar because no one came forward to
substantiate the charges. Surprisingly, he was allowed to continue to preach.
The final confrontation came in September 1803 before the Synod of Kentucky
was even one year old. The Synod chided the Washington Presbytery for failing
to follow up on the charges made against McNemar. In a series of lopsided
votes it was clear that the anti-revivalists were firmly in control. The revivalists
withdrew from the deliberations but made a dramatic return a few days later
when Robert Marshall read a paper to the Synod on their behalf.

The paper declared their intention to remove themselves from the jurisdiction of the Synod and its Presbyteries. Furthermore, they claimed the privilege
of interpreting Scripture with the aid of the Holy Spirit, but without human
doctrines, citing the Confession of Faith as particularly harmful. The document
concluded with these words: "...we bid you adieu until, through the providence
of God it seems good to your rev. body to adopt a more liberal plan, respecting
human Creeds and Confessions." It was signed by Marshall, McNemar, John
Dunlavy, Barton W. Stone, and John Thompson.[34] After three days of fruitless
negotiations to close the rift, the Synod suspended all five men from its membership.

It is clear that both sides understood that the Confession of Faith was a critical stumbling block on which neither could afford to compromise. Because it was so critical it would be well to examine at least the disputed part of the Confession and the revivalist's objection to it.

The Confession in question was the Westminster Confession. During the English Civil War the Long Parliament passed an act, in 1643, calling for an assembly of divines to eliminate "false aspersions and interpretations" from the Church of England. In 1647 they completed their work. The assembly had been dominated by Presbyterians which may explain why the Scottish General Assembly approved the Confession within a few months. In 1690 the Scottish Parliament approved this action. In 1729 the Synod of Philadelphia, the first Presbyterian synod in the American colonies, adopted the Westminster Confession as "the Confession of our Faith." With a few revisions it remained the Confession of American Presbyterianism until the time of Stone.

One of the parts of the Westminster Confession with which the revivalists surely disagreed was Chapter XII, "Of Effectual Calling":

> All those whom God hath predestinated unto life, and those only, he is pleased, in his appointed and accepted time, effectually to call, by his word and Spirit, out of that state of sin and death in which they are by nature, to grace and salvation by Jesus Christ: enlightening their minds, spiritually and savingly, to understand the things of God, taking away their heart of stone, and giving unto them an heart of flesh; renewing their wills, and by his almighty power determining them to that which is good; and effectually drawing them to Jesus Christ; yet so as they come most freely, being made willing by his grace.
>
> II. This effectual call is of God's free and special grace alone, not from anything at all foreseen in man, who is altogether passive therein, until, being quickened and renewed by the Holy Spirit, he is thereby enabled to answer this call, and to embrace the grace offered and conveyed in it...
>
> IV. Others, not elected, although they may be called by the ministry of the word, and may have some common operations of the Spirit, yet they never truly come to Christ, and therefore cannot be saved...[35]

The revivalists objected to the stark predestination of the Confession which limited the ability "to understand the things of God," presumably including the the Gospel, to the elect. Moreover, they rejected the complete passivity of the sinner whose regeneration is the result of God's free grace alone: the elect must rely completely on the Holy Spirit to enable them to answer God's call. Others can never be called, can never be saved. The emphasis on predestination, on a small number of the elect, on the inability of man to initiate his own regeneration was recognized as inimical to the revival. The Confession of Faith had to be rejected.

The Springfield Presbytery

The immediate result of the confrontation was the expulsion of the revivalists by the Synod of Kentucky and the formation of a new presbytery by Stone and his associates. The Springfield Presbytery was organized sometime after September 1803. It represented a conscious effort on the part of the five revivalists to demonstrate that although they had withdrawn from the Synod they had not renounced Presbyterianism. In January 1804 the Springfield Presbytery published *An Abstract of an Apology for Renouncing the Jurisdiction of the Synod of Kentucky, Being a Compendious View of the Gospel and a Few Remarks on the Confession of Faith.* As the title indicates, the work was divided into three parts. The first, written by Robert Marshall was an account of the events leading up to separation. The second, written by Stone, was intended to show where the Confession had erred in its interpretation of Scripture. The third part, written by John Thompson, argued that creeds and confessions divided Christians and were therefore harmful.

Within that second part, authored by Stone, is contained some of the fundamental ideas of the Restoration Movement. The first of these is the idea that the origin of division within the Church is rooted in creeds.

> Through the subtilty of the enemy, the Christian church has long been divided into many different sects and parties. Each has a *creed, confession of faith,* or brief statement of doctrines, as a bond of union among its members, or rather a separating wall between itself and other societies. This is generally called the *standard* of such a church.... The people have the privilege of reading the scriptures to *prove the standard to be right;* but no privilege to examine it by Scripture, and prove it to be *wrong.* For if any should do this, he forfeits his privilege in that church, and must be cast out as a *heretic.*[36]

Creeds become dangerous and divisive when they cease to be considered human opinion and instead replace the word of God:

> It is an established maxim, that when any law, or rule of conduct is *authoritatively* explained, the explanation is the law; and we are necessarily bound to understand the original according to the ex-

planation. A creed, or confession of faith, is considered both as a summary of the doctrines taught in the Bible, and an explanation of them. If it were left in its own place, to occupy the low ground of human opinion, it might do some good. But the moment it is received and adopted as a *standard*, it assumes the place of the Bible; it is the explanation, according to which we must understand the original law, the *word* of the living God.[37]

Stone's solution to this division is the rejection of human creeds for the divine word of God as contained in the Bible:

> Is it not better to clear away all the rubbish, of human opinion, and build the church immediately on the rock of ages, the sure foundation, which God has laid in Zion?...Thus these *creeds, help* to split the real church of Christ, keep asunder the truly pious, and prevent that union, which would otherwise take place among the real lovers of religion. That real Christians would be united, if *human creeds* were laid aside, is evident; because we find, that such do agree, on practical religion, when they enjoy the Spirit of Christ.[38]

Much of Stone's confidence in Christian union is derived from his recent experience with the Great Revival. Revivals are useful because they enhance the power of the Spirit and decrease the influence of creeds:

> And wherever this revival is going on with life and power, as in Cumberland, and some other places, there Christians of different societies, losing sight of their *creeds, confessions, standards, helps,* and all those speculations which enter not into the religion of the heart, flock together, as members of one body, knit by one spirit.[39]

The idea that creeds and confessions divide Christians, that they need to be abolished for a Bible-centered faith, is central to the Restoration Movement.

On June 28, 1804, less than ten months after separation from the Synod, and only five months after the publication of the *Apology,* the Springfield Presbytery met at Cane Ridge and decided on its own dissolution. The *Last Will and Testament* of the Springfield Presbytery is a whimsical but serious document considered to be one of the basic charters of the Restoration Movement.[40]

It is probable that the *Last Will and Testament* was written by Richard Mc-Nemar. According to Robert Marshall and John Thompson, two other signatories, McNemar came to the meeting with the text already prepared. No one had planned to dissolve the Presbytery but after some discussion it was agreed to accept the document. Presumably the members came to realize that it was somewhat inconsistent to decry the existence of sects while creating still another religious party.

The *Last Will and Testament* reiterates some of the ideas found in previous documents. While it does not explicitly promote the idea of a united church, it does, in the very beginning, call for the dissolution of the presbytery so that it may "...sink into union with the Body of Christ at large...." Similarly, it does not call for a general return to the primitive church, but it makes clear that the Bible is the ultimate Christian authority and it puts forward a rather pure congregationalism in which each particular church has complete authority to choose its own preacher and to govern itself. The Presbyterian origins of the group are clearly revealed in the amount of space devoted to the procedure and criteria for licensing preachers, which had been a dominant issue in American Presbyterianism since the Great Awakening.

> We will, that candidates for the Gospel ministry henceforth study the Holy Scriptures with fervent prayer, and obtain license from God to preach the simple Gospel, with the Holy Ghost sent down from heaven, without any mixture of philosophy, vain deceit, traditions of men, or rudiments of the world.

The influence of the revival is just as clear in the following section:

> We will, that the church of Christ resume her native right of internal government - try her candidates for the ministry, as to their soundness in the faith, acquaintance with experimental religion, gravity and aptness to teach; and admit no proof of their authority but Christ speaking in them.

At the same time that the revivalists were renouncing sectarianism they adopted the name "Christian" for their enterprise. The choice of the term is attributed to Rice Haggard who published an *Address on the Import of the Christian Name* at this same time (1804). Haggard, it seems, had also been instrumental in having both the O'Kelly Republican Methodists and the New England movement under Elias Smith and Abner Jones adopt the name "Christian Church."[41] But it was Barton Stone who identified the term "Christian" with the Restoration Movement, a quarter century before Alexander Campbell suggested the alternative term "Disciple."

The *Last Will and Testament* was signed by the original five revivalists and David Purviance, a candidate for ordination by the West Lexington Presbytery, who had been attracted to the movement. Of the six, John Dunlavy and Richard McNemar shortly joined the Shakers, while in 1812 Robert Marshall and John Thompson returned to the Presbyterian fold. Only Stone and Purviance remained faithful to the ideals of the *Last Will and Testament*.

Despite these defections the Christians grew quickly. Almost all of the Presbyterian Churches in southwestern Ohio became Christian and with the influx of Christians from the East there were at least eight Christian churches in Kentucky and seven in southwestern Ohio.[42]

Stone's Theology

We have already seen that Barton Stone's theology led him in the broad direction of seeking the simple essentials of original Christianity. This was the basis of his opposition to supracongregational organizations and to creeds. He rejected creeds because he felt that they divided Christians into parties, but he also rejected specific doctrines in traditional creeds as either unreasonable or unrevealed. Stone rejected the orthodox doctrine of substitutionary atonement which held that Christ's sacrifice purchased reconciliation. This made Stone vulnerable to the charge that he reduced the death of Christ to a natural event and robbed it of its efficacy.[43] Stone also became embroiled in a public debate over the nature of Christ. He believed that Christ was not God but the Son of God. This assertion led his opponents to accuse him of Arianism, a charge he denied.[44] Nevertheless, Stone's writings on the Trinity were certainly less than fully orthodox.

Stone was frequently attacked for his deviation from orthodoxy, a reaction which he had invited because of his public statements on doctrine. He generally declined to counterattack and refused to enter into lengthy debate over doctrine, because he felt that it undermined the unity of the Church of Christ. He sometimes disputed specific doctrines because he felt that they undermined the primacy of revelation. But if Stone concluded that a doctrine was the product of the human mind it became something relatively unimportant and unworthy of dispute. Responding to a correspondent who asked why he rejected the doctrine of the Trinity, Stone replied:

> This query is founded on the supposition that we deny the trinity because of its mysteriousness....No, sir, we deny the doctrine for better reasons, and the greatest of all is that it is not a doctrine of revelation....All of God you love and adore is his character revealed; you know nothing more. His being or essence, or the mode of his existence, you know not....That same character in God I love and adore; his being or essence I know not; It is not revealed, and therefore not necessary for us to know.[45]

Barton Warren Stone's greatest contribution to the Restoration Movement was his recognition that stress on doctrinal differences was the greatest cause of Christian disunity. Perhaps as a Presbyterian, in a tradition which particularly emphasized right doctrine in the guise of the Westminster Confession, Stone was able to perceive that while doctrine was the principal means of maintaining the identity of each denomination, in so doing it also tended to divide the Church of Christ into self-defined and mutually exclusive doctrinal groups.

In attempting to devise a "theology" of Christian unity, Stone went to the Bible but presented his "Bible ideas" in a context of Christian love and trust without which there could be no true union.[46] Stone was convinced that no creed which reduced Christianity to a few essential doctrines could form the basis of union. While he wanted to go back beyond creeds, beyond what he called the apostasy in the age of Constantine, to the Bible, he warned his own followers that they must not attempt to make their own interpretations of the Bible essential to salvation. This, he maintained, would be hardly different from union proposed on a creedal basis. He went still further and rejected any attempt at union through a simple amalgamation of a heterogeneous mass of sectarian people by means of discarding wrong doctrine. Instead, Stone suggested that union ought to be modelled on the unity existing between the Father and the Son, who were one in character, one in operation, and one in the spirit of love. Put another way, he spoke of four types of union: book union, head union, water union, and fire union. He defined book union as unity founded on authoritative creed or confession of faith. Head union he defined as union founded on common opinion. Stone recognized that some enthusiasts asserted that their creed was the Bible alone. He saw a danger in this since different interpretations of the Bible were inevitable. Making any opinion, whether creedal or in the form of a personal interpretation of the Bible, the basis of fellowship was wrong. Water union, based on the immersion of believers into water, he rejected as too easily dissolved. Finally there was union of fire or of the spirit. This is the only true union, founded by faith not in opinions but in Jesus Christ and in obedience to his commands. Christian unity is the result of the activity of both God and humanity. Stone felt that humans could initiate union. Certainly it is necessary to pray to God to effect union, but there could never be unity unless there was unity in each individual; each one is to begin in himself or herself and correct his or her own errors. Through God and mankind true Christian unity can be achieved:

> Let every Christian begin the work of union himself. Wait upon God, and pray for the promise of the Spirit. Rest not till you are filled with the Spirit. Then, and not till then, will you love your God and Savior - then and not till then will you love the bretheren, who bear the image of the heavenly - then you will have the spirit of Jesus to love the fallen world. ...Every one in this spirit flow

together and strive together to save the world. The secret is would this, the want of this Spirit, the Spirit of Jesus is the grand cause of division among Christians: consequently, this spirit restored will be the grand cause of union. Let us, dear bretheren, try this plan; it will injure no one. God is faithful who has promised - has promised to give the Holy Spirit to them that ask him. With this spirit, partyism will die - without it anti-partyism in profession only, will become as rank partyism as any other, and more intolerant.[47]

Stone was a rationalist, even a Lockian. He could write that "faith depends not on the will, inclination, or disposition, but on testimony. Were I from home, and a messenger should come and inform me that my wife was dead, I should believe it; not because I was willing, but because of the testimony of the messenger."[48] But Stone was also a bit of a mystic rooted in perfectionism. He derived from the Great Revival a deep trust in the Spirit and in individual reformation. Ultimately, for Stone, the unity of Christians depended on love. These revivalist tendencies were much less pronounced in the thought of the leaders of a second strain of American Restorationism, Thomas and Alexander Campbell.

Chapter Three

From Scottish Presbyterianism
to American Restorationism

If the founders of the Restoration movement were affected by the philosophical currents of their time, even more influential was their religious environment. That religious environment was Presbyterianism. In fact it is remarkable
that each of the principal founding figures of the Restoration Movement,
Thomas and Alexander Campbell, Barton Stone and Walter Scott were
originally all Presbyterians. It is difficult to dismiss this fact as a mere coin-
cidence.

Lynn A. McMillon suggests that Scotland was such a fertile environment for
the Restoration Movement because in that country "...more than any other place
in the world there was a strong climate for religious groups to develop independent of any official church authority."[1] This assertion is apparently based on
the Declaration of Indulgence issued in April 1687 by James II, which
suspended the penal laws against Catholics and dissenters in Britain. The relative religious freedom which undoubtedly did exist in Scotland was therefore
also to be found in England as well, which first of all makes Scotland less unique
than McMillon suggests. It might also be suggested that in the eighteenth century at least some of the North American English colonies enjoyed even greater
religious freedom than did Scotland, which would indicate, once again, that
Scotland did not occupy such a unique place "in the world." While the independence of the local congregation needs to be recognized, a contrary principle
better explains the important connection between Presbyterianism and the
Restoration Movement.

If religious groups were indeed permitted to develop independent of
church authority, then precisely the opposite would have occurred: they could
and would have remained in the Presbyterian Church. In fact, John Glas, Barton Stone and Thomas Campbell were all forced to account for themselves and
their ideas before official church authorities. Their refusal to submit to those institutions is what stimulated the development of a new religious organization.

So it is not so much that "church authority" was lacking as the fact that Protestantism in general and Presbyterianism in particular attempted to maintain a dual source of authority: Scripture, as the ultimate God-given authority for all Christians, but also an earthly authority which Christ handed down to his Church. In the seventeenth century, a very authority-conscious age indeed, and in a Presbyterian context, church authority tended to manifest itself in a creed, namely the Westminster Confession.

The tension implicit in this division of authority (and of course it was not viewed as divisive but rather as complementary) was that individuals were encouraged to read the Bible for themselves but were also expected to adhere to the creedal statement. In practice the system worked very well, but there was always the possibility that someone might not see creedal authority as having the proper basis in scriptural authority.

Stated another way, Presbyterianism can be traced back to its Calvinist origins as embodying a rather radical theology and ecclesiology which rejected sacramental Catholicism, a hierarchical episcopacy and medieval devotional practice for a much simpler, Bible-centered New Testament Church. This is true of most Protestantism. What distinguished Presbyterianism was the rather conservative polity and organizational genius which Calvin devised, which, while different in structure from the episcopate, was nevertheless very effective in developing and enforcing a rigid orthodoxy. That orthodoxy was heavily doctrinal and creedal; deviation was not tolerated for very long. As a result there was a tension within Presbyterianism which fostered both an interest in New Testament Christianity and a fair amount of local autonomy to practice it, together with an orthodoxy and enforcing agent, the synod. Therefore, there was an environment which encouraged Restoration ideas rooted in a strict evangelical spirit, but which forced adherents of those more radical ideas out of the church because they conflicted with the accepted orthodoxy.[2] In a more relaxed congregational organization these more radical ideas might have coexisted with orthodoxy for a time until one was absorbed by the other. In a less evangelical context, the conflict between Scripture on the one hand, and creed and practice on the other may never have surfaced at all. But in Presbyterianism, a lively dynamic between a strict biblicism and a strong church organization formed a fertile environment for the development of the Restoration Movement.

Robert Richardson, the first biographer of Alexander Campbell, had a much less sanguine view of Scottish Presbyterianism:

> No despotism, indeed, could be more complete than that sought to be established by the Church of Scotland, which exercised, by means of its clerical machinery, a real inquisitorial authority over men's minds and consciences...[3]

The tyranny of the presbyterial system, as Richardson saw it, was responsible for the growth of various reform movements.[4] These "Scotch Independents" were a diverse group which nonetheless were precursors of the Restoration Movement and which certainly influenced the thought of the Campbells.

How influential were dissenters such as Glas, Sandeman and the Haldanes on the Restoration Movement? This is a matter of debate. Alexander Campbell himself gave indications both that he was and was not influenced by them. The real value of examining these men and their ideas is to demonstrate that the Restoration Movement had deep European roots and that a good many of Campbell's most important ideas were known and had been debated for some time. In effect, the ideas of these eighteenth-century reformers provide the historical context for the Restoration Movement.

John Glas

John Glas was born on September 21, 1695 at Auchtermuchty, Scotland. He attended school in Perth and college at St. Andrews and Edinburgh. Glas' father was a minister in the Church of Scotland and Glas himself was ordained and became minister of the Tealing parish in the Presbytery of Dundee.

Glas' ministry went well until he came upon the question in the Presbyterian Catechism, "How doth Christ execute the office of a king?" The answer in the Larger Catechism reads in part, "Christ executeth the office of a king, in calling out of the world a people to himself; and giving them officers, laws, and censures, by which he visibly governs them;..."[5] The controversy in which Glas was to become enmeshed revolved around the relationship between church and state. In the Scottish context the debate was over the covenants.

Early in the Scottish Reformation confessions of faith were ratified by the king and imposed on all his subjects. In 1638 the National Covenant defended the reformed religion and pledged resistance to innovations. In 1643, at the beginning of the English Civil War, the Solemn League and Covenant was signed. This covenant agreed to establish a uniform religion for England, Scotland and Ireland. Moreover, since the Assembly which drafted the covenant was dominated by Presbyterians, it concluded that government by Presbytery is "expressly instituted or commanded" in the New Testament as the proper polity of the Church. In Scotland, as illustrated in the excerpt above from the Larger Catechism, a strong majority of Presbyterians came to believe that the "Lord Jesus is the sole King and Head of the Church, and has appointed a spiritual government in the hands of chosen representatives."[6]

During the first few years of his ministry Glas was moving towards a position that rejected the covenants and replaced them with a new idea of the nature of the Church. This view of church was manifested by the local congregation which was made up of believers who had experienced God's saving grace. As he made these ideas known, the congregation at Tealing split and Glas and some of the members founded an independent congregation nearby. Glas' position was not widely known until circumstances brought him together with John Willison, an ardent supporter of the covenants, in 1726. The public debate that ensued brought Glas and his ideas to the attention of the Presbyterian authorities.

As Glas' case was wending its way through the Presbytery of Dundee and various synods, he wrote *The Testimony of the King of Martyrs Concerning His Kingdom* in 1727. It denounced state religion as unscriptural. A year later the Synod of Angus and Mearns submitted twenty-six questions to Glas. When asked if it was warrantable to carry on reformation by national covenanting, he replied: "It is my opinion, that the covenants commonly called the National Covenant, and the Solemn League and Covenant were without warrant in God's word; and that all the true reformation that has been in these lands, was carried on by the word and Spirit of the Lord Jesus, by the New Testament."[7] And when asked if there is no warrant for a national church under the New Testament or not, he replied: "It is my opinion: for I can see no churches instituted by Christ, in the New Testament, beside the universal, but congregational churches."[8] Based on his replies, the Synod suspended Glas from any exercise of his ministry. Subsequently he was deposed from the ministry, a decision which was confirmed by the General Assembly of the Church of Scotland in 1730.

Robert Sandeman

Robert Sandeman possessed a more dynamic personality than Glas and became the disseminator of Glas' ideas in Scotland, England and in the North American colonies. Born in Perth, Scotland in 1718, Sandeman was introduced to the ideas of John Glas at an early age through his father's membership in Glas' fellowships at Tealing and Dundee. Robert's father planned a career for him in the Church of Scotland, and around 1734 Robert was sent to Edinburgh to begin his studies. Shortly after entering the university, Sandeman met Glas and was won over to his teachings. By 1735 he had abandoned the idea of a career in the Church of Scotland and returned to Perth where he established a weaving business with his brother William. Both Robert and his youngest brother Thomas married daughters of Glas and by the 1740's Robert was devoting himself fulltime to promoting the establishment and growth of congregations devoted to Glas' ideas.

Sandeman's fame rested on his response to James Hervey's popular book *Dialogues Between Theron and Aspasio* published in 1755. Hervey had been a student of John Wesley and a member of the Oxford "Holy Club."[9] Sandeman communicated directly with Hervey for a time and then issued a reply in 1757 entitled *Letters on Theron and Aspasio*. Both Hervey's and Sandeman's books are quite lengthy and treat diverse subjects. Among them emerges one which is particularly relevant because it foreshadowed an important aspect of Alexander Campbell's theology.

The controversy over the nature of "saving faith" was a lively one well into the nineteenth century. In 1888, for example, a debate began between W. H. Whitsitt, a Baptist, and G.W. Longan, a Disciple, over whether or not the Disciples were an offshoot of "Sandemanianism," in this subject and in many other matters.[10] This was but one chapter of the sometimes heated debate between Baptists and Disciples.

Simply put, the debate between Hervey and Sandeman can be summed up by the question, "Does a miraculous change of heart precede faith, or does faith come first by a simple intellectual act of accepting the Gospel as true?" Sandeman begins his critique of Hervey by defining faith as the "entrance into the Christian religion." He expresses surprise that Aspasio finds Theron in hopeful circumstances because the latter has repented his sins although he has not yet expressed his faith in Jesus Christ. Sandeman suggests that mercy, especially divine mercy, is not related to misery. In other words, we do not merit saving grace through our very sincere awareness of our sinfulness. Saving grace is a free gift from God.[11] The influence of Calvin's theology can hardly be overlooked here.

A good deal of Sandeman's argument focuses on Luke's account (23: 39-43) of the good thief, which he concedes illustrates how a change of heart won the dying thief a place in Paradise. Sandeman argues, however, that such a change was extraordinary since it depended on the death of the Savior himself which cannot reoccur. He continues: "We are left to conclude, then, that the ordinary way of attaining good hope, is by endeavouring to make our hearts beat time to the moving addresses of a fervent preacher."[12] It is difficult to escape the conclusion that Sandeman is attacking the "fervent preaching" of contemporaries such as George Whitefield, whose preaching was such an important part of the emotional Great Awakening in America.[13]

Somewhat later, immediately preceding an extensive quotation from *Theron and Aspasio* of a description of a classic conversion experience, Sandeman makes a telling critique of the psychology of the "popular preachers":

> I proceed now to take notice of another notable artifice, by which they set aside the divine sovereignty. They urge the hearer to believe, that Christ is as *willing* to save him as he is *able*. This, at first view, seems somewhat plausible; and the hearer is led to think it would be impious to move any objection. But here it must be considered, that so soon as any man knows that Christ is willing to save him, he knows that he shall infallibly be saved, seeing it is simply impossible, that the divine will can be frustrated. Here the preachers, who seldom fail to find some subterfuge or other,

are ready to extricate themselves, by giving us to understand, that Christ is willing to save him, whose will is previously well disposed to accept of him in all his offices, so is ready to obey all his commandments. Thus the divine willingness to save him, which the hearer is called to believe, and which is displayed before him, with many high-sounding words of divine grace, turns out to no more account than the above-mentioned grant or deed of gift.[14]

After refuting what he considers to be the pretensions of the "popular preachers," who use the example of the good thief to buttress their argument, Sandeman attempts his own explanation of saving grace:

We may now proceed to take notice of the capital absurdity of the popular doctrine. It leads us to read the New Testament backwards. It sets before us the several effects or fruits of faith, or rather certain operations of its own, under the sacred names of these effects; and then prompts us to work our way to faith, by first attaining or feeling these effects. Hence it is, that we have so many treatises describing to us the previous steps necessary to be taken in order to conversion.[15]

In attempting to reverse the "New Testament backwards," Sandeman appeals to revelation. He states that the first apostolic converts began by believing, or coming to the knowledge of the truth. This is a key point in Sandeman's thought. He rejects conversion for what he calls "bare faith":

Thence it will appear, that justification comes by bare faith. Ask a Christian, What's his faith, the spring of all his hope? and he answers you in a word, The blood of Christ. Ask a proficient in the popular doctrine the same question, and he immediately begins to tell you a long-winded story, how grace enabled him to become a better man than he was, and this he calls *conversion*. Thus we see what a wide difference there is betwixt the false and true grace of God.[16]

If justification comes from faith, then what is faith? At one point Sandeman responds simply that "If they hold the gospel to be true, this is faith."[17] A bit later on Sandeman writes more fully on the subject. He asserts that faith and belief are essentially synonymous. We believe, for example, what a person says when we are persuaded that what he or she says is true. Faith, then, is closely related to truth. "When once a man believes a testimony, he becomes possessed of a truth; and that truth may be said to be his faith. Yea, we have no idea of truth, but with reference to its being believed."[18] Sandeman continues, "As the whole efficacy of faith flows from the nature and importance of the thing testified, he who is justified by faith, is justified by what he believes. He has peace with God; not conscious of any difference betwixt himself and others; but hearing that Jesus is the Christ, or that he hath fulfilled all righteousness, which now becomes to him a truth, so his faith."

Just as faith is linked to truth, truth is the same truth which the Apostles believed and is therefore associated with the truth of the early Church:

> Every one who believes the same truth which the apostles believed, has equally precious faith with them. He has unfeigned faith, and shall assuredly be saved. If any man's faith be found insufficient to save him, it is owing to this, that what he believed for truth, was not the very same thing that the apostles believed, but some lie connected with or dressed up in the form of truth. So this faith can do him no good; because, however seriously and sincerely he believes, yet that which he believes is false, and therefore it cannot save him. There is but one genuine truth that can save men.[19]

The saving truth which the apostles believed was that "Jesus is the Christ." The apostles had but one uniform fixed sense of these words and that sense is contained in the New Testament, "...faith comes by hearing, and hearing by the word of God."[20] We can do nothing to contribute to truth and so faith does not come by human endeavors.[21] We return to the notion of "bare faith":

> Every one who believes that *Jesus is the Christ* in a different sense from the apostles, or who maintains any thing in connection with these words subversive of their real meaning, believes a falsehood; so his faith cannot save him. In the days of the apostles many affirmed along with them, that *Jesus is the Christ,* who yet meant very differently from them. The far greater part of Christendom will affirm in like manner; yet we shall not easily find many who, when they come to explain themselves, have the same meaning with the apostles.[22]

In this way Robert Sandeman presented a very rational idea of faith, synonymous with truth, revealed in the "gospel-history" and believed simply because God himself is the historian.[23] Similar tendencies toward a "head religion" can be found in the theology of Alexander Campbell along with a proclivity to speak of "truth" as possessing only one possible sense. [24]

The Haldanes

With the Haldane brothers we come still closer to the world of Thomas and Alexander Campbell. Robert was born in 1764 and James, his brother, in 1768.

Orphaned at an early age, the brothers were raised by their maternal grandmother and their uncles. The boys received a good education and then followed in the footsteps of their uncle, Admiral Duncan, by entering the Royal Navy. By the time they were in their thirties, both brothers had married, given up their naval careers and found themselves drawn towards the ministry.

Robert initiated two philanthropic missionary efforts. The first was an attempt to go as a missionary to India; the second to educate some children from Sierra Leone and return them to Africa as missionaries. With the failure of both enterprises, the brothers turned their attention towards home.[25] In 1797 they became involved with John Campbell of Edinburgh in the establishment of Sunday Schools for the children of the poor. The following year they began in Edinburgh a society for the propagation of the faith at home. Notably unconcerned about doctrine, the brothers stated in their first address:

> It is not our desire to form or to extend the influence of any sect. Our whole intention is, to make known the evangelical gospel of the Lord Jesus Christ. In employing itinerants, schoolmasters or others, we do not consider ourselves as conferring ordination upon them or appointing them to the pastoral office. We only propose, by sending them out, to supply the means of grace wherever we perceive a deficiency.[26]

James began a career as an itinerant preacher while Robert continued to support various enterprises from his personal fortune. In 1799 he founded his own seminary in order to train men as evangelists. Around this time the brothers came into intimate contact with several men who were in the process of breaking their ties with the official Church of Scotland. In 1798 they invited Rowland Hill, an English evangelist, to tour Scotland. They leased the Edinburgh Circus in which Hill preached several times, sometimes to as many as ten or fifteen thousand people.

One of the most influential of the Haldanes' associates was Greville Ewing. Ewing, a native of Edinburgh, was ordained a minister in the Church of Scotland in 1793. Early on he became a key participant in the missionary enterprise to India and in the home mission effort. Ewing resigned from the Church of Scotland in 1798 and shortly thereafter he was one of the ministers who ordained James Haldane. When Robert Haldane established his seminary in Edinburgh in January 1799 he appointed Ewing its head. A few months later both Ewing and the school moved to Glasgow, but the arrangement did not last long. Disagreements over the financial support of the seminary — aggravated, no doubt, by a growing dispute over the proper administering of baptism — led to the resignation of Ewing and the removal of the seminary back to Edinburgh.

Ewing was particularly important in the development of many of the ideas associated with the Haldanes, and was responsible for their acceptance of the writings of Glas and Sandeman, especially regarding the simplicity of faith and the primacy of the Scriptures.[27] The Haldanes rejected, however, the Sandemanian intellectual definition of faith. They adhered to a congregational form of church government, the practice of celebrating the Lord's Supper every Sunday, and the baptism of believers only, by immersion.

The controversial names Glas, Sandeman, and the Haldanes were often invoked by critics of Alexander Campbell in attempts to trace his ideas back to some old "heresy." In response to this technique of criticism he responded in 1827:

> To call me a Sandemanian, a Haldanean, a Glasite, an Arian or a Unitarian, and to tell the world that the Sandemanians, Haldaneans, etc., etc., have done so and so, and have been refuted by such and such a person, is too cheap a method of maintaining human traditions, and too weak to oppose reason and revelation. You might as well nickname me a Sabellian, an Anthropomorphist, a Gnostic, a Nicolaitan, or an Anabaptist, as to palm upon me any of the above systems. I do most unequivocally and sincerely renounce each and every one of these systems.[28]

Campbell felt sincerely and probably accurately that he was not beholden to any one thinker for his views on the Christian religion. But no person thinks in isolation. Without labeling Thomas and Alexander Campbell, it seems certain that many of the ideas attributable to the Restoration Movement can be traced back to the historical context in which the Campbells lived. John Glas emphasized the separation of church and state, a dislike for creeds and a preference for the authority of Scripture to which, he believed, nothing could be added. Robert Sandeman developed a theology which emphasized the precedence of faith and tended to equate faith with truth. The Haldanes instituted the celebration of the Lord's Supper each Sunday, insisted on baptism of believers by immersion and were certainly less aggressive and confrontational than Sandeman in their approach to Christian unity. All of these men insisted on a strict congregationalism which they saw as scriptural; that only deacons and elders were scripturally authorized church offices; and on the plurality of elders in each congregation. All of these ideas play an important role in the Restoration Movement.

Certainly Alexander Campbell had close contact with some of these men and their ideas. Rowland Hill preached at Rich Hill, Campbell's village, on one of his evangelistic tours. James Haldane preached there as well. During the time he studied at Glasgow, Alexander Campbell developed a very intimate relationship with Greville Ewing and was frequently to dinner or tea at Ewing's home.[29]   Moreover, Glas, Sandeman, and the Haldanes established an American presence which may be considered a forerunner of the Restoration Movement. Sandeman himself came to New England in 1764. He had been invited by some New England Congregationalists who had become interested in Sandeman's ideas after the publication of an American edition of *Letters on Theron and Aspasio.* Sandeman created as much controversy in New England as he had in Great Britain. By the time he died at Danbury Connecticut in 1771 he had created a good many opponents and a few congregations that espoused his ideas. This movement grew despite a split in its ranks, and one of these factions eventually affiliated itself with the movement headed by Alexander Campbell in 1817.[30]

Restoration connections with the Haldanes are even more obvious. Walter Scott, who was to become the famous evangelist of the Restoration Movement, was hired to teach in a Pittsburgh academy founded by George Forrester who was deeply influenced by the ideas of the Haldanes.[31] Scott later visited a congregation of "Scotch Baptists" in New York City led by Henry Errett. Henry's son, Isaac, later became perhaps the most influential leader of the Restoration Movement after the death of Alexander Campbell.[32] Finally, Alexander Campbell himself traveled to England and Scotland in 1847 and made personal contact with many of the congregations which had a close association with Glas, Sandeman and the Haldane brothers.[33] All this leads to the conclusion made by Robert Richardson regarding the "reformatory movement then progressing in Scotland", "... a movement from which Mr. Campbell received his first impulse as a religious reformer, and which may be justly regarded, indeed, as the *first phase* of that religious reformation which he subsequently carried out so successfully to its legitimate issues."[34]

To return to an earlier theme, the one trait which Glas, Sandeman, the Haldanes and the Campbells all had in common was Scottish Presbyterianism. But the Campbells were members of a particular subgroup of Scottish Presbyterianism. The Campbells came originally from Argyl in western Scotland. At some point they relocated to northern Ireland. Archibald Campbell, Alexander's grandfather, was born a Catholic but converted to Anglicanism some time in mid-life. Alexander's father, Thomas, was born in 1763 in County Down, Ireland. He became a Presbyterian.

Thomas Campbell

In 1712 the Church of Scotland attempted to enforce the existing laws of patronage, depriving the congregations of the privilege of choosing their own pastors and instead giving that responsibility to the local landlords. Protests went unheeded and by 1733 a split was formalized with the formation of a new presbytery which became the nucleus of a new group known as "Seceders." The Seceders spread throughout Scotland and into northern Ireland as well.[35] Thomas Campbell became a member of this Secession Church.

Although the separation was based on a dispute between church and state, there were some theological ramifications as well. W.E. Garrison has called the Secession of 1733 "a counter-reformation of Calvinism" and has suggested that it was a movement comparable to the Wesleyan revival in England. Presumably he is alluding to the fact that both were movements away from the official church but which maintained ties to Presbyterianism and Anglicanism, respectively, for some time. In actual fact they were quite different in spirit as illustrated in this story cited by Garrison:

> The difference between the two, as regards their view of the Scriptures, was exhibited in a conference between Whitefield and Moncrieff, one of the leaders of the Secession, during an evangelistic tour by the former in Scotland. In discussing a point of church polity, Whitefield dissented from an opinion which had been expressed. Laying his hand over his heart, he said with emotion, "I do not find it here." Moncrieff replied, as he slapped the Bible that lay before him, "But, sir, I find it here!"[36]

These kinds of differences were maintained on the American frontier between Methodists and "Christians."

The Secession Church itself split into two parties in 1747. The issue this time was whether members of the Church should swear an oath to adhere to the "religion presently professed in this realm." The question, therefore, was whether the oath referred to Presbyterianism in general (including Seceders) or to the established Church of Scotland. Those who supported the oath became known as Burghers, those who opposed it, Anti-burghers. Finally, in 1795 still another division developed among both Burghers and Anti-burghers over the power of civil magistrates in religion. Thus there were "Old Lights" and "New Lights" in both parties.

Thomas Campbell was an Old Light, Anti-Burgher, Seceder Presbyterian. In its historical context this was a radical position because of its vehemence in rejecting any connection between church and state. Another insight into the Campbells' thought can be gleaned by the fact that Thomas Campbell was active in promoting union between the Burghers and Anti-Burghers. In fact, Campbell took his plea for reunification to both the Synod of Belfast and the General Synod of Scotland.[37] We do not have to go much beyond the personal experiences of Thomas and Alexander Campbell in order to understand their rejection of sectarianism and their interest in the unity of the Church of Christ. Radicalism with a strong unity motive were "Restoration" ideas with strong roots in elements of Scottish Presbyterianism.

The narrative history of the life of Thomas and Alexander Campbell has been told many times. What follows is simply a brief synopsis of events which lead to the founding of the Restoration Movement in the United States.

Thomas Campbell was born on February 1, 1763 in County Down, Ireland. After a few years of schoolteaching, Thomas was drawn to the Seceder Presbyterian Church and to the ministry. He studied at the University of Glasgow from 1783 to 1786 and then attended the theological school of the Anti-Burgher division of the Seceder Presbyterian Church. Shortly after completing his theological studies, he returned to Ireland and married Jane Corneigle. Their first son, Alexander, was born in 1788. After teaching and preaching in the vicinity of his father's home in Sheepbridge, Thomas Campbell became minister to a congregation in Ahorey in 1798. Ahorey was a small town about two miles from Rich Hill and thirty miles southwest of Belfast.[38]

In April 1807 Thomas Campbell left Ireland, his wife, and seven children for America. Most authors cite ill health as the reason for his departure, his doctor having recommended a sea voyage. Disappointment over his failure to heal the breach in the Seceder Church might have been a contributing factor. Certainly the route from northern Ireland to America had been made easier by decades of migration and Thomas Campbell may have been motivated like those before him by the poverty of his native country and the opportunity of the New World.

On May 13, 1807 Thomas Campbell landed in Philadelphia and learned that the Associate Synod of North America was in session at that very time in the city. The Synod was in reality the organization of the Anti-Burghers, but since the Burghers had never organized in America it was in effect the organization of all Seceder Presbyterians. Campbell presented his credentials and was cordially welcomed into the Synod. He specifically requested and was granted assignment to the Presbytery of Chartiers because its jurisdiction included Washington, Pennsylvania, where many of his friends had relocated from Ireland. Campbell received preaching assignments in Pittsburgh and in points between that town and Washington beginning July 1, 1807. Within a few months, however, he was facing serious charges before the Synod.

On October 27, 1807 charges were brought against Thomas Campbell which cast doubt on his orthodoxy. Not long after he was admitted into the Chartiers Presbytery, Campbell was given the task of visiting some of the widely scattered Anti-Burgher Presbyterians up the Allegheny River. He was accompanied by William Wilson, a fellow minister. One of the principal purposes of the trip was to observe the Lord's Supper among the scattered faithful in this remote part of the frontier. Here is the origin of Campbell's difficulties in the words of Robert Richardson:

...Mr. Campbell's sympathies were strongly aroused in regard to the destitute condition of some in the vicinity who belonged to other branches of the Presbyterian family, and who had not, for a long time, had an opportunity of partaking of the Lord's Supper, and he felt it his duty, in the preparation sermon, to lament the existing divisions, and to suggest that all his pious hearers, who felt so disposed and duly prepared, should, without respect to party differences, enjoy the benefits of the communion season then providentially afforded them.[39]

At the time of this trip Wilson said nothing of any disgreement with Campbell. However, rumors began to spread and a short time later a Reverend Anderson refused to accept an appointment by the Presbytery to assist Campbell in administering the Lord's Supper. He offered as his excuse Campbell's alleged deviation from orthodoxy. At the regular meeting of the Presbytery in October 1807, a committee was formed to investigate the accusations and if necessary to draw up formal charges in the form of a "Libel." Less than four months after beginning to preach in the United States, Thomas Campbell was involved in a controversy with the Seceder Prebyterians over questions of both doctrine and discipline.

It is surprising that previous writers have not commented much on why, apparently, Thomas Campbell evoked no accusations of heterodoxy during all the years he ministered in Ireland, and yet how almost immediately he stirred considerable opposition on the Pennsylvania frontier. Richardson has suggested that the action of the Synod was motivated by personal envy.[40] John Anderson, who began the controversy by his refusal to serve with Campbell, was appointed to the committee created to investigate the charges. The other three members of the committee were all former students of Anderson. In effect, then, the principal accusers of Thomas Campbell were also his judges. It is entirely possible that at least part of the hostility toward Thomas Campbell was rooted in a personal resentment on the part of a small group of frontier ministers toward a newcomer with all the credentials of a European university education.[41]

A more general analysis can be attempted. It is true that one of the notable influences on Thomas Campbell was the Independent congregation at Rich Hill, which was located just a few miles from his own congregation at Ahorey, Ireland. It was at Rich Hill that Campbell heard the preaching of Independents such as Rowland Hill, Alexander Carson, John Walker, and James Haldane. Some of the attitudes which Campbell would have encountered at Rich Hill were a certain liberality in allowing preachers of all opinions the use of the meeting house, an emphasis on the right of private judgment combined with the independence of the local congregation, and a hostility towards the close connection between church and state. All of these ideas came into play during Campbell's confrontation with the Presbytery of Chartiers.

It is plausible to suggest that one of the reasons that Campbell left Ireland for the United States is that he felt he would have greater freedom in America to practice some of these unorthodox ideas. He may have become more aggressive in openly expressing these ideas in the United States than he had previously. This would explain why he had not had similar difficulty with the synod in Ireland. Instead it is likely that Campbell was confronted with a Seceder Presbyterianism which was motivated by an impulse contrary to his own. It is likely that the Seceders, confronted with the greater diversity of denominationalism on the frontier, instead drew inward and sought to protect their identity. After all, the whole history of Secederism was marked by a willingness to split and split again to preserve a strict orthodoxy. In 1796, for example, the Associate Synod had passed an act prohibiting "occasional communion," or communion with other bodies of Christians. Thomas Campbell and the Chartiers Synod were travelling in opposite directions which was bound to lead to strain and perhaps a break. In other words the origin of the Restoration Movement in the United States was intertwined with the history of the Presbyterian Church.

In 1935 William H. Hanna published a biography of Thomas Campbell. In the course of his research Hanna had discovered the minutes of the Chartiers Presbytery and the Seceder Synod and much of his book is devoted to the controversy between Campbell and the Seceder Presbyterians. It remains the definitive account of this episode in Campbell's life. What follows here is a brief summary of that account for the purpose of understanding the origins of some of the principal ideas of the Restoration Movement.

At the meeting of the Presbytery in January 1808, a Libel was produced which charged Thomas Campbell with seven errors. The Libel charged that the accused:[42]

1. Holds that "...a person's appropriation of Christ to himself as his own Saviour, does not belong to the essence of Saving Faith; but only to a high degree of it."

2. Asserts "...that a church has no divine warrant for holding Confessions of Faith as terms of communion."

3. Asserts "...that it is the duty of ruling elders to pray and exhort publickly in vacant congregations."

4. Asserts that it is permissible to "...hear ministers that are in stated opposition to our testimony."

5. Asserts that "...Our Lord Jesus Christ was not subject to the precept as well as the penalty of the law in the stead of his people or as their surety."

6. Asserts that "... any man is able in this life to live without sin in thought, word and deed."

7. Has preached "... in a congregation where any of our ministers are settled, without any regular call or appointment."

Mr. Campbell's response to the fifth and sixth charges were found to be basically acceptable, his views on the others were not. The first article of the Libel dealt with "saving faith." Basically, Campbell refused to accept the idea that any sort of mystical or emotional experience resulting in the assurance of salvation was an essential element of saving faith. In his response to the charge Campbell testified: "But that this faith may be in lower degrees of it where the assurance is not; that therefore this assurance can not be of the essence of faith: for if it were, then none that had true faith, could be possibly without it."[43] A few sentences above Campbell testified that "...it is the right of all that hear the gospel so to believe upon the bare declaration, invitation and promise of God..." There is some justification for detecting a connection between this statement and the idea of an intellectual "bare faith" espoused by Robert Sandeman in the previous century.

It is significant that this charge was the first listed against Thomas Campbell because it is anticipatory of the theological divergences which were to separate the Campbells from other religious groups on the American frontier. Actually it is not surprising that the nature of faith became a source of disagreement when it is considered that Dr. Anderson, Campbell's principal antagonist, wrote a book entitled *The Appropriation Which is The Nature of Saving Faith.* This same Anderson and the rest of the committee composed the Libel. They cite as part of their authority the *Larger Catechism,* Question 72, which in part reads: "Justifying faith is a saving grace, wrought in the heart of a sinner, by the Spirit and word of God; whereby he, being convinced of his sin and misery, and of the disability in himself and all other creatures to recover him out of his lost condition, not only assenteth to the truth of the promise of the gospel, but receiveth and resteth upon Christ and his righteousness... for pardon of sin...[44] This passage above all reveals that Thomas Campbell, and later the Restoration Movement, was in large part a rejection of the predominant form of frontier religion which was above all a repository of Calvinism.

The second article of the Libel was more straightforward. Regarding the use of Confessions of Faith as terms of communion, Campbell responded that it is lawful to use them for such a purpose "insofar as our testimony requires." Suspecting quite correctly that Campbell was being too diplomatic, he was asked what he meant when he said at Monture's Run "that we have neither precept nor example in Scripture for Confessions of Faith and Testimonies." He answered "that there was no formal nor express precept to that purpose."[45]

Like the first, Campbell was found guilty of the second charge. Rejection of Confessions of Faith as terms of communion was to become one of the central ideas of American Restorationism.

Campbell did not dispute the third article and admitted that he held that it was the duty of ruling elders to pray and exhort publicly in vacant congregations. Once again he echoes an idea found in both Glas and Sandeman who, unlike orthodox Presbyterians, made no distinction between ruling and teaching elders.[46] Campbell's opinion anticipates the Restoration idea of making little distinction between clergy and laity.

The fourth article touched on another doctrine which was to become an important tenet of Restorationism and Campbell made no effort to hide his opinion from the Presbytery. He answered: "I believe that in the present broken and divided state of the church, when Christians have not an opportunity of hearing those of their own party, it is lawful for them to hear other ministers preach the gospel where the publick worship is not corrupted with matters of human invention."[47] Campbell's opinion that the divisions within the Church were scandalous and that the origin of the division lay mostly in humanly contrived creeds was rightly discerned by the Presbytery who found Campbell guilty of the charge.

Finally, as to the charge that he invaded Reverend Ramsey's parish Thomas Campbell replied: "...I acknowledge that I preached at Canonsburg, but not in a congregation where any of our ministers is settled, nor yet without a regular call, as I conceive I have appointment to preach the gospel and the call of some of the most regular and respectable people of that vicinity to preach thereof which I can produce sufficient testimonials if required."[48] The Presbytery recognized that this response was insufficiently respectful of its authority and found Campbell guilty of the charge.

On February 12, 1808 the Presbytery of Chartiers suspended Thomas Campbell from preaching. Campbell appealed to the Associate Synod of North America which functioned as the highest court of the American Seceders. The deliberations of the Synod were largely technical. Basically, the Synod found Campbell guilty of the charges, observing that his answers to them were "...so evasive, unsatisfactory and highly equivocal upon great and important articles of revealed religion as to give ground to conclude that he has expressed sentiments very different upon these articles from the sentiments held and professed by this church; and are sufficient ground to infer censure."[49] On the other hand, the Synod reversed the decision of the Presbytery to suspend Campbell, voting instead to "rebuke and admonish" and to lift the suspension if he submitted.

Mr. Campbell did submit and he was given preaching assignments in Philadelphia for two months before being sent back to his own presbytery. But all was not well. When he returned to western Pennsylvania he found that no appointment for him to preach had been made. It was perfectly clear that there was great personal animosity towards him in the presbytery and that they accepted him as a member only because they had been ordered to do so by the synod. Within a few weeks the break was complete. On September 13, 1808 the minutes of the Chartiers Presbytery read: "...then in his own name and in the name of all who adhered to him, he declined the authority of this Presbytery for reasons formerly given, the authority of the Associate Synod of North America and all the courts subordinate thereto; and all further communion with them."[50] On May 23, 1809, it is recorded in the minutes from a meeting of the Synod that Mr. Campbell had returned the sum of fifty dollars which had been given to him on his arrival from Ireland two years before. On April 18, 1810 the Presbytery deposed its suspended member from the ministry, which was a formality since Thomas Campbell had already made his break with Seceder Presbyterianism.

The Christian Association and the "Declaration and Address"

We really do not know Thomas Campbell's state of mind in the months following his separation from the Seceder Presbyterians. It would be surprising if he had not been filled with self-doubt. In a very short period of time he found himself in a still strange country, cut off from the church in which he had ministered all his adult life, and separated from his wife and children. In one sense he was very much alone; in another he found himself at the center of a unique fellowship.

It seems very clear that Thomas Campbell continued to preach in the vicinity of Washington, Pennsylvania. He spoke to whomever wanted to hear him: Seceder Presbyterians, members of other denominations, the unchurched. Sometime in the early summer of 1809 a group of sympathizers met with Campbell at the home of Abraham Altars to discuss plans to form some kind of organization. Two important decisions emerged out of this meeting. The first was Campbell's decision to announce a guiding principle or rule: "That rule, my highly respected hearers, is this, that WHERE THE SCRIPTURES SPEAK, WE SPEAK AND WHERE THE SCRIPTURES ARE SILENT, WE ARE SILENT."[51] The implication of such a principle was apparent to those in attendance. Almost immediately one member of the group asserted that adoption of the rule would eliminate infant baptism. After an emotional discussion he left the group. Others would follow. The significance of Thomas Campbell's general principle is perhaps best and most dramatically summed up by Robert Richardson's comment: "It was from the moment when these significant words were uttered and accepted that the more intelligent ever afterward dated the *formal and actual commencement of the Reformation* which was subsequently carried on with so much success, and which has already produced such important changes in religious society over a large portion of the world."[52] The second decision was to conduct a second meeting.

On August 17, 1809 a meeting was held at "the head-waters of Buffalo Creek." It was resolved that they would form themselves into a regular association under the name "The Christian Association of Washington [Pennsylvania]." A committee was formed which determined the need to compose a written statement of the purposes and objectives of the association. Thomas Campbell was entrusted with the task.

The document which Thomas Campbell composed is known as the *Declaration and Address*. Along with *The Last Will and Testament of the Springfield Presbytery*, it is the most important document of the Restoration Movement because it contains at least the germ of nearly all the basic ideas of Restorationism.

The *Declaration and Address*, as first published, was fifty-six pages long and was divided into three parts. The first (three pages) was a Declaration of the reasons and purpose for the formation of the Christian Association; secondly, an Address (eighteen pages) which amplified the arguments of the previous section especially for the unity of all Christians; and thirdly, an Appendix (thirty-one pages) a series of explanations offered "to prevent mistakes," that is, possible criticisms. The original edition is dated September 7, 1809. Three months after this date a Postscript was written offering suggestions for the implementation of the Association's program. The most important sections are the first two because they contain the most succinct version of principles which were to guide the movement.

The Declaration contains four basic ideas. The first is the right of private judgment: "We are also persuaded that as no man can be *judged* for his brother, so no man can *judge* for his brother; every man must be allowed to judge for himself, as every man must bear his own judgment - must give account of himself to God."[53] With this statement Campbell places himself firmly in the Protestant tradition of personal accountability first articulated by Luther.

The right of private judgment is linked to the idea of the sole authority of the Scriptures: "We are also of opinion that as the Divine word is equally binding upon all, so all lie under an equal obligation to be bound by it, and it alone; and not by any human interpretation of it; and that, therefore, no man has a right to judge his brother, except in so far as he manifestly violates the express letter of the law."[54]

Thirdly, a condemnation of sectarian division: "Moreover, being well aware, from sad experience, of the heinous nature and pernicious tendency of religious controversy among Christians; tired and sick of the bitter jarrings and janglings of a party spirit, we would desire to be at rest; and, were it possible, we would also desire to adopt and recommend such measures as would give rest to our bretheren throughout all the churches: as would restore unity, peace, and purity to the whole Church of God."[55]

Finally, that the source of division among Christians is human opinion and the solution to division lies in the Scriptures alone:

> Our desire, therefore, for ourselves and our brethren would be, that, rejecting human opinions and the inventions of men as of any authority, or as having any place in the Church of God, we might forever cease from further contentions about such things; returning to and holding fast by the original standard; taking the Divine word alone for our rule; the Holy Spirit for our teacher and guide, to lead us into all truth; and Christ alone, as exhibited in the word, for our salvation; that, by so doing we may be at peace among ourselves, follow peace with all men, and holiness, without which no man shall see the Lord.[56]

The Declaration concludes with nine resolutions including the intention to form The Christian Association of Washington; for each member to subscribe to a certain sum to support the ministry; to form a Standing Committee; to meet at least twice a year, and so on. One further resolution makes it clear that the Association is not to be considered a church but that its members should be considered "...as voluntary advocates for Church reformation..."[57] The aspiration that ministers and members could join in the work of the Association while remaining members of their own churches was not realized since no other ministers joined, no missionaries were sent forth and no similar organizations were established.

The second part, the "Address," is essentially a plea for Christian unity and contains some of Thomas Campbell's most eloquent statements on the subject. Although they constitute only a small portion of the document, the thirteen propositions in the middle of the Address give a very clear delineation of the principles which were to become the Restoration Movement.

The first proposition is brief and so basic to understanding the thought of Thomas Campbell and his son that it may be quoted completely:

> That the Church of Christ upon earth is essentially, intentionally, and constitutionally one; consisting of all those in every place that profess their faith in Christ and obedience to him in all things according to the Scriptures, and that manifest the same by their tempers and conduct, and of none else; as none else can be truly and properly called Christians.[58]

Proposition Two recognizes the necessity of the existence of separate congregations, but asserts that there must be no uncharitable divisions among them and that they must be "perfectly joined together in the same mind."

Proposition Three is important because it offers the formula to accomplish unity:

...nothing ought to be inculcated upon Christians as articles of faith; nor required of them as terms of communion, but what is expressly taught and enjoined upon them in the word of God. Nor ought anything to be admitted, as of Divine obligation, in their Church Constitution and managements, but what is expressly enjoined by the authority of our Lord Jesus Christ and his apostles upon the New Testament Church; either in express terms or by approved precedent.

Although Proposition Four asserts that the Old and New Testaments are "inseparably connected" it makes the following distinction: "...the New Testament is as perfect a constitution for the worship, discipline, and government of the New Testament Church, and as perfect a rule for the particular duties of its members, as the Old Testament was for the worship, discipline, and government of the Old Testament Church..." This distinction was later to be amplified by Alexander Campbell and became one of the points of division between the Reformers and other Christian groups.

Proposition Five flows out of the previous two and is quite straightforward. "Nothing ought to be received into the faith or worship of the Church, or be made a term of communion among Christians, that is not as old as the New Testament."

Propositions Six and Seven are refinements of the previous proposition. The first states that while inferences and deductions from Scripture may be true doctrine, they cannot be made binding on the consciences of Christians "farther than they perceive the connection." They cannot be made terms of communion nor do they have any place in a church's confession. The second states that creeds ("doctrinal exhibitions") may be "highly expedient" but cannot be made terms of communion.

Proposition Eight states that it is not necessary for admission to the Church for people to have a knowledge and understanding of "all Divinely revealed truths." What is essential is a consciousness of sin, faith in Jesus Christ as savior, a profession of faith, and obedience to the word of God. The proviso that upon admission to the church no one should be required "to make a profession more extensive than their knowledge" may reflect just a certain simplicity or it may well indicate a rejection of the requirement to relate an experience of conversion which was common to the frontier religion of the time.[59]

The ninth proposes that all members of the Church "should love each other as brethren, children of the same family and Father." The tenth condemns divisions among Christians as "a horrid evil" and as antichristian, antiscriptural, and antinatural. The eleventh blames division on the neglect of the will of God and on the creation of human inventions as terms of communion.

The twelfth proposition is particularly important because it comes close to defining what the Church of Christ is. As such it provides a basis for discussion of the propositions as a whole:

> That all that is necessary to the highest state of perfection and purity of the Church upon earth is, first, that none be received as members but such as having that due measure of Scriptural self-knowledge described above, do profess their faith in Christ and obedience to him in all things according to the Scriptures; nor, secondly that any be retained in her communion longer than they to manifest the reality of their profession by their temper and conduct. Thirdly, that her ministers, duly and Scripturally qualified, inculcate none other things than those very articles of faith and holiness expressly revealed and enjoined in the word of God. Lastly, that in all their administrations they keep close by the observance of all Divine ordinances, after the example of the primitive Church, exhibited in the New Testament; without any additions whatsoever of human opinions or inventions of men.[60]

Proposition Twelve can be reduced to three principles. The first is that the Church is comprised of members who profess their faith in Jesus Christ and obey his scriptural commands. The second is that the Church is modeled on the example of the primitive Church. The third is that no human opinion or invention is to be added to that which is exhibited in the New Testament Church.

The thirteenth and last proposition states that if absolutely necessary to observe the divine ordinances, "expedients" may be adopted. It is important, however, that it be made clear that these expedients are of human not sacred origin so that they may be altered as needed without causing division.

The very first thing one notices about the Address is that, not surprisingly, it reflects Thomas Campbell's Protestant background. It tends to speak, for example, of church in an exclusively scriptural and congregational context and makes it clear that the Scriptures are the supreme and ultimate source of authority. Another Protestant characteristic is that the right to private interpretation of the Scriptures is again and again affirmed. Moreover, the Address adopts a radical Protestant perspective since it maintains that the New Testament contains a perfect model of Christian faith, life, worship, ordinances and government. In other words nothing was left to devise that had not already been established by Jesus and the apostles. Proceeding from this principle is the idea that all post-apostolic devices are merely "human opinions" or "deductions" and therefore function on a different and much lower level of authority than the New Testament.

Thomas Campbell's most apparent contribution to Protestant thought may have been the distinction he drew between the personal faith of the believer and the theological faith embodied in creeds.[61] By making the explicit rejection of creeds a central tenet of the Movement, Campbell moved beyond Reformation Protestantism. It should be kept in mind that the systematic theologies which the Reformation had developed were still very much operational in most denominations at the beginning of the nineteenth century, certainly in Presbyterianism. Once the unifying tendencies of these systematic theologies as manifested in creeds was lost, a new source of unity had to be designed. This 'new" source of unity was the New Testament and the practices of the primitive church.

While most of these ideas regarding the authority of the Scriptures can be found among other evangelical Protestant groups both in Scotland and in the United States, what distinguishes the Restoration Movement and in particular the *Declaration and Address* is the strong presence of a unity motive. Others certainly stressed the importance of the unity of the Church of Christ in Europe and in North America, but none combined evangelical Protestantism and the unity motive more powerfully than Thomas Campbell. What distinguishes Restorationism from Protestant ecumenism is that the Restoration Movement soon became an effort to eliminate denominations and to substitute an actual unification of the Church of Christ. Of course, it tended to define that unity in its own terms.

First of all, Campbell is actually advocating a "re-unification" since the unity motive is also related to the second and more general evangelical motive, which reveals that the Church which Jesus instituted in the New Testament was undisputedly singular. In other words, the unity of Christ's Church is not just a good deed; it is a scriptural necessity. As the very first proposition states, the apostolic church was essentially one. Its oneness is prescribed by the New Testament itself and therefore is binding on all Christians.

The means of effecting the reunification of the Church of Christ is also thoroughly evangelical, that is, it is to be accomplished by means of the New Testament. This too is an idea which has precedent, but which plays a unique and defining role in the Restoration Movement not found in other Protestant groups.

By the time Campbell was writing, evangelical Protestantism had already done away with the greater part of Catholic church structure. Therefore, when Thomas Campbell rejects creeds as inappropriate bases for communion he is left with very little alternative than to turn to Scripture alone as a means of restoring the unity of the Church. And since he has already made an important distinction between the Old and New Testaments (Proposition Four) he concludes that the path to unity lay through a strict adherence to the New Testament and to the model of the primitive church, what his son, Alexander, was to call the restoration of the ancient order of things.

If the New Testament is to be the means of unifying the Church (while purifying it as well), then clearly it is important that the Scriptures provide a clear basis for agreement. Therefore, Thomas Campbell is careful on several occasions to address the subject of the nature of the Scriptures. He categorizes the Bible, for example, as "the self-same thing to all" and Scripture as the "matter-of-fact evidence of the things referred to."[62]

In other words, Scripture ought to convey the same ideas to all. Campbell acknowledges that differences of opinion do exist but he explains that they originate not in Scripture itself but rather in deductions made from Scripture: "...there is a manifest distinction between an express Scripture declaration, and the conclusion or inference which may be deduced from it; and that the former may be clearly understood, even where the latter is but imperfectly if at all perceived."[63] Campbell is more circumspect subsequently when he admits that a perfect state of unity is not likely to result from the restoration of New Testament principles:

> Should it be further objected, that even this strict literal uniformity would neither infer nor secure unity of sentiment; it is granted that, in a certain degree, it would not; nor indeed, is there anything either in Scripture or the nature of things that should induce us to expect an entire unity of sentiment in the present imperfect state.[64]

It is clear that by "imperfect state" Campbell is referring to sectarianism.

There is in fact a large degree of ambiguity in Campbell's argument. He proposes that the New Testament can unite all Christians because it provides principles which are perfectly clear and impossible to disagree on. At the same time he acknowledges a certain imperfect reality which will prevent a perfect union. More important, he clearly embraces a reductionist argument. He distinguishes between essentials on which all can agree and which are the means of restoring the unity of the Church of Christ; and non-essentials, deductions or inferences about which we can agree to disagree without affecting unity. The problem, of course, is determining what is essential and what is non-essential and who distinguishes between the two. At still another point Campbell seems to back away from this question and refuses to distinguish between essentials and non- essentials.

> We dare neither assume nor propose the trite indefinite distinction between essentials and non-essentials, in matters of revealed truth and duty; firmly persuaded, that, whatever may be their comparative importance, simply considered, the high obligation

of the Divine authority revealing, or enjoining them renders the belief or performance of them absolutely essential to us, in so far as we know them.[65]

Thomas Campbell has reached an impasse. He perhaps realized this when in the Appendix, written "to prevent mistakes," he tried to answer the anticipated charge of latitudinarianism. Specifically, he lays out the accusation that he is willing to allow each person to profess belief in the Bible but practice what it contains in his or her own way. Campbell responds to this hypothetical accusation by repeating his belief that if people practice exactly what is in the Bible then there will be no disagreement since the Bible exhibits the same things to all. He rejects creeds as "a mere uniformity of words," as he rejects catechisms. And he steadfastly maintains that no one may judge or condemn a professing brother or sister.[66] He proposes a middle way between "a vague indefinite approbation of the Scriptures" and creeds:

> ...It must be a plain way, a way most graciously and most judiciously adapted to the capacity of the subjects, and consequently not the way of subscribing or otherwise approving human standards as a term of admission into his Church...It must be very far remote from logical subtilties and metaphysical speculations, and as such we have taken it up, upon the plainest and most obvious principles of divine revelation and common sense - the common sense, we mean, of Christians...Hence we have supposed, in the first place, the true discrimination of Christian character to consist in an intelligent profession of our faith in Christ and obedience to him in all things according to the Scriptures...[67]

The great difficulty presented by the *Declaration and Address* is that it proposes the New Testament as the means of restoring both the purity and the unity of the ancient Church without specifying how that was to be accomplished and without even acknowledging that it might be a difficult task. Despite clear indications that judgments would have to be made about what comprises "express Scripture declaration" and what comprises deduced inference, there is no attempt either to make those judgments or to construct a mechanism which would facilitate making such a determination. In fact it is quite clear that Thomas Campbell took great pains to stake out a position pointing in the opposite direction, namely that each individual had the right to interpret Scripture.

It is difficult to explain why Thomas Campbell did not understand the dilemma presented by making Scripture the means of effecting unity and purity without also establishing a means of interpreting certain passages or resolving contradictions. Presumably, the most logical method would have been to reduce essential beliefs to a minimum. While in some places Campbell seems to be leaning in this direction, in other places he specifically rejects this alternative. Another solution could have focused on the tension between the obligation to agree on essentials and the proposition that no one may judge another. In this case neither the individual nor the group as a whole but rather a part of the group, a minority or a majority, would determine what is sanctioned by the New Testament. This group would then force others to adhere to their decision or else would leave and form another group. This is very close to what did happen in the Restoration Movement, though it is difficult to believe that Thomas Campbell or even his more dynamic son Alexander could have advocated this path, given their great emphasis on the unity of the Church of Christ. In effect a choice needed to be made between the restoration of the New Testament and *int.* the unity motive.

Ultimately, it seems that a good deal of idealism must be read into the *Declaration and Address* and into the Restoration Movement as a whole. Thomas Campbell was a visionary. This is indicated by the fact that he quickly handed over leadership to his son, Alexander, declining involvement in the implementation of his ideas. He was content to announce and develop an idea which he believed to be true, and then to leave it to Providence to guide that idea to fruition. It is this idealism tempered by rather vague prose which is the legacy of the *Declaration and Address,* and it was a very unstable legacy indeed.

One of the keys to understanding the *Declaration and Address* is the philosophical background of Thomas Campbell. Campbell had attended Glasgow University from 1783 to 1786 where he may have heard Thomas Reid lecture. Reid published his most important works late in life. In fact his *Essays on the Intellectual Powers of Man* was published in 1785 while Campbell was still attending the university. It is significant that in the reference cited above Campbell uses the term "common sense, the common sense of Christians," language which is so reminiscent of Thomas Reid. Of course Reid was primarily interested in refuting Berkeley and Hume, but he did so by going back to Locke, who provides the real philosophical context for the *Declaration and Address.*

The points of contact between the thought of Locke and Thomas Campbell are several, even to the point where they sometimes share the same language. A good starting point is Locke's definition of church as a free and voluntary society. Because of this emphasis on freedom, the individual possesses the liberty to interpret Scripture according to personal conscience, or as Locke puts it, the right to join and withdraw from any church as one sees fit.[68]

Scripture occupies a central role in Locke's vision of Christianity. Because of its importance it is necessary to establish the possibility of agreement over the meaning of the New Testament. So Locke, like Campbell, argues that the proper interpretation of Scripture rests in "the plain direct meaning of the words and phrases,"[69] what Campbell would call the "matter of fact evidence" found in the Bible.

For similar reasons Locke tends towards a minimalist Christianity, and writes of "propositions" about which no one will disagree: "I know there are some propositions so evidently agreeable to scripture, that no-body can deny them to be drawn from thence: but about those therefore than [sic] can be no difference." The following section speaks in terms which are remarkably similar to those chosen by Thomas Campbell more than a century later. Although Locke is principally interested in promoting the idea of toleration, it is also clear that he traces the division of Christendom to deductions from Scripture imposed on people by the "sects":

> This only I say, that however clearly we may think this or the other
> doctrine to be deduced from scripture, we ought not therefore to
> impose it upon others, as a necessary article of faith, because we
> believe it to be agreeable to the rule of faith; unless we would be
> content also that other doctrines should be imposed upon us in
> the same manner; and that we should be compelled to receive
> and profess all the different and contradictory opinions of
> lutherans, calvinists, remonstrants, anabaptists, and other sects
> which the contrivers of symbols, systems, and confession, are ac-
> customed to deliver unto their followers as genuine and neces-
> sary deductions from the Holy Scripture. I cannot but wonder
> at the extravagant arrogance of those men who think that they
> themselves can explain things necessary to salvation more clear-
> ly than the Holy Ghost, the eternal and infinite wisdom of God.[70]

Both Locke and Campbell shared a distaste for the "arrogance" of deducing from Scripture, and an inclination to reduce Christianity to a very simple set of beliefs. Locke put it this way: "St. John knew nothing else required to be believed, for the attaining of life, but that 'Jesus is the Messiah, the Son of God.'"[71] Adding non-essential propositions to Scripture and making them terms of communion are the causes of disunity, an argument echoed by Campbell in Proposition Eleven of the *Declaration and Address*. Here is Locke:

> For when they have determined the Holy Scriptures to be the only
> foundation of faith, they nevertheless lay down certain proposi-
> tions as fundamental, which are not in the scripture; and because
> others will not acknowledge these additional opinions of theirs,
> nor build upon them as if they were necessary and fundamental,
> they withdrawing themselves from the others, or expelling the
> others from them.[72]

Locke's program for the unification of the Church of Christ is all but identical to the third Proposition in Campbell's *Declaration and Address*, namely to restore the purity of the Gospel. In fact the language used by Locke is so similar that it could well have been written by Thomas Campbell.

> But since men are so solicitous about the true church, I would only ask them here by the way, if it be not more agreeable to the Church of Christ to make the conditions of her communion consist in such things, and such things only, as the Holy Spirit has in the Holy Scriptures declared, in express words, to be necessary to salvation? I ask, I say, whether this be not more agreeable to the church of Christ, than for men to impose their own inventions and interpretations upon others, as if they were of divine authority; and to establish by ecclesiastical laws, as absolutely necessary to the profession of Christianity, such things as the Holy Scriptures do either not mention, or at lest [sic] not expressly command? Whosoever requires those things in order to ecclesiastical communion, which Christ does not require in order to life eternal, he may perhaps indeed constitute a society accommodated to his own opinion, and his own advantage; but how that can be called the church of Christ, which is established upon laws that are not his, and which excludes such persons from its communion, as he will one day receive into the kingdom of heaven, I understand not.[73]

Although their ultimate purpose may have varied, both John Locke and Thomas Campbell shared a common agenda for Christianity. They wanted to reduce it to a minimalist religion comprising only the express commands of Scripture. By eliminating human deductions, the purity of Scripture would be restored and the causes of sectarian division removed. In one sense, the Restoration Movement was in its origin a meditation on the religious philosophy of John Locke.

Chapter Four

Alexander Campbell and the Restoration Movement

It was probably in June or July 1808, just after Thomas Campbell had been reinstated by the Seceder Synod, that he sent word to his family to join him in the United States. Campbell's assumption that all was now well and that his affairs with the Synod had been settled was, of course, erroneous. Nevertheless, Thomas Campbell's wife and seven children set off from Londonderry on October 1, 1808. The ship was wrecked almost immediately on the coast of the island of Islay, one of the Hebrides, though all the passengers were taken to safety. Because it was already very late in the season to make a transatlantic crossing, it was decided that Campbell's wife and children would spend the winter in Glasgow.

There were other reasons for staying in Glasgow. The eldest child, Alexander, had been born in 1788. He had been almost completely educated by his father and when Thomas left for America he entrusted his academy at Rich Hill to his nineteen-year-old son. However intelligent and well-read, Alexander had lacked the opportunity to study formally. It seemed as if Providence had provided an opportunity which was too valuable to pass up and Alexander and his family set off for Glasgow so that he could study at the university.

Alexander pursued a classical curriculum typical of his time. He studied Greek, Latin, logic, belles lettres, French and the New Testament. As noted, Greville Ewing exerted a powerful influence on Campbell during his stay in Glasgow. Not only did he become better acquainted with some of the ideas associated with Sandeman and the Haldanes, he also became more favorably disposed towards the principles of congregationalism as practiced by Ewing. According to Richardson, the influence of Ewing and his religious independence was reinforced by extensive contact with preachers from various religious groups, which had the effect of freeing Alexander from the "denominational influences of his religious education."[1]

Whatever the causes, Alexander Campbell was approaching a momentous decision. As the semi-annual communion season for Seceder Presbyterians approached, he was torn between his growing inclination to reject religious systems and his desire to fulfill the religious obligations which his father had been so careful to nurture in him. His indecision is well illustrated by a story related by Richardson. Alexander applied for the metal token which everyone who wished to communicate had to obtain. Since he lacked a letter of introduction, he had to submit to an examination, passed, and received a token. Uncertain even as the communion tables were being prepared, Alexander waited until the last table to be served hoping to overcome his scruples:

> Failing in this, however, and unable any longer conscientiously to recognize the Seceder Church as the Church of Christ, he threw his token upon the plate handed round, and when the elements were passed along the table, declined to partake with the rest. It was at this moment that the struggle in his mind was completed, and the ring of the token, falling upon the plate, announced the instant at which he renounced Presbyterianism for ever the leaden voucher becoming thus a token not of communion but of separation.[2]

When he departed Glasgow he asked, as usual, for a certificate of good standing as he had done nothing to violate any rule of the church. Perhaps his decision to leave was not as definite as Richardson suggests. Most likely, Alexander was concerned about how his father would react to his son's decision to leave a church in which he, Thomas, was a minister of good standing. The father and son had much to tell each other.

The Campbells left Glasgow in early August 1809, and after brief stops in New York and Philadelphia they were reunited with Thomas somewhere on the road to western Pennsylvania. Father and son must have been embarrassed at first and then amazed that their paths separated by thousands of miles had led them to the same decision to abandon the Seceder Church and to seek a united Church of Christ. Alexander read and approved the *Declaration and Address,* and then informed his father that he intended to devote himself to a life in the ministry. A very powerful partnership had been formed.

Father and Son

Over the next year Alexander studied for the ministry, and began to preach to small gatherings at his home or at the homes of sympathetic friends. In the fall of 1810 Thomas Campbell, identifying himself as a representative of the Christian Association of Washington, applied for ministerial communion with the Synod of Pittsburgh. This was not a Seceder institution but a unit of the main Presbyterian body. It is a little puzzling that Thomas Campbell after separating rather harshly from his own branch of Presbyterianism would seek communion with a rival segment. One writer suggests that Campbell had been encouraged by members of the Synod who assured him of acceptance.[3] Perhaps psychologically he was uncomfortable without a church connection. Perhaps he wanted to demonstrate, by specifically seeking communion with an ecclesial body, that the Association was, as he claimed, not a church but an organization of churches dedicated to the unity of the Church of Christ. Perhaps he suspected in his own heart that the road he was travelling could well lead to separation instead of unity.

Most Restoration writers have written derisively of the rejection by the Synod. To be sure, the denial could have been phrased less harshly. But truthfully, the reasons given are remarkably perceptive of the ideas contained in the *Declaration and Address* and of the eventual effects of the Restoration Movement:

> ...the Synod unanimously resolved, that however specious the plan of the Christian Association and however seducing its professions, as experience of the effects of similar projects in other parts has evinced their baleful tendency and destructive operations on the whole interests of religion by promoting divisions instead of union, by degrading the ministerial character, by providing free admission to any errors in doctrine, and to any corruptions in discipline, whilst a nominal approbation of the Scriptures as the only standard of truth may be professed.[4]

The rejection by the Pittsburgh Synod was significant because it represented the final attempt to execute the ideas of the *Declaration and Address* within the confines of existing church structures. Several developments followed quickly. At the semiannual meeting of the Christian Association, held just a few weeks after the Synod's rejection, Alexander Campbell delivered a discourse where he replied to the criticisms of the Synod and defended the program of the Association. Alexander Campbell, eloquent debater and aggressive defender of Restoration ideas, was beginning to emerge. At the next meeting in May 1811 the Association constituted itself a church, known by the name of its location in western Pennsylvania, as the Brush Run Church. Thomas Campbell was chosen elder, four deacons were elected and Alexander Campbell was licensed to preach. All this was done on the "congregational" authority of the church itself. The Lord's Supper was observed on the next day and every week thereafter. On the following New Years Day 1812, Alexander was ordained to the ministry seven months after he accepted a license to preach. This is surely indicative of the opinion held by the Campbells that there was no essential distinction between clergy and laity and that laymen had the right to preach. The direction of the Restoration Movement had shifted towards restoring Christian unity through the creation of a church separate from the "sects."

The Campbellite Restoration Movement had to pass through another phase, which was introduced through the question of immersion. There is no evidence that immersion was a serious topic of discussion among the Campbells until 1812, but certainly the issue was familiar to both men. There was a branch of Sandemanians known as "Scotch Baptists" and shortly before Alexander reached Glasgow the rift between the Haldanes and Greville Ewing was finalized due to their disagreement over immersion and infant baptism. Ewing was an ardent supporter of paedobaptism and one would suppose that he would have influenced Alexander Campbell to accept his point of view. Finally, when the Christian Association of Washington was being formed it adopted the motto "Where the Scriptures speak, we speak; and where the Scriptures are silent, we are silent." This had immediately provoked disagreement over whether infant baptism had to be abandoned. The issue, therefore, was probably never very far from the surface. Despite indications of disagreement during this period of time, it seems as if Thomas Campbell wanted to keep the issue from becoming a point of division. For example, the Synod of Pittsburgh offered as a reason for rejecting the request for communion, the assertion that some in the Christian Association denied the scriptural authority for infant baptism. Almost certainly then, there was debate about baptism among members of the Association.

The crucial event which affected how the Campbells viewed immersion seems to have been the birth of Alexander Campbell's first child, Jane, on March 13, 1812. In the succeeding months Alexander gave the subject much thought and study. He concluded that the Greek word baptism could only be translated as immersion. Moreover, he concluded that believers and believers only could be subject to this ordinance. When he felt sufficiently certain Campbell acted. He decided to contact an acquaintance, a Baptist preacher named Matthias Luce who lived nearby, and ask to be immersed. On his way to call on Luce, Alexander stopped at his father's house to present his conclusions and decision to act. Before he could find his father, he was intercepted by his sister Dorothea who confided in him that she could find no scriptural authority for infant baptism. Heartened by this confidence, Alexander told his father of his intention to call on Mr. Luce. Thomas responded only that Alexander and Luce should call on him on their way back. On June 12, 1812 on their way to Buffalo Creek for the immersion, Luce and Alexander called on Thomas Campbell and were surprised to learn that he and his wife had decided to be immersed on that day as well. In fact, seven persons were immersed that day, Alexander, his wife, his mother and father, a sister and two other members of the Brush Run Church. These are the simple events that led to the decision to adopt immersion, a decision which marked a real turning point in the Restoration Movement.

First of all, it is quite clear that it was Alexander Campbell's decision to adopt immersion, and that Thomas followed his son's lead. This event, therefore, marks the succession of Alexander Campbell to the leadership of the (Campbellite) Restoration Movement. It also marks a very different direction for that movement, one which reflects the personality of Alexander and not Thomas Campbell. The *Declaration and Address* was pervaded by the naive gentleness of Thomas, who thought that religious denominations would promote their own demise as they became convinced of the superior logic of the unity of the Church of Christ. This was an approach based on the gentlemanly art of persuasion and the reasonableness of human nature. In this sense it represented a mentality which was distinctly imbued with eighteenth century ideas. On the other hand, the new campaign plotted by the younger Campbell was filled with a different spirit. It was the spirit of "truth" and carried a conviction that the old guard would never participate in its own end. The falseness, indeed the baseness of sectarianism had to be exposed and once this was accomplished denominationalism would collapse from its own dead weight. This was the cry of youth and revolution and very much reflected the spirit of the early nineteenth century.

Leadership fell quickly to Alexander Campbell, and Thomas assumed the role of an elder statesman no longer involved in the day-to-day affairs of the movement. The two impulses of Restorationism, unity and truth, derived from the thought and personalities of father and son, were never fully resolved and continued to foster tension within Restorationism. The ascendant impulse during this next phase of the Restoration Movement was very definitely in restoring the ancient order of things, that is, of primitive Christianity.

The method and principles by which Alexander Campbell committed the Restoration Movement to immersion are instructive.

Probably because he had been brought up in an atmosphere of relative freedom and because he had never been ordained into a particular church, Alexander Campbell was better able to break the bonds which held his father. It must have been difficult for Thomas Campbell, who had always been a paedobaptist and who had been a minister all his adult life in a church which accepted infant baptism, to reject the doctrine. For his son it was less a question of renouncing his past than of accepting the logic of his convictions that the supreme religious authority was the Bible. Quite simply, immersion was adopted because it was the only true scriptural baptism and infant baptism was rejected because it was a human invention. Similarly, Alexander had stipulated with Mr. Luce that the ceremony should reflect strictly the pattern given in the New Testament. There was to be no testifying of a "religious experience" as was common among the Baptists because this was a modern custom without scriptural authority. Candidates should be admitted on the simple confession that "Jesus is the Son of God" which is strikingly similar to the notion of "bare faith" espoused by Sandeman who defined faith as the confession that "Jesus is the Christ."

In general, Alexander Campbell adopted immersion based on the Restoration principles found in his father's *Declaration and Address*. But to be more accurate, he embraced one of the guiding principles of that document but forsook another. When confronted with the real likelihood that his decision to adopt immersion would not in fact foster further unity but would instead force people to leave the Brush Run Church he did not hesitate to embrace a greater principle, namely the restoration of the New Testament Church. It was this principle which was to win Alexander fame on the frontier as a formidable partisan for his cause. It was this principle which was to guide the Restoration Movement through controversy for the next twenty-five years.

The Redstone Baptist Association

In the fall of 1813 the Brush Run Church was accepted into the Redstone Baptist Association. For seventeen years the Campbells and other members of the church were in effect Baptists. They were Baptists because they were members of a Baptist association, but there was always some tension between the two groups. Most obviously, the two groups shared a commitment to believer's baptism and immersion. But differences manifested themselves even before union. The Redstone Association had formally adopted the Philadelphia Confession of 1742. The Brush Run Church, therefore, stipulated as a condition for union "that we should be allowed to teach and preach whatever we learned from the Holy Scriptures, regardless of any creed or formula in Christendom."[5]

It is difficult to determine exactly why the two groups decided to embrace each other. Alexander Campbell very definitely recalled that it was the Baptists who sought him out and asked him to preach to them. This may be self-aggrandizement, but it may also reflect a certain level of respect for the European-educated Campbell. On a more general level then, most Baptists, but certainly not all, may have been pleased to welcome educated men like the Campbells into their association. From the perspective of the Brush Run Church, joining the Baptists restored them to communion with other Christians. In this regard Thomas Campbell may have heavily influenced the decision. In effect, then, joining the Baptists put the Brush Run Church in the position envisioned by the *Declaration and Address*, that of an individual and independent congregation, which in communion with others could effect the restoration of the New Testament Church and the unity of the Church of Christ. In this sense they had traded their Presbyterian identity for a Baptist one.

By 1816 Thomas Campbell was running a school in Pittsburgh and Alexander was preaching from the Brush Run Church. In August of that year the Redstone Association met at Cross Creek in what is today West Virginia. John Pritchard was the elder at Cross Creek Church and he was associated with the most strident opposition to Alexander Campbell. Pritchard's efforts to prevent Campbell from preaching were thwarted, however, when one of the other preachers was taken ill and Campbell was asked to take his place. On August 30, 1816 Alexander Campbell preached what came to be known as the "Sermon on the Law."

The Sermon on the Law

The "Sermon on the Law" is one of the most important historical documents of the Restoration Movement. It is important not as a mature statement of Campbell's thought — that would evolve considerably over the next three decades — but rather as the point of origin of the separation from the Baptists and the development of a distinctive Restoration theology.

The sermon itself is quite long and the arguments are often rather complex. What follows is a very brief synopsis which focuses on the conclusions at the end of the sermon.[6] The point of departure is Romans 8:3 and the sermon begins with the very Lockian sentence, "Words are signs of ideas or thoughts."[7] The word that Campbell is concerned with is "law." Campbell is interested in demonstrating that "the law" signifies the Mosaic dispensation, a distinct and peculiar institution designed by God for a special people and for a limited time. His method is made clear by this passage:

> We would observe that there are two principles, commandments, or laws, that are never included in our observations respecting the law of Moses, nor are they ever in holy writ called the law of Moses; these are 'Thou shalt love the Lord thy God with all thy heart, soul, mind, and strength; and thy neighbor as thyself.' These our Great Prophet teaches us, are the basis of the law of Moses, and the Prophets.[8]

Campbell, therefore, judges the Mosaic Law by New Testament standards. In fact he states that all Jewish Law is but a modification of the two commandments handed down by Jesus. The principles found in both collections of law are rooted in universal and immutable obligation which God has engraved on the hearts of his creatures, angels and men, Christians and heathens. The law of Moses, then, can be swept away without weakening the moral obligations which they contain.

Once he has established what the law is, Campbell makes four additional points: 1) those things which the law could not accomplish; 2) the reason why the law failed to accomplish those objects; 3) how God has remedied those relative defects of the law; and 4) conclusions. The first conclusion is that "there is an essential difference between law and gospel - the Old Testament and the New. He minces no words about this opinion. The law is called "the letter;" "the ministration of death;" it is "abolished, and vanished away." The New Testament is "the Spirit"; "the ministration of righteousness;" it "lives and is everlasting."

Campbell concludes that since the law and the gospel are essentially different, there is no necessity for preaching the law in order to prepare men for receiving the gospel. This is an idea which was contrary to contemporary Baptist theology. In the fourth conclusion Campbell is more concrete and it is easier to see the revolutionary nature of his opinion. He rejects the idea that Old Testament practices can be integrated into Christianity. Therefore, infant baptism, tithes, holy days, fasting, national covenants, the establishment of religion, even the sanctification of the seventh day "...and all reasons and motives borrowed from the Jewish law, to excite the disciples of Christ to a compliance with or an imitation of Jewish customs, are inconclusive, repugnant to Christianity, and fall ineffectual to the ground; not being enjoined or countenanced by the authority of Jesus Christ."[9]

The rejection of these adaptations from the Old Testament caused quite a stir. Campbell himself participated in three debates with Presbyterian ministers which focused largely on the question of infant baptism, the most prominent issue which separated Baptists from more conservative Protestants. The radicalism of Campbell's thought, however, also caused tension between "Christians" and Baptists. Although Baptists also emphasized restoring the New Testament church, they were not so rigorous in applying the logic of that argument. This can be seen clearly through the Baptist confessions of faith.

It will be recalled that the Redstone Association had formally adopted the Philadelphia Confession of 1742. This confession was itself an adaptation of the Second London Confession of 1689.[10] All of Chapter XIX entitled "Of the Law of God" is imbued with a different attitude regarding the Law. Paragraph seven states that the uses of the Law are not "contrary to the Grace of the Gospel; but do sweetly comply with it."[11] In the beginning of the "Sermon on the Law," Campbell speaks of three classifications of the Law: the moral, ceremonial and judicial. This is exactly the same terminology used by the Confession. It is likely then, that Alexander was refuting, very specifically, the official confession of the Redstone Association, whose members he was addressing. Little wonder that some members took offense at the sermon. Within a few years of coming to the United States, Alexander Campbell was already applying a rigorous logic to Restoration ideas which was placing him on the cutting edge of American Protestant theology.

The Theology of Alexander Campbell

It is beyond the scope of this study to present a comprehensive discussion of the theology of Alexander Campbell or of any other figure in the Restoration Movement. Nevertheless, it is useful to examine certain ideas of the Movement because they represent some of the most original thinking in American religion. One part of Campbell's thought, a very important part, revolves around the related issues of faith, baptism and regeneration. To obtain an understanding of these subjects is to gain an appreciation for the importance of the Restoration Movement as an American religious phenomenon.

James Hervey, author of *Dialogues between Theron and Aspasio,* maintained a view which described faith as a state of feeling and which placed it at the end of a process of emotional conversion. Robert Sandeman countered with a view of faith which was distinctly intellectual in which any change of heart and feeling was the effect of faith. Alexander Campbell could not have escaped this controversy about the nature of faith which dominated religious thought in eighteenth-century Britain. Campbell developed his own opinion of the nature of faith which saw, for example, the Methodist view as something akin to a Protestant mysticism. In order to rectify what he viewed as abuses, Campbell developed a different concept of faith, one related to the intellectualism of Sandeman but with some important differences.

Campbell's view of the nature of faith is perhaps his most important theological concept. This is so, in large part, because it ran counter to ideas on the subject which had become the accepted norm on the American frontier by the end of the first quarter of the nineteenth century.

Alexander Campbell was a very logical thinker and it is often difficult to excerpt his ideas out of the carefully crafted constructions of his thought. In the *Christian System,* most of Campbell's ideas on faith will be found in a section called "Foundation of Christian Union." Campbell begins this section with a familiar condemnation of creeds as mere opinions which serve only to divide Christians. He wants to replace creeds with the Bible; a revelation not based on opinion but on fact. Fact means something done, and the gospel facts are the recording of the sayings and doings of Jesus Christ from his birth to his ascension. The intellectual nature of faith becomes apparent as Campbell speaks of the gospel facts as a moral seal which delineates the image of God upon the human soul. "All the means of grace are, therefore, only the means of impressing this seal upon the heart, of bringing these moral facts to make their full impression on the soul of man. Testimony and faith are but the channel through which these facts, or the hand of God, draws the image on the heart and character of man."[12]

It is testimony which conveys the moral seal to the intellect. The influence of Locke is most obvious here. Testimony is evidence gathered by the five senses or witnesses. These witnesses constitute the five avenues through which the human mind learns about the material world. Testimony concerning any fact brings that fact into contact with the mind and allows it to impress itself or to form its image upon the intellect or mind of man. Through the five senses we acquire all information about the objects around us; we receive information about facts not immediately objects of our senses, through human and divine testimony. This kind of testimony is just another name for history or narrative. It is at this point that Campbell introduces the idea of faith.

"No testimony, no faith: for faith is only the belief of testimony...Where testimony begins, faith begins; and where testimony ends, faith ends...Faith never can be more than the receiving of testimony as true, or the belief in testimony;

and if that testimony be written it is called history."[13] It is in these stark terms that Alexander Campbell introduces his views on faith. Since faith is the acceptance of testimony as true, faith is an extension of sense perception. In sum: "All our pleasures and pains, all our joys and sorrows, are the effects of the objects of sensation, reflection, faith, etc. apprehended or received, and not in the nature of the exercise of any power or capacity with which we are endowed."[14] Campbell then writes at length demonstrating that the efficacy of faith is not in the nature of our faith but in the truth believed.

Regeneration

The process of confirming belief, really an epistemology of belief, has important consequences since it becomes a process of regeneration. There is a connection of cause and effect which begins with fact and proceeds through testimony and faith to feeling. Paramount is *fact* since the whole process is based on it. It is fact which produces the change in the frame of mind. *Testimony,* or the report of fact is essential to belief and *belief* is necessary to bring the thing said or done to the heart. The change of heart is the end of a process of regeneration which was probably the most important contribution of Alexander Campbell to American Christian theology.

The "fundamental fact" which is the basis of Christianity is that Jesus is the Christ. Belief in this one fact and submission to baptism is all that is required for admission into the church. The evidence is provided by the testimony of the apostles and confirmed by prophecy, miracles, and spiritual gifts. The person who believes and is baptized is saved.[15] As faith is simply belief in testimony, it is useless to try to make people believe by threats, persuasion, or emotional excitement. Faith is completely natural and the recipient is completely passive in receiving it. Faith is dependent solely on adequate testimony, so it is unnecessary, even inappropriate to pray for it. If faith is desired all that is necessary is to lay aside prejudice and accept the evidence and testimony.

Probably the most important consequence of Campbell's conception of faith is its relationship with the process of conversion.[16] In the classic frontier version this process commenced with the penitent being broken down by a sense of sinfulness. Filled with remorse, there was little choice but to wait for God to grant the gift of faith. Sometimes this took an excruciatingly long period of time. Even after receiving faith, the penitent often waited further for an assurance of pardon. Only after being assured of forgiveness could the process of reformation be completed.

Campbell changed the traditional order so that faith began the process of conversion. In another section of the *Christian System* entitled "Faith in Christ," he speaks of faith much more in personal and less in intellectual terms: "that faith in Christ which is essential to salvation is not the belief of any doctrine, testimony, or truth, abstractly, but belief in Christ; trust or confidence in him as a

person, not a thing."[17] Repentance is an effect of faith. Campbell does not
make a distinction between repentance and reformation. Repentance is sorrow
for sins committed, and it is also resolution to foresake them. But it is still more;
it is "repentance unto life," it is reformation, the actual amendation of life.[18]
The principal thrust of Alexander Campbell's thinking was against the
emotionalism that dominated the frontier of his day. He opposed faith as a
psychological turning to God. His own Lockian sensationalism rooted faith in
experience, or in this case in its extension, testimony. Ultimately, though, faith
was rooted in the Word alone. He argued against repentance as mere feeling,
giving it a more practical foundation by insisting that it must lead to an actual
change of life.

Baptism and the Remission of Sins

Most of these ideas were more fully developed by Campbell in his thinking
about baptism, which was developed over many years in a series of debates.[19]
Responding to a general challenge by Rev. John Walker in 1820, a Seceder
Prebyterian minister of Mount Pleasant, Ohio, Campbell took up the challenge
and met Walker to debate the subject of baptism. Walker argued in favor of infant baptism and sprinkling, and based his argument on an analogy between circumcision and baptism. Thus there was a continuity in covenants where
circumcision was the seal of the old for Jews and baptism was the seal of the new
for Christians. Campbell countered with an argument honed from his *Sermon
on the Law* which made a sharp distinction between covenants.

During the Walker debate Campbell mentioned the idea that baptism is
connected with the remission of sins, but it was hardly developed. In 1823, in
another debate held in Kentucky with Rev. W. L. McCalla, a Presbyterian minister, Campbell made a distinction between real remission and the formal remission which occurs in baptism. He made it clear that he was speaking of the
remission of the personal sins of the individual and not original sin which per-
tains to infants.

In 1843 Alexander Campbell met in debate with still another Presbyterian,
Rev. N. L. Rice in Paris, Kentucky.[20] This was Campbell's longest debate, last-
ing a full two weeks, and one of his most famous, moderated by no less distin-
guished a debater than Henry Clay. In this debate, in his writings in the *Christian
Baptist* and *The Christian System,* and under the influence of Walter Scott,
Campbell developed his mature views on baptism.

Baptism is an ordinance established by the direct command of Jesus Christ.
Using the divisions employed by Campbell himself, the *action* is immersion in
water in the name of the Father, Son, and Holy Spirit. The *subjects* of baptism
are not infants or adults, males or females, but penitent believers. In other
words, the proper subjects of baptism are those who already believe, that is have
faith, and have repented their sins. The *design* or meaning of baptism is for the

remission of sins. Campbell was able to attach a rather subtle meaning to remission by distinguishing between real and formal remission. Real remission refers to the forgiveness of past sins because of a change of character effected through faith and repentance. Formal remission is based on a change in the sinner's state as he or she enters the state of citizenship in the Kingdom of God.[21] The analogy Campbell used is that of political citizenship. The aspiring citizen must first be naturalized or made an adopted citizen. This is accomplished by renouncing all political allegiance and vowing to adopt and submit to the Constitution of the United States. Once this is done then a change of state is possible. The person can now formally become a citizen of the United States. This change of state is not effected in any change of views and affections.[22]

> [Baptism] has no abstract efficacy. Without previous faith in the blood of Christ, and deep and unfeigned repentance before God, neither immersion in water, nor any other action, can secure to us the blessings of peace and pardon. It can merit nothing. Still to the believing penitent it is the *means* of receiving a formal, distinct, and specific absolution, or release from guilt. Therefore, none but those who have first believed the testimony of God and have repented of their sins, and that have been intelligently immersed into his death, have the full and explicit testimony of God, assuring them of pardon.[23]

It could be said that Alexander Campbell's opinions on baptism was a *via media* between the evangelical Protestant and Roman Catholic views on the subject. Regarding both form and subject, Campbell was entirely in agreement with the Baptists, since he advocated immersion of penitent believers only. His whole reasoning up to a point was representative of Protestant orthodoxy. This is especially true of its emphasis on personal faith and repentance, although as we have seen there were important differences about whether faith came first or after repentance. But onto this orthodoxy Campbell grafted an opinion, namely the remission of sins through baptism. In other words, he advocated that a real change of state is effected by the sacrament and ordinance, which at first glance seems very Catholic. In fact he was at great pains to deny any principle of baptism as "magic" (as were, of course, Catholics) and emphasized the importance of faith, but he was constantly accused of promoting a view of baptismal regeneration.

"Campbellism" and Controversy

Alexander Campbell was a controversial and divisive religious figure on the American frontier. It is a tribute to him that his ideas were so well understood by his contemporaries. One Methodist writer in 1835 recognized well that

"Campbellism" rejected "Divine Agency on the heart" and that the theory of remission of sins through baptism was "the principal arch in the superstructure of Campbellism."[24] Another Methodist writer, T. McK. Stuart, correctly perceived that the doctrine of the remission of sins through baptism was based on reversing the traditional order of repentance first, then faith.[25] He also recognized that Campbell espoused an intellectual conception of faith and denied the immediate operation of the Spirit.[26] But he goes further, attacking the Lockian basis of Campbell's thought as entirely subjective. Because there is no immediate witness of the Holy Spirit he criticizes the "Campbellite" as relying on a subjective assurance of pardon, namely the infallible interpretation of Scripture. The unfortunate consequence is that "the advocate of this faith is sure he is right and all others wrong; for his conviction that he is a child of God depends upon the certainty that he is not mistaken in his interpretation."[27] This is an observation made by many others from various denominations.

Stuart calls the Campbellite doctrine of baptism "papistic," citing canons from the Council of Trent. He concludes that there is a difference of words only between advocates of "baptismal regeneration" and the Campbellites. Then he makes an interesting accusation, that Campbell's doctrine teaches justification by works, since baptism is an act or work to be performed. The Restoration Movement, therefore, becomes in the eyes of one cleric a repudiation of the Reformation idea of justification by faith alone, indeed of Protestantism itself.[28]

Restoration historians often cite the debate between Campbell and Bishop Purcell in order to depict the former as a defender of Protestantism. However, it is clear that many contemporary American Protestants viewed the Movement not as within the mainstream, but rather as a radical force which was introducing ideas foreign and inimical to Protestantism. This is an important point to remember when considering the Restoration Movement within the context of Southern religion.

The Mahoning Baptist Association

The theology which Alexander Campbell developed out of the "Sermon on the Law" affected his relationship with his own Baptist religious organization. In the years following the Sermon his opponents in the Redstone Association never ceased to agitate for his excommunication. Finally, in August 1823 Campbell acted, perhaps because he wearied of the battle, perhaps because he realized that his opponents had mustered enough votes to expel him. Richardson contends that Campbell cared little about the possibility of expulsion itself, but that since the debate with McCalla was only two months away he feared that expulsion might affect his success or cause cancellation of the debate.[29]

Only days before the meeting of the Redstone Association, on August 31, 1823, Campbell and thirty other members withdrew from the Brush Run Church. They founded a new church at Wellsburg, Virginia (now West Virginia) on the Ohio River. The church applied for admission and was accepted into the Mahoning Baptist Association of northeast Ohio. This association had been formed in 1820 under the influence of Adamson Bentley, a Baptist minister who had been deeply impressed by Alexander Campbell in his debate with Walker.[30] Campbell's opponents were foiled since the Wellsburg church was not a member of the Redstone Association and was not subject to its authority.

Why did Campbell and his followers make the effort to remain Baptists? Certainly their relationship with the Baptists was ambiguous. As a result of the "Sermon on the Law" and the two debates with Walker and McCalla, Campell had become both an eloquent defender of immersion of believers and the remission of sin through baptism. Thus at the same time he became one of the foremost defenders of Baptist practice on the American frontier and, at least according to some, a purveyor of heresy. Campbell remained a Baptist because he opposed "sectarianism" and did not want to be responsible for founding a new sect. He also desired the freedom to publicize his views.[31] While he was able to accomplish both ends he was content to remain a Baptist, though one does have to question just how "Baptist" he really was.

The Christian Baptist

The period from the delivery of the "Sermon on the Law" in 1816 until separation from the Baptists in 1830 was distinguished by the most radical and iconoclastic Alexander Campbell who was in the process of developing his own mature thought. The principle organ by which he disseminated his ideas was the journal *Christian Baptist*. Campbell purchased presses, type, and everything else necessary to run the enterprise independently, and published it for seven years. The title itself indicates the ambiguity of Campbell's position during these years. "Baptist" aligned the journal with that religious party, while "Christian" betrayed the non-sectarian interest of the publication. Despite its name, the prospectus which Campbell circulated indicated clearly the nature and goals of the journal:

> The "Christian Baptist" shall espouse the cause of no religious sect, excepting that ancient sect "called Christians first at Antioch." Its sole object shall be the eviction of truth and the exposing of error in doctrine and practice. The editor, acknowledging no standard of religious faith or works other than the Old and New Testament, and the latter as the only standard of the religion of Jesus Christ, will, intentionally at least, oppose nothing which it does not enjoin. Having no worldly interest at stake from the

adoption or reprobation of any articles of faith or religious practice, having no gift nor religious emolument to blind his eyes or
to pervert his judgment, he hopes to manifest that he is an impar-
tial advocate of truth.[32]

The "Christian Baptist" was a vehicle designed to expose three basic errors
endemic to modern sectarianism. They were: 1) the use of creeds as standards
of orthodoxy; 2) unscriptural usurpation of power by the clergy; 3) and un-
authorized organizations in the churches. The first, as we have seen has a long
tradition going back to the thought of Thomas Campbell. The second, the clergy, was extremely important and was the focal point of Campbell's criticisms
during this time. According to Richardson, Campbell completely denied the
validity of any distinction between clergy and laity. He wished to take the New
Testament out of the hands of the clergy and place it in its rightful place with the
people. This would be difficult since the clergy had lorded it over the people for
so long and so effectively. "They [the clergy] have, in order to raise the people's
admiration of them for their own advantage, taught them in creeds, in sermons,
in catechisms, in tracts, in pamphlets, in primers, in folios, that they alone can
expound the New Testament—that, without them, people are either *almost* or
altogether destitute of the means of grace."[33]

This hostility to the clergy is very important because it forms one of the bases
of Campbell's opinion on church organization. In a famous series of articles
under the general title, "A Restoration of the Ancient Order of Things," he set
down a strict criteria of judgment which he applied with remorseless logic: he
opposed all practices which could not be specifically validated as in use among
the early Christians, and he urged the adoption of everything sanctioned by
apostolic practice. Therefore, he urged the abandonment of creeds, confessions, unscriptural words and phrases, and the use of ecclesiastical titles. Organs were forbidden in public worship because the early Christian churches did
not have them. He denounced synods, presbyteries, conferences, general as-
semblies, Sunday-schools, missionary, education, and even Bible societies. His
reasoning here was very much linked to his hostility to the clergy, who he felt had
perverted these organizations into organs of denominational aggrandizement in
order to perpetuate their domination of the people.[34] Later on, once the clergy
had been purged from a non-denominational church of Christ, his attitude sof-
tened somewhat on church organizations.

On the other hand, he wrote in support of everything sanctioned by primitive practice: the weekly breaking of the loaf, the simple order of public worship,
and the independence of each congregation under the care of its elders and
deacons.[35]

During this period of time Campbell tended towards "closed communion" or rejecting communion with the unimmersed. This was a new phase of the Restoration. The principles of the *Declaration and Address* had failed to bring the "sects" around to abandon the idea of denominationalism. There was no longer the expectation that this would ever happen. Instead, at least one congregation could be established which participated fully in the "ancient order of things." However, this created a certain feeling of exclusivism which could always be detected in the movement:

> I have no idea of seeing, nor one wish to see, the sects unite in one grand army. This would be dangerous to our liberties and laws. For this the Savior did not pray. It is only the disciples of Christ dispersed among them, that reason and benevolence would call out of them. Let them unite who love the Lord, and then we shall soon see the hireling priesthood and their worldly establishments prostrate in the dust.[36]

The years of the publication of the *Christian Baptist* created many enemies and many devoted followers. In throwing down the gauntlet to the bulk of American religion, Alexander Campbell rewrote the more gentle "ecumenism" espoused by his father in the *Declaration and Address*. The dialectic between "unity" and "truth," which was always present, continued, though the balance was tipped in favor of the "eviction of truth and the exposing of error." The unity motive persisted, but was transformed into a faithful remnant who would destroy the perversions of the "sects" and restore an authentic, apostolic Christianity. The unity motive, therefore, became a motive of separation as well, both between the restored and the unrestored and ultimately among those within the Restoration Movement as well.

Chapter Five

Separation, Unification
and Independence

Walter Scott

A fourth person who played a crucial role in the development of the Restoration Movement was Walter Scott, who was born in Moffat, Scotland on October 31, 1796.[1] His father, John, was a music teacher and his mother, Mary, was known as a pious woman whose greatest desire was that her son become a minister in the Church of Scotland. Walter was a student of great intelligence and his parents resolved to send him to the University of Edinburgh where it is presumed he earned a degree. Scott was sent in July 1818 to join one of his uncles who was working in New York. He secured a position teaching Latin in an academy in Jamaica, New York. Within a year, however, he left for the frontier and arrived in Pittsburgh on May 7, 1819.

In Pittsburgh he obtained a position teaching at an academy run by George Forrester, a fellow Scotsman. Forrester was also a preacher and pastor of a small church which viewed human standards of religion as imperfect and which derived its practices and beliefs strictly from the Bible, including baptismal immersion, foot washing, and the "holy kiss." Scott was greatly impressed with Forrester's piety and dedication to the Bible. He was baptized by immersion and became a member of the small church. Forrester eventually resigned his position with the academy, so that the school fell into the hands of Walter Scott.

As he was administering the academy, Scott was drawn deeper into a study of Scripture and of the writings of Glas, Sandeman, the Haldanes, and Locke.[2] He also found in Forrester's library a tract written by Henry Errett, father of Isaac Errett who became one of the most prominent second-generation Restoration leaders.[3] Henry Errett was the pastor of a small congregation of "Scotch Baptists" (Sandemanian immersionists) in New York City, and his tract closely connected immersion with the remission of sins. Scott was so impressed with this and other ideas that he sold the Pittsburgh academy and moved to New York City to gain further instruction from this church. Apparently he was discouraged by conditions there for he left before long and wandered, ministering to various Haldanean groups in Paterson, New Jersey; Baltimore; and Washington. Finally, he decided to accept an offer to return to Pittsburgh.

The offer to return to Pittsburgh was tendered by Nathaniel Richardson, an Episcopalian and prominent citizen who wanted Scott to tutor his son Robert. This Robert Richardson eventually became a professor at Bethany College, founded by Alexander Campbell, and became Campbell's first biographer. The information he provides on Campbell and Scott is all the more valuable because it was the result of many years of intimate contact with both men. Richardson does not specify how the two men met, but it is relatively simple to form a likely hypothesis. Richardson had been tutored by Thomas Campbell, who at this time was residing in Pittsburgh.[4] Subsequently, the boy was taught by Walter Scott at Forrester's academy and then again when Scott returned to Pittsburgh. Although Baxter suggests that Scott came to know Thomas Campbell only after he first met his son, Alexander,[5] it is obvious that the Richardsons, Scott, and Thomas Campbell traveled in the same circles in Pittsburgh. Richardson is specific that during the winter of 1821-22 Alexander Campbell came to Pittsburgh to visit his father and at that time first met Walter Scott.[6]

By all accounts Walter Scott and Alexander Campbell became friends and collaborators almost immediately. The story goes, for example, that Campbell wanted to call his new journal "The Christian" and that it was Scott who persuaded him to call it instead "The Christian Baptist" in order to gain the support of the Baptists.[7] Scott wrote an article for the very first issue in 1823 and was a steady contributor for many years thereafter.

The reasons for this friendship are not difficult to uncover. Both men came from very similar backgrounds. Both were Scots, both had been raised as Presbyterians, and both were influenced by the writings of Locke, Glas, Sandeman, and the Haldanes. More importantly, both men independently came to similar conclusions about the central tenets of their Christian faith. Very simply, both men shared a desire to "restore the ancient order of things" by searching the Bible for the beliefs and practices of the primitive church. On a more complex level both men concluded that baptism was properly administered to believers by immersion, and that it secured the remission of sins and, ultimately, salvation for the immersed. But at the heart of their collaboration was a remarkably compatible view of religion which can be seen through an examination of Scott's opinions on the nature of faith:

> Jesus having died for sin and arisen again to introduce the hope of immortality, the great fact to be believed, in order to be saved, is that he is the Son of God; and this being a matter-of-fact question, the belief of it as necessarily depends upon the evidence by which it is accompanied as the belief of any other fact depends upon its particular evidence....We shall see by and by that to preach the gospel is just to propose this glorious truth to sinners, and support it by its proper evidence. We shall see that the heavens and the apostles proposed nothing more in order to con-

vert men from the error of their ways and to reduce them to love
and obedience of Christ.... In short, the apostles proceeded thus:
they first proposed the truth to be believed, and secondly, they
produced the evidences necessary to warrant belief.[8]

The similarity of language with Campbell's writings on the same subject is
striking.   "Fact," "evidence," "truth," "belief" constitute a Campbellian
vocabulary. But of course the argument is Lockian and Sandemanian as well. In
answer to the very crucial question, "How does a person become a Christian?,"
Scott answered with a simplicity worthy of Locke: the central idea of Christianity is the Messiahship of Jesus. "Jesus is the Christ," is the single truth which
Scott called the "Golden Oracle."
    If Scott and Campbell shared similar ideas about Christianity, they were
very different personalities. Richardson, who knew both men very well, con-
trasted their characters in an extended passage of his biography of Alexander
Campbell:

> the different hues in the characters of these two eminent men
> were such as to be, so to speak, complementary to each other,
> and to form, by their harmonious blending, a completeness and
> a brilliancy which rendered their society peculiarly delightful to
> each other. Thus, while Mr. Campbell was fearless, self-reliant
> and firm, Mr. Scott was naturally timid, diffident, and yielding;
> and, while the former was calm, steady and prudent, the latter
> was excitable, variable and precipitate....in Mr. Campbell the un-
> derstanding predominated, in Mr. Scott the feelings; and, if the
> former excelled in imagination, the latter was superior in brillian-
> cy of fancy. If the tendency of one was to generalize, to take wide
> and extended views and to group a multitude of particulars under
> a single head or principle, that of the other was to analyze, to
> divide subjects into their particulars and consider their
> details....In a word, in almost all of those qualities of mind and
> character, which might be regarded differential or distinctive,
> they were singularly fitted to supply each others wants and to
> form a rare and delightful companionship.[9]

The complementary personalities of Scott and Campbell would be merely
interesting if it were not for the fact that the nature of their relationship had a
crucial and lasting effect on the Restoration Movement. Walter Scott stayed in
Pittsburgh until 1826 when he moved to Steubenville, Ohio. This placed him
close to Campbell's church at Wellsburg and in the immediate vicinity of the
Mahoning Baptist Association. On his way from Wellsburg to New Lisbon,
Ohio for the association's annual (1827) meeting, Campbell stopped at
Steubenville and invited Scott to accompany him. The minutes of the associa-

tion reveal the formation of a committee to nominate a person "to travel and labor among the churches." Later in the meeting Walter Scott was chosen to fulfill this task.

Scott was not a member of the Mahoning Association, he did not reside in the association's district, and, in fact he was not even a Baptist. But Association members hoped he would address some problems. According to Baxter the association was suffering from a deep malaise, caused by the "ultra Calvinist views then prevalent."[10] The association was hardly growing at all. In 1827 fifteen churches reported only thirty-four baptisms and eleven of these were from Campbell's Wellsburg church. In the previous year seventeen churches reported only eighteen baptisms while there were twenty-three exclusions and deaths.[11]

The apathy was a result of the kind of Calvinist theology which had come to dominate the American frontier. It was rooted in a firm conviction that individuals could do nothing to save themselves, but rather had to wait for the direct influence of the Holy Spirit. This was coupled with a stress on a religious experience, an agitation of the feelings rather than a change of conduct. The result was often an apathy, an inability to resolve conflict or to effect change in one's life except during periods of great excitement which tended to rise and fall in cycles of short duration. This was the context of the growth of the Restoration Movement, where the ideas of Alexander Campbell were applied with great success by Walter Scott because they resolved satisfactorily the question, "How does one become a Christian?"

This was the question. The solution, some realized, lay in the ordinance of baptism. Some of the prominent preachers including Scott "were indeed aware that Mr. Campbell had spoken of it [i.e. baptism] at the McCalla debate as a pledge of pardon, but in this point of view it was, as yet, contemplated only *theoretically*, none of them having so understood it when they were themselves baptized, and being yet unable properly and practically to realize or appreciate its importance in this respect."[12] This was Walter Scott's contribution to the Restoration Movement: to transform the intellectual insights of Alexander Campbell from theory to the practice of a new evangelism.

Scott's genius lay in his ability to arrange various facets of the gospel in their proper order, and to do it simply and effectively.[13] Scott's theory of salvation rests on the presupposition that faith is attainable by man through reason. The most basic principle of the Christian faith is that Jesus is the Messiah and this can be proved simply by applying man's reason to the evidence supplied by revelation. Once reason convinces one that Jesus is the Christ then it simply follows that everything else in the Christian system rests upon Christ's authority. To restore the original process of conversion it is necessary to go back to the New Testament to see what Jesus commanded and the apostles did.

The emphasis was, therefore, very different from the system of conversion heretofore prevalent on the American frontier. Men and women did not have to wait for the intervention of the Holy Spirit, nor was a frenzy of emotion necessary or even desirable. Rather there was an appeal to reason and authority. In short there were three things that a person could do, in fact should do, to foster the process of salvation: believe that Jesus is the Messiah, based upon the scriptural evidence; repent personal sins with the resolve to sin no more; and be baptized. Then there were three things that God could do and promised to do if conditions were fulfilled: forgive repented sins; bestow the gift of the Holy Spirit; and grant eternal life.

Walter Scott developed this formula for salvation over a period of years, particularly in a series of articles published in the *Christian Baptist* entitled, "A Divinely Authorized Plan of Preaching the Christian Religion." This formulation was largely complete by 1827[14] and if it seems very similar to the method employed by Alexander Campbell in his *Christian System* it may well be that the latter incorporated the arrangement into his own theology. But the real genius of Walter Scott lay in his ability to preach and to make the most complicated arguments intelligible to the average person on the frontier. So the six points described above became, in practice, five with either the ultimate or penultimate being omitted or combined to yield an arrangement such as: 1. faith; 2. repentance; 3. baptism; 4. remission of sins; 5. Holy Spirit. In this fashion it became known as the five-point formula or the five-finger exercise. Scott liked to meet children after school, introduce himself and ask the children if they would like to learn a new five-finger exercise. It only took a few minutes to teach it to them, as they ticked off "faith," "remission" etc. on each of their five fingers. Then he would tell them to go home and teach it to their parents. This almost always gave him entry into the neighborhood at large.[15]

At the same time that Scott was chosen as evangelist for the Mahoning Association he had already developed his method of evangelizing, but now it was necessary to put his ideas into practice. At first he met with failure as he introduced his new method of explaining the gospel outside the association. After laying before the audience his analysis of scripture he invited those disposed to come forward to be baptized for the remission of sins. No one, however, came. Richardson offers an analysis of that initial failure, with a view of the consternation which must have been widespread among a frontier people used to a very different process of conversion:

> The whole community were [sic] filled with the notion that some special spiritual influence was to be exerted upon men's hearts - that some supernatural visitation must occur before any one could be a fit subject for baptism. This spiritual operation, too, all had been taught to regard as the evidence of acceptance and pardon, and hence when they were simply invited to come direct-

ly forward and be baptized for the remission of sins, they were filled with amazement that any one should thus propose to dispense with all the usual processes to which "mourners" and pentitents were subjected. Like the Syrian noble, they were offended because the usual ceremonies were not observed, and because they were merely directed to "wash and be clean." None of them had ever witnessed or heard of such a proceeding. They could find no precedent for it among all the rites and ceremonies of the religious parties, and hence, being without the authority conferred by usage, they could regard it only as an innovation.[16]

Here is a concrete example just how revolutionary the Restoration Movement was within the context of nineteenth-century American religion.

Walter Scott was not deterred by this initial failure. Instead he was determined to try again at New Lisbon, Ohio where he had received his appointment as evangelist. In one of the most oft-repeated stories of the Restoration, Scott decided to give notice that he was going to deliver a series of discourses on the "Ancient Gospel."[17] The subject of his first discourse was Matthew 16:16 and Acts 2:38. This was the theological heart of the Restoration Movement because these passages revealed the Messiahship of Jesus and the doctrine of baptism for the remission of sins. Just as Scott was about to conclude his long discourse, a stranger entered the church and stood in the back among the overflowing crowd. The preacher gave a brief summary and invited anyone present to come forward and to be baptized for the remission of sins. To everyone's surprise the stranger immediately stepped forward and presented himself. Upon being questioned carefully, he seemed to understand the matter perfectly and so was baptized for "the remission of sins" according to the formula used by Peter in Acts 2:38. The stranger was William Amend who through his own study of Scripture had come to the same conclusions as Walter Scott. He had resolved to wait until he heard the gospel preached in the same words as Peter had preached it, and when he heard Scott do that very thing he did not hesitate to heed his call to baptism.

The event was a real turning point in the Restoration Movement. According to Richardson the ordinance of baptism was restored to its proper place for the first time since the primitive church: "The people were filled with bewilderment at the strange truths brought to their ears, and now exemplified before their eyes in the baptism of a penitent for a purpose which now, on the 18th of November, 1827, for the first time since the primitive ages was fully and practically realized." In effect, then, the ancient order of things had been restored.

The baptism of William Amend was a turning point for another reason. Here again are the words of Robert Richardson:

A great excitement at once ensued; the subject was discussed everywhere through the town, and Mr. Scott, continuing daily to address increasing audiences and developing his views of the gospel in all its parts, succeeded, before the close of the meeting, in inducing in all seventeen persons to accept the primitive faith and baptism. Thus the charm was broken; the word of God had triumphed, and the veil which theology had cast over men's hearts was removed. Henceforth the Reformation, which had already restored to the Church the ancient order of things and the simplicity of the primitive faith, was enabled to make a practical application of the gospel to the conversion of the world.[18]

With the conversion of large numbers of people, the Restoration Movement was being transformed from an intellectual movement into a church.

It was probably not immediately apparent just what had happened at New Lisbon. But within a few months the growing number of converts was beginning to present the movement with some problems. Since the Mahoning Association was a Baptist organization and since practices of the Regular Baptists were being increasingly abandoned, the conversions were creating much controversy. After consulting with his father, Alexander Campbell requested that the former visit the Western Reserve and evaluate the progress that Walter Scott was making there. It is remarkable that Thomas Campbell understood so quickly and clearly the implications of what Walter Scott was doing:

I perceive that theory and practice in religion, as well as in other things, are matters of distinct consideration....We have spoken and published many things correctly concerning the ancient gospel, its simplicity and perfect adaptation to the present state of mankind, for the benign and gracious purposes of its immediate relief and complete salvation; but I must confess that, in respect of the direct exhibition and application of it for that blessed purpose, I am at present, for the first time, upon the ground where the thing has appeared to be practically exhibited to the proper purpose. 'Compel them to come in,' saith the Lord, 'that my house may be filled.'[19]

Thomas Campbell is saying quite clearly that he and his son had developed certain theoretical principles for the reunification of the church of Christ based on the restoration of primitive Christianity. But they had not been able to devise a means of getting people to join that church. Now, for the first time, Walter Scott had come up with a way to accomplish just that.

Separation from the Baptists

The practical consequences of Walter Scott's evangelism manifested themselves quickly. Within three years of Scott's appointment, the Mahoning Association had been transformed. The association had probably always harbored a certain sympathy towards restorationism since it had, in effect, provided a refuge for Alexander Campbell from the hostility of the Redstone Baptist Association. With the influx of new converts, who were attracted by the message of Scott, the association effectively ceased to be a Baptist organization. At its annual meeting in August 1830, at Austintown, Ohio, there was overwhelming sentiment to dissolve the Mahoning Association. There was a conviction that such an association violated the principle of adhering to the practices of the early church, which they professed, and also that such an organization had a tendency to exercise arbitrary power. It was unanimously decided to end the Mahoning Association as "an advisory council" or an "ecclesiastical tribunal" and to convert it into an annual meeting "for worship, and to hear reports of the progress of the gospel."[20]

The dissolution of the Mahoning Association was but one step in the process of separation from the Baptists. In retrospect separation seems almost inevitable even at the time the Brush Run Church joined the Redstone Association in 1813. One must question just how "Baptist" the Reformers ever were. Of course the Mahoning Association must have been even less orthodox to accept Campbell and his followers. So there were always differences and tensions between the Baptists and the Reformers, but the process of separation certainly accelerated after 1830.

Most writers agree that there were several differences in faith and practice between the Baptists and Reformers among which were:[21]

1. Baptists and Reformers shared a dedication to restore primitive Christianity, but there was much less sustained interest among the former in restoring the unity of the church.

2. Baptists and Reformers agreed that creeds ought not to be made tests of Christian fellowship. But whereas Reformers were sometimes opposed even to their existence, Baptists were willing to use creeds as general guidelines.

3. Both Baptists and Reformers agreed that no ecclesiastical body had the right to exercise authority over any congregation. But Baptists were generally united in associations that exercised a certain amount of influence over their members; Reformers almost always disbanded such associations.

4. Baptists saw no reason to question their name; Reformers regarded it as sectarian and non-biblical.

5. Baptists observed the Lord's Supper periodically but almost never more often than quarterly; Reformers observed the ordinance every Sunday.

6. To be accepted into the membership of a Baptist congregation, a believer had to make a confession of faith, relate a personal experience which gave credibility to that confession, receive a favorable congregational vote, and submit to baptism. Both groups held to baptism by immersion but the Reformers required only a confession of faith and baptism.

7. The item above reveals a significant theological difference between Baptists and Reformers. Experiential religion was far more important among Baptists, whereas the Reformers emphasized a more rational concept of faith.

8. The theological differences were focused especially on the subject of baptism. Baptists generally regarded baptism to be a sign that the Holy Spirit had operated on the mind and heart and that the remission of sins and regeneration had already transformed the believer. Reformers believed in baptism for the remission of sins.

9. Baptists restricted the administration of baptism and the Lord's Supper to ordained ministers whereas the Reformers held that all baptized persons have the right to administer the ordinances. Both groups de-emphasized the difference between clergy and laity, but the Reformers to a greater degree.

10. Alexander Campbell made a radical distinction between the Old and New Testaments. The Baptists made no such distinction.[22]

It is instructive to pause for a moment and consider the split between Baptists and Reformers from the Baptist point of view. Here is what one Baptist historian, H. Leon McBeth, has written recently:

> For Baptists Alexander Campbell has significance far beyond the antimission movement. In the 1820's, he led an ultraconservative "Reformation" which challenged historic Baptist teachings and ultimately split the denomination. Hundreds of Baptist churches left the denomination to line up with Campbell's "Reformers," who after 1830 formed a new denomination known as Disciples of Christ or Church of Christ. Historians estimate, for example, that fully half the Baptist churches of Kentucky switched to the new Disciples movement.[23]

Quite obviously from the Baptist perspective the separation was a traumatic and deeply divisive experience.

McBeth's list of disagreements between Baptists and Reformers would be basically the same as those mentioned above. In one area—different views of Scripture—he makes an illustrative remark: "Campbell embraced a stark literalism which required that all church practices have precept or precedent in scripture. By that hermeneutic, he rejected missionary societies, instrumental music in worship, the use of written confessions, regular salaries for ministers, the use of ministerial titles, and many other practices."[24] It is interesting to read a Southern Baptist historian using terms such as "ultraconservative" and "stark literalism" to describe a contemporary religious movement. This illustrates that while Baptists and Reformers shared many ideas and practices, they came from different Reformation traditions. The Baptists were more influenced by the institutional emphasis of Calvin's thought, while the Reformers were more affected by a primitivism derived from the radical Reformation.

The Consequences of Separation

The evangelism of Walter Scott and the separation from the Baptists was a real watershed in the history of the Restoration Movement. The years following 1830 marked the transition of the movement from a small minority among the Baptists to an independent religious group. This transition had widespread effects. One of these was a shift in emphasis within the movement from the construction of ideas to organizational development. This is not to suggest that the intellectual history of the Restoration Movement ended in 1830. Certainly, ideas continued to develop and new problems had to be confronted. But the fundamental ideas which identify and define the Restoration Movement such as the emphasis on the unity of the Church, the restoration of primitive Christianity, and baptism for the remission of sins, were largely in place by the time of separation. After the 1830's, the formative years of the movement came to an end. These years had been distinguished by almost purely intellectual activity. Once the Reform ceased to be only a movement of ideas and became also an institution with thousands of members spread over a geographic area of great and growing diversity, then other, different problems arose which occupied much of the attention of the movement's leadership.

Alexander Campbell was at the forefront of this transition. In 1830 he began to publish the *Millennial Harbinger.* He abandoned the *Christian Baptist* certainly because it was an inappropriate title after separation from the Baptists, but also because he felt that it was time to present his ideas with a milder tone.[25] With independence came the responsibility not only to criticize but also to develop a model for a truly reformed church. It is in this direction that

Alexander Campbell in particular and the Restoration Movement in general began to move in the 1830's. It is almost as if the movement had struggled to define itself for two decades and with that task in hand, could now afford to shift its concern towards bringing like-minded people together under the aegis of the primitive faith.

The most immediate consequence of the separation from the Baptists was that independence allowed the Reformers to unite with other religious groups. Heretofore the Restoration Movement had been embodied, for the most part, in two separate groups. Because these two groups so emphasized the autonomy of the local congregation and were so deeply suspicious of "sectarian structures," they were slow to coalesce into definable entities. The terms which those in the movement preferred were "Christians" and "Reformers" respectively. The contemporary shorthand, with connotations of derision and hostility, was "Stoneites" and "Campbellites," the followers of Barton Stone and Alexander Campbell.

The two groups elaborated a remarkably similar set of ideas considering that they had developed separately. The first personal contacts came as a consequence of Alexander Campbell's debate with the Rev. W. L. McCalla which took place in October 1823 at Washington, Kentucky. After the debate Campbell traveled to Lexington where he preached, and although his writings and ideas had preceded him, this visit was a real catalyst for communication between the Stone and Campbell movements. In 1824 Campbell returned to Kentucky for a three month tour. By this time he had begun publishing the *Christian Baptist* and had written an article on "Experimental Religion," denying that the notion was scriptural. The idea provoked much debate in Kentucky, which had been the site of the great Cane Ridge meeting. Richardson includes a long section on the first meeting between Campbell and "Racoon" John Smith which focuses on their discussion of "experimental religion." Both men emerged from this discussion in complete agreement.[26]

John Smith was to become one of the principal architects of the union of the Reformers and Christians. Smith's life was a typical one on the American frontier. Just a few months before he was born in October 1784, Smith's family had crossed the mountains and settled in eastern Tennessee. He grew up in a log cabin, the ninth of thirteen children, in a devoutly religious family. They were dedicated Calvinists, Baptists who felt that no one was saved until they had received a mysterious call from the Holy Spirit.[27] Smith received only the barest rudiments of an education, but by the time the family relocated to Kentucky he could read the New Testament.

Typical of his time and place, John Smith anguished over his own depravity and salvation. Finally, he felt convinced that he was saved, went to the local Baptist church, related his experience and was accepted into membership. He struggled for years about becoming a preacher before finally taking an examination and being ordained a Baptist minister in 1808. Smith married and bought some land near Huntsville, Alabama. Several years later, two of his children burned to death when their cabin caught fire. Smith's wife died of grief and he contracted a fever and nearly died as well. He returned to Kentucky in an effort to carry on with his life but he was deeply disturbed by the assumptions of popular Calvinism which suggested that his children were doomed to eternal damnation because they had not yet had a religious experience.

It was around this time that Alexander Campbell began publishing the *Christian Baptist* and Smith became a subscriber. He met Campbell during his 1824 trip to Kentucky and gradually came to accept most of his ideas concerning creeds, baptism, and the clergy. Smith was enormously successful as an evangelist earning the nickname the "Dipper" because of the number of immersions he had performed. As the Reformers and Baptists were splitting, Smith emerged as one of the most effective leaders of the reform in Kentucky.

John T. Johnson also played an important role in the unification of the Reformers and Christians. He was born in Kentucky in 1788 to a family with close ties to the military. Both his father and brother were colonels in the army and the latter was elected a United States senator and vice-president of the United States under Martin Van Buren. John T. received an unusually good education for the time. He studied at a private academy run by a Presbyterian minister and then attended Transylvania College, receiving a degree in law. Johnson was a successful farmer, businessman, and politician. He was elected to the Kentucky State Legislature and was a Congressman for ten years. In 1830 he retired from Congress and devoted himself to his long-standing interest in religion. He began to study the writings of Alexander Campbell of whom he said: "My eyes were opened, and I was made perfectly free by the truth. And the debt of gratitude I owe to that man of God, Alexander Campbell, no language can tell."[28] In 1821 Johnson had joined the Baptist church at Great Crossings. By 1831 he was attempting to introduce Restoration ideas into the church, which were rejected. Johnson and a few others withdrew and founded their own congregation which grew quickly. In the same year Barton W. Stone, who was editing the *Christian Messenger* in nearby Georgetown, Kentucky, invited Johnson to become co-editor. This was perhaps just what the movement needed: an ex-Baptist "Campbellite" editor of a "Christian" journal.

This editorial union of Christians and Reformers was augmented by an agreement between the two congregations in Georgetown to worship together. They found that they shared so many beliefs and practices that a complete union was soon considered.[29] At a meeting held in Lexington on January 1, 1832, John Smith spoke for the Reformers and Barton Stone represented the Christians. After each delivered poignant speeches, Stone extended his hand to Smith who grasped it warmly. Representatives from both sides rose and joined hands with each other. Hymns were sung, the Lord's Supper was observed; unity seemed imminent. Unfortunately, within a few weeks difficulties became obvious. The Christians believed that only ordained ministers could officiate at the Lord's Supper. The Reformers made no distinction between clergy and laity. It took an additional three years to work out a complete merger.[30]

The Union of Reformers and Christians

Part of the difficulty lay in how to effect a merger. While the Christians were perhaps slightly more structured, both groups identified themselves by rejecting non-scriptural institutions. As a result there could be little structural merger of agencies or organizations. Congregations could be consolidated; ministers could preach at sister congregations. But the idea of merger was reduced to the type of ecclesial activity which had already been taking place. The Lexington meeting, therefore, created a team consisting of John Smith (Reformer) and John Rogers (Christian) which went out to visit each of the churches, held meetings, and carried the message of union. This effort was supported financially by contributions from both groups. Journalism always played an important role in the Restoration Movement, so that joint editorships and circulation of journals across group lines was another means of cooperation. In such an ultra-congregational context little more could be done.

The whole question of union is an important one, especially in light of subsequent divisions in the Restoration Movement. Robert Richardson offers a shrewd evaluation of the approaches of the leading figures of their respective movements, Alexander Campbell and Barton Stone:

> Both Mr. Campbell and Mr. Stone were alike devoted to the great end of uniting the true followers of Christ into one communion upon the Bible, but each regarded the method of its accomplishment from his own point of view. Mr. Campbell, contemplating the distinct congregations with their proper functionaries as the highest religious executive authority on earth, was in doubt how a *formal* union could be attained, whether by a general convention of messengers or a general assembly of the people. Barton W. Stone, on the other hand, looking at the essential spirit of the gospel, exclaimed, "Oh, my bretheren let us repent and do the first works, let us seek for more holiness, rather than trouble ourselves and others with schemes and plans of union. The love of God, shed abroad in our hearts by the Holy Ghost given unto us, will more effectually unite than all the wisdom of the world combined."[31]

The differences between Campbell and Stone were deeply rooted in their own personalities and intellects. The former always leaned towards a more rigorous logic, a tendency to explore all the possibilities before arriving at a definite conclusion which he was always ready to defend vigorously. Stone was milder by nature and not so inclined to be consistent or to argue his case. More a visionary than an organizer, Stone had a proclivity to trust in God to resolve disagreements, which manifested itself in a tendency to blur specific differences in favor of general agreement.

It is hardly surprising, therefore, that very soon after the Reformers broke with the Baptists, Barton Stone began to urge the union of the two groups. In 1831 he wrote in the *Christian Messenger:*

> In spirit we are united, and that no reason existed on our side to prevent the union in form. It is well known to those bretheren, and to the world, that we have always from the beginning declared our willingness, and desire to be united with the whole family of God on earth, irrespective of the diversity of opinion among them.[32]

Typically, Alexander Campbell was much more cautious, and thought a union was premature. He noted Stone's lack of precision and questioned how a "union in form" could be effected without some sort of meeting. Was it to be a meeting of messengers or a general assembly of the sum total of both groups? Stone's proposal lacked a precision which Campbell's mind demanded. More precisely, Campbell felt that a union had to be based firmly on Restoration principles. Because he had only just discovered those principles, more time was needed to discuss and disseminate them:

> To us it appears the only practicable way to accomplish this desirable object, is to propound the ancient gospel and the ancient order of things in the words and sentences found in the apostolic writings: to abandon all traditions and usages not found in the record, and to make no human terms of communion. But on this theme much must yet be said before all the honest will understand it. One thing, however, is already sufficiently plain to all, that a union amongst Christians can be obtained only upon Scriptural grounds, and not upon any sectarian platform in existence.[33]

It is quite clear that the idea for the union of Reformers and Christians was initiated by Barton Stone. But the determination of Campbell to better define the grounds for union was not laid to rest. In effect, Campbell forced Stone to participate in a series of correspondences to settle various disagreements that he thought should have been resolved before union. This debate continued until 1840. A brief review of this debate will be of help in understanding the diversity of opinions that were contained in the Restoration Movement.

The Christians and Reformers shared both similarities and differences. It is fair to say that the similarities greatly outweighed the differences or else union would have been impossible. Certainly both groups emphasized a Biblical primitivism and the necessity of uniting all Christians. Both rejected creeds as tests of fellowship; both recognized only two ordinances, the Lord's Supper and baptism; and both practiced believers' baptism by immersion. Both rejected sectarian and non-scriptural names.

On the other hand there were differences. Probably the most obvious, though in the end one of the less important disagreements, revolved around the name for the church. Stone chose the name "Christian," while Campbell preferred the designation "Disciples of Christ." The controversy was carried on in the opponents' respective journals over a period of almost ten years and at times degenerated into legalisms. Campbell chose "Disciples" because the term was more ancient, (the disciples were called "disciples" in the Bible before they were called "Christians" at Antioch); because it is more descriptive; because it is more "scriptural," (since the Acts of the Apostles uses the term "Disciple" thirty times but "Christian" only twice); and because it is more unappropriated, (other groups use the term "Christian" but no one else uses "Disciples.") Stone responded "that 'Disciples' is a common, not a proper noun, and not even a patronymic, while 'Christian' is a proper and patronymic name because it is derived from Christ the founder. Campbell replied that Christian is not a patronymic because Christ is not a proper name."[34] And so the arguments went.

Both Thomas Campbell and Walter Scott joined with Stone in preferring "Christian," but Alexander Campbell was adamant. Eventually both sides were persuaded to drop the discussion as harmful to the common good. Failing to reach a decision on a name has had some practical consequences. All three religious bodies which share a Restoration heritage, the Churches of Christ, the Christian Church and Churches of Christ, and the Christian Church (Disciples of Christ) also share similar names which are derived directly from this controversy. Names become even more confusing on a local level where, for example a particular congregation called a Church of Christ could be associated with any of the three groups. Then there are groups with similar names such as the United Church of Christ, which have nothing to do with the Restoration Movement, and which compound the confusion, especially to an outsider.

Genuine theological issues such as Christology were also grounds for disagreement,[35] but for the most part differences rested on the degree to which principles were to be applied. Both Reformers (Disciples) and Christians shared a commitment to the restoration of primitive Christianity and to the unity of the Church of Christ. Alexander Campbell had shifted the balance between these two tendencies in favor of the "truth motive." Relatively speaking, Barton Stone emphasized more the "unity motive." This can be seen in several specific instances. For example, the two groups agreed that there were two ordinances, baptism and the Lord's Supper, but disagreed on the details. Both Stone and

Campbell agreed that the correct mode of baptism was immersion and that it was for the remission of sins, but Stone could not bring himself to consider that all of the unimmersed, regardless of character, would be condemned. Similarly, Stone was opposed to excluding the unimmersed from communion and fellowship. Campbell, on the other hand, thought Stone was too latitudinarian and tended to restrict salvation to the immersed alone.[36] At the time of union the Reformers practiced closed communion and the Christians open communion. Regarding the Lord's Supper, the Reformers observed the ordinance weekly, the Christians somewhat less frequently. It will be recalled that the union of the two groups at Lexington foundered over the issue of who could administer the Lord's Supper. The Christians had a "higher" concept of the clergy than the Reformers who were adamant in maintaining that there was no difference between clergy and laity.

Finally, the Reformers and Christians differed over methods of evangelism. Alexander Campbell had not developed an explicit method of evangelism. That task fell to Walter Scott, but his method, which was very clear and rational, fit perfectly with the ideas of both Campbells. This was a system in which emotion had no place. Barton Stone, on the other hand, came out of a tradition which was altogether different. The Christians were deeply rooted in frontier revivalism and their emphasis on "conversion" was one of the principle sources of their separation from the Presbyterians. Typically, Barton Stone accepted Scott's five-finger exercise while continuing also to hold the opinion that the gifts of the Holy Spirit could come before immersion.

Alexander Campbell's opinion of revivalism was perfectly clear. Rooted no doubt in his Lockian rationalism and in a metaphysics which separated moral from physical power, (e.g. that the Spirit works through the Word alone) he thought revivalism was unscriptural at best and fanatical at worst. The theological differences centered on the Holy Spirit. Campbell wrote quite openly on those differences:

> in the rage for sectarian proselytism, "the Holy Ghost" is an admirable contrivance. Every qualm of conscience, every new motion of the heart, every strange feeling or thrill, - all doubts, fears, despondencies - horrors, remorse, etc., etc., are the work of this Holy Ghost.

and

> We must occasionally notice the fanaticism of this age on the subject of *mystic impulses*; for, in our humble opinion, the constant proclamation of "the Holy Ghost" of the schoolmen, and all its in-

fluences, is the greatest delusion of our age, and one of the most prolific causes of the infidelity, immorality, and irreligion of our contemporaries.[37]

Most historians of the movement indicate that no real conflict ensued over programs of evangelism, but with differences so clearly delineated it is difficult to believe that tension did not exist. Perhaps the tension eased over time and was lessened by changing attitudes. Perhaps though, it was one of the bases of division.

The differences, indeed acrimony, between Barton Stone and Alexander Campbell were such that union of their respective movements would never have occurred if it had depended on a personal coming together of these two leaders. The union was promoted largely out of the spirit of Barton Stone and only by effectively bypassing Campbell was unity effected. Barton Stone was a man caught in the middle. Deeply committed to Christian unity he wanted to unite not only with the Reformers but also with the "Christian Connection" in the East. This was a union of three separate groups which had divided from the Baptists, Methodists, and Presbyterians, respectively. They emphasized Christian unity and the independence of each congregation.[38] He labored long and hard to realize this union, but ultimately failed.

There was considerable animosity between Alexander Campbell and the leaders of the Christian Connection. The Christian Connectionists accused Campbell of limiting the work of the Holy Spirit to the Word. They felt that Campbell's religion was "spiritless," and unlike Stone, they refused to compromise their heritage in "experimental religion."[39] Closely connected was the doctrine of baptism. The Eastern Christians described Campbell's position as the "soul chilling doctrine of water baptism." They accused the "Campbellites" of denying the efficacy of prayer since the Spirit could not operate before baptism.[40] The Trinity was yet another source of disagreement. The Christian Connectionists were convinced that Campbell was a Trinitarian and Calvinist just as Campbell was certain that the Christians in the East were Unitarians.[41]

The union between "Campbellite" Reformers and "Stoneite" Christians was a turning point in the Restoration Movement. The 1830's were crucial because, thanks to the merger and to the evangelism of Walter Scott, the Restoration Movement became an independent religious organization of significant size. It ceased to be a movement within Presbyterianism or among the Baptists and became an independent religious body. Leaders such as Alexander Campbell found their roles changing from iconoclasts and prophets to shepherds whose primary obligation was to maintain unity and cooperation. In many instances this impetus towards greater organization was in direct confrontation with the centrifugal forces of the movement and with the character of the American frontier in which it thrived.

The differences in personalities, socioeconomic status, and educational background between Barton Stone and Alexander Campbell were profound, and despite many common ideas, the union of the forces each led was, at first, tenuous indeed. Alexander Campbell was not a personality who fostered unity. The strength of his character and the force of his ideas were such that while many found him an inspirational leader, many others found him repugnant. Although there were signs of significant growth just after the union of Reformers and Christians, by 1834 the movement was in difficulty. The rate of conversion had slowed and by June 1835 there were indications that many were withdrawing from the leadership of Barton Stone.[42] Undoubtedly, this withdrawal can be traced in large part to the rejection of Campbell as a leader of the movement. The 1830's were replete with steady controversy between Campbell and Stone and between Campbell and the Christian Connection. Outside of the movement Campbell continued his practice of debating his opponents. In 1837 he debated John B. Purcell, Catholic Bishop of Cincinnati, and in 1843 Campbell debated Rev. N. L. Rice, a Presbyterian minister, in Lexington, Kentucky.

Finally, the union of Reformers and Christians represented the merger of two groups which had developed separately and which had produced diverse ideas which went beyond the personality differences of their respective leaders. The different role which emotional revival played in each movement comes quickly to mind. Perhaps the most significant result of the union was the internalization of these differences within what was to be a united religious body. In other words, the roots of division within the Restoration Movement can be traced to the separation from the Baptists, the union between Christians and Reformers, and institutional growth.

By 1840, then, the Restoration Movement was in the process of becoming a religious body of significant size, which faced the question of how and to what extent cooperation was to be pursued. It was now spread out over a large and growing geographical area, and contained within it deep internal divisions, all during a time in American history in which sectional and societal divisions were increasing. The intellectual development of the Restoration Movement was largely done. All of the principal precepts of unity and biblical primitivism which still mark the movement were identified and developed. The next issue which had to be faced was no longer what the movement was to be, but rather how, in fact whether, the Restoration Movement was able to systematize a method to sustain simultaneously its two organic principles — unity and biblical truth.

Chapter Six

Intellectual and Social
Origins of Division

It may seem somewhat odd to end the history of the Restoration Movement in the 1840's and 1850's, when arguably it had only begun two decades before with the separation of the Reformers from the Baptists. Even the "Christians" associated with Barton Stone can trace themselves back as a group only to the first decade of the nineteenth century. It hardly seems warranted to end an account of a movement before the outbreak of the Civil War when in fact that movement was only just beginning.

However, concluding in the 1850's can be justified by recalling the purpose of the study: the intellectual origins of the Restoration Movement. The Campbells, Stone, and Scott were beginning to pass from the scene. Many of their ideas remained and in fact were accepted as the heritage of the movement by a vast majority of its adherents. This phase of intellectual development — introduction and acceptance of basic tenets — was complete. The dynamic of the evolution of those ideas continued, especially as affected by the peculiar American environment. But a new phase in the history of the movement was beginning. This phase was marked by institutional and membership growth, greater diversity, and ultimately division. What remains to be accomplished is to summarize the characteristics of this phase, especially in light of the intellectual origins of the Restoration Movement. This new phase of restoration history extends approximately from 1840 until the end of the century, although I will be emphasizing the first twenty years.

This summary will focus on organizations and on instrumental music, two issues which were particularly controversial. But first it is necessary to understand better the institutionalization of the movement which was occurring during these crucial decades.

Membership Growth

The gathering of church membership statistics has been and continues to be an inexact science. Nevertheless, some estimates are possible. It has been suggested that at the time of merger in 1832 the "Campbellite" reformers had at least twelve thousand members and the "Stoneite" Christians about ten thousand, for a total of twenty-two thousand.[1] Most authorities agree that after some initial adjustments and a loss of membership, membership growth was extraordinarily rapid. Garrison and DeGroot estimate that by 1860 there were at least 192,000 members.[2] The states with the largest memberships were, in descending order: Kentucky, Ohio and Indiana (tied), Missouri, Illinois, Tennessee, Iowa, and Virginia. A few deductions are obvious. States where the movement began, Kentucky (Stone) and Ohio-West Virginia (Campbell) had large memberships. The movement was concentrated on the secondary frontier and not the primary frontier, which by 1860 was well into the Great Plains. Membership followed migratory patterns from Tennessee, Kentucky, and Ohio into Indiana, Illinois, and Missouri. Finally, the membership was neither primarily northern nor southern but was concentrated along the border states, most of which sided with the North during the Civil War, but which contained large minorities with Southern sympathies. Looked at another way, these eight largest states were evenly divided in number between slave states and free states.

Rapid growth continued for the rest of the century. By 1900 there were an estimated 1,120,000 members,[3] which would have made the Restoration Movement one of the largest religious groups in the United States.[4]

Organizational Growth

With such rapid membership growth it is hardly surprising that this period of time was also marked by organizational growth. It is one of the truisms of the Restoration Movement that its leaders were also editors, that given the hostility toward "denominational structures," publishing was the principal means of organizing the movement. Each of the early leaders edited his own journal. Of course, Alexander Campbell founded the *Millennial Harbinger,* to which his father often contributed. Barton Stone published the *Christian Messenger* from 1826 to 1837 and then again from 1839 to 1845. Walter Scott's periodical *The Evangelist* began publication in 1832 and closed in 1844.

As the movement grew, more and more individuals established periodicals which published weekly, monthly, or quarterly.[5] As disagreements became more prominent, particularly just before and after the Civil War, more and more publications were founded to express a particular point of view. Among more than a score of such publications a few were particularly influential. By the beginning of the Civil War the *Millennial Harbinger,* which had dominated the movement for thirty years, began to wane. In 1856 Benjamin Franklin (1812-1878) began publishing the *American Christian Review* in Cincinnati. Through the *Review,* Franklin became the spokesman for opposition to the missionary society and to the "liberal digression" in general. For twenty years until his death in 1878 the *American Christian Review* was perhaps the most influential and popular publication in the movement.

In 1866 the *Christian Standard* was established for the purpose of counteracting the conservative influence of Franklin. The editor from its founding until his death in 1888 was Isaac Errett who by the 1880's was the most influential figure in the movement. Because it had been founded explicitly as an alternative to the *Review,* the *Standard* could be classified as liberal, though it was far from radical and tended to express the views of the center of the Restoration Movement. By the 1890's several journals well to the left of the *Christian Standard* began to appear.

Similarly, many journals sprang up to the right of the *Standard* and to the *Review* as well. The most influential of these was the *Gospel Advocate.* Founded in 1855 by Tolbert Fanning, it ceased publication during the war but resumed in 1866. By this time Fanning was well on in years and soon resigned editorial control to David Lipscomb and Elisha Sewell. For the next forty years, David Lipscomb, in particular, became the predominant spokesman for the conservative wing of the party. Published in Nashville, the *Advocate* became a voice for the defeated South as well as an advocate for the type of restorationism which flourished in central Tennessee. Although it was clearly conservative, over the second half of the nineteenth century many publications were established which were to the right of the *Gospel Advocate.*

Institutions of higher education were also founded in great numbers at this time. All of the early leaders of the Restoration Movement had unusually good educations. Barton Stone had attended David Caldwell's academy in North Carolina, both Campbells had attended the University of Glasgow, and Walter Scott was educated at the University of Edinburgh. All of these men, especially Thomas Campbell, taught a great deal during their lives and were particularly interested in education.

The first institution of higher learning associated with the movement was Bacon College at Georgetown, Kentucky, which was organized in 1836. Its origin lay in the expulsion of a professor of mathematics, Thornton F. Johnson, from Georgetown College which was a Baptist institution. The first "Christian" college thus paralleled the separation of the "Campbellites" from the Baptists. It is interesting that the new college was named for Francis Bacon, the so-called founder of the scientific method who is associated with empirical thought, which was so important to the intellectual origins of the movement. Walter Scott became the first president, though he only served for one year.[6]

Alexander Campbell had long been interested in founding a college which would devote itself to the propagation of moral culture based on the Bible. It seems that the unexpected genesis of Bacon College delayed his plans somewhat, since he did not want to interfere in the endowment of that institution. But by 1840 he was ready to act. Previously he had written extensively on the subject of education and in the winter of that year he obtained a charter. Campbell himself presented the board with a deed of land for the use of the institution and was elected president.[7] Bethany College became one of the most important educational institutions associated with the Restoration Movement, in large part due to the active role played by Campbell who was also professor of moral sciences until just before his death.

The third institution was Franklin College near Nashville, Tennessee. It was largely the work of Tolbert Fanning who managed to finance and staff the school in time to open in January 1845. Franklin prospered despite Fanning's refusal to accept an endowment. In 1861 it closed, however, a casualty of the Civil War. Attempts to revive it after the war were short lived. Despite its rather brief history, Franklin College established Nashville as an important center of learning for the Restoration Movement.

By the 1850's many more colleges were established; some failed, but many exist today. Too numerous to name, it might suffice to mention that Eureka College, founded at Eureka, Illinois in 1855 came to have a famous alumnus: Ronald Reagan.

Intellectual Developments

A new intellectual climate accompanied the membership and institutional growth of this period. In 1835 Alexander Campbell published *The Christian System*. In the Preface Campbell refers to the publication of his debates and to his writings in the *Christian Baptist* and *Millennial Harbinger*. He then turns to his purpose in writing the book: "our aim is now to offer to the public a more matured view of such cardinal principles as are necessary to the right interpretation of the Holy Scriptures..." and "I undertake this work with a deep sense of its necessity, and with much anticipation of its utility, in exhibiting a concentrated view of the whole ground we occupy, of rectifying some extremes, of furnishing new means of defence to those engaged in contending with this generation for primitive Christianity."[8] Campbell wants to lay out the principles contained in his effort to reform Christianity. Of course he had been doing just that for more than twenty years. Now, however, he speaks of offering a "more matured view" of those principles; in other words he has changed his views somewhat from the early days of the movement. Secondly, he wants to offer a "concentrated view," that is, a more comprehensive and logical and less extreme exposition of the principles of the Restoration Movement as he saw them. Campbell recognized a new stage in the movement, one which required a better organized and more moderate compilation of guiding principles.

Campbell was roundly criticized from outside the movement for at last providing a "creed" for his purportedly creedless movement. In the Preface to the second edition of *The Christian System* [9] Campbell responded: "We speak for ourselves only; and, while we are always willing to give a declaration of our faith and knowledge of the Christian system, we firmly protest against dogmatically propounding our own views, or those of any other fallible mortal, as a condition or foundation of church union and co-operation."

While Alexander Campbell reaffirmed his rejection of creeds as a condition for church union and presented *The Christian System* as his opinions alone, the writing of such a work illustrates the more moderate direction of his thought. It also illustrates his recognition that the movement was entering a new phase of development.

The Lunenburg Letter

The famous "Lunenburg Letter" is a good means of examining the shift in Alexander Campbell's thought and for introducing the problem of controversy within the movement, which became more and more predominant over the course of the century.

Baptism was one topic which had received careful and lengthy discussion by Campbell. In fact it was the combination of immersion and the doctrine of baptism for the remission of sins which distinguished the Restoration Movement from most other Christian bodies. The importance of baptism to Restoration thought (in fact to all Christian thought) rested on the relationship between baptism and becoming a Christian. In essence the question being posed was,"Who is a Christian?"

A "conscientious sister" from Lunenburg, Virginia took notice in Campbell's writings that he had admitted the possibility of Christians existing among the "sects." She wrote to Campbell and asked: "Will you be so good as to let me know how any one becomes a Christian?" and "Does the name of Christ or Christian belong to any but those who believe the gospel, repent, and are buried by baptism into the death of Christ?"

Campbell was responding in large part to questions raised by John Thomas, an English physician who had immigrated to the United States and who had established a gospel ministry in eastern Virginia in the vicinity of Lunenburg. By the time of the composition of the Lunenburg Letter Campbell had already engaged Thomas in a discussion of several issues. Undoubtedly Campbell wrote the Lunenburg Letter to counteract some of the opinions of Thomas and his followers. One of those opinions centered on baptism. Thomas had written that baptism, even in the "correct" form of immersion, if performed by denominationalists such as Presbyterians, Episcopalians, and Catholics was invalid because they preached a gospel different from that contained in the scriptures.[10] He also denied the validity of Baptist immersion because it was not for the remission of sins. Campbell replied with a broader interpretation of baptism which acknowledged that baptism could still be valid even if the baptized had an imperfect understanding of the meaning of baptism. This is the background for the Lunenburg Letter and Campbell's reply.

Alexander Campbell responded in an article published in the 1837 volume of the *Millennial Harbinger* entitled "Any Christians Among Protestant Parties?" The article is crucial to understanding the basis of division within the Restoration Movement and its intellectual history:

> Who is a Christian? I answer, Every one that believes in his heart that Jesus of Nazareth is the Messiah, the Son of God; repents of his sins, and obeys him in all things according to his measure of knowledge of his will. *A perfect man in Christ,* or a perfect Christian, is one thing; and "a babe in Christ," a stripling in the faith, or an imperfect Christian, is another. The New Testament recognizes both the perfect man and the imperfect man in Christ...

> I cannot, therefore, make any one duty the standard of Christian state or character, not even immersion into the name of the Father, of the Son, and of the Holy Spirit, and in my heart regard all that have been sprinkled in infancy without their own knowledge and consent, as aliens from Christ and the well-grounded hope of heaven...

> Should I find a Pedobaptist more intelligent in the Christian Scriptures, more spiritually minded and more devoted to the Lord than a Baptist, or one immersed on a profession of the ancient faith, I could not hesitate a moment in giving the preference of my heart to him that loveth most. Did I act otherwise, I would be a pure sectarian, a Pharisee among Christians. Still I will be asked, How do I know that any one loves my Master but by his obedience to his commandments? I answer, *In no other way.* But mark, I do not substitute obedience to one commandment for universal or even general obedience. And should I see a sectarian Baptist or a pedobaptist more spiritually-minded, more generally conformed to the requisitions of the Messiah, than one who precisely acquiesces with me in the theory or practice of immersion as I teach, doubtless the former rather than the latter, would have my cordial approbation and love as a Christian. So I judge, and so I feel. It is the image of Christ the Christian looks for and loves; and this does not consist in being exact in a few items, but in general devotion to the whole truth as far as known...

> There is no occasion, then, for making immersion, on a profession of the faith, absolutely essential to his sanctification and comfort. My right hand and my right eye are greatly essential to my

usefulness and happiness, but not to my life; and as I could not be a perfect man without them, so I cannot be a perfect Christian without a right understanding and a cordial reception of immersion in its true and scriptural meaning and design. But he that thence infers that none are Christians but the immersed, as greatly errs as he who affirms that none are alive but those of clear and full vision.[11]

Much to Campbell's surprise the response to the Lunenburg Letter evoked considerable reaction. Even today it functions as a guidepost to one's position in the movement. For example, the liberal critique focuses on the Alexander Campbell of the Lunenburg Letter:

This correspondence reveals an important aspect of Campbell's thought that must be taken into account if the basic witness of the man is to be understood. A significant number of his followers, particularly one and two generations later, adopted his inflexible Christian primitivism but virtually ignored the Lunenburg Letter which he wrote at the height of his powers. Their distorted view of Campbell contributed to the rise of Disciples scholasticism and multiplied the problems of a developing denomination.[12]

The conservative response has been either to ignore the Lunenburg Letter,[13] or to place it in historical context. Through the latter technique, Campbell's letter can become not a turning point in his thought but an aberration which ought not to shift focus from the early Alexander Campbell of the *Christian Baptist*. Others depict Campbell as the first person to ask the vital question of who is Christian, but who by himself was unable to supply a complete answer.

Of the "contextualists" David Roper is the most complete and convincing and has produced the most insightful conservative interpretation of the "Lunenburg Letter."[14] He sees three factors which explain the nature of Campbell's response to the letter. The first was the relative infancy of the movement. After all the movement began as an effort to unite all Christians who were defined at that time as anyone who believed in Jesus Christ. The design of baptism had not yet been clearly articulated, so Campbell's response was in the context of a new movement which still had many ties to the old ways. Secondly, Campbell was replying to the ideas and influence of Thomas which were reflecting badly on the Restoration Movement. Finally, only a few months before, Campbell had participated in a debate with Bishop Purcell where he functioned as a defender of Protestantism against the Catholic prelate. Campbell, feeling that a "breakthrough" was in the offing, wanted to court the favor of Protestants who he thought were now willing to join his movement. For this reason Campbell used the term "Christian" in an "accommodative" sense, that is, in a way in which the denominations used the term.[15]

It will serve no purpose to reproduce Roper's excellent analysis. It will suffice to make a few important points. The first appearance of "Any Christians among Protestant Parties" in the September issue of the *Harbinger* was barely four pages long. There is no evidence that Campbell thought he was saying anything new or particularly controversial. He was, in fact, surprised that the Lunenburg Letter evoked such a quick and clamorous response. In the November issue he responded with a two-page clarification invoking, significantly, I think, Paul and a Pauline frame of reference. This did not have the desired effect. The matter would not be put to rest and Campbell was forced to issue a seven-page article in December.

In this response Campbell attempted to defend himself from charges of inconsistency by citing from his past writings similar opinions on the question. He also defended his opinion from "the sectarian application of it" by dividing the unimmersed into two classes. Some who are ignorant of the obligation to be immersed for the remission of sins can be called Christians and can be saved. But those who know better, those who know Campbell's opinion, for example, which reflects the teaching of the Bible, can take no comfort because they have knowingly substituted the opinion of men for the will of God.

Finally, Campbell offered his reasons for delivering his original opinion in the September article. He suggests, as Roper observes, that he was addressing a larger Protestant audience:

> We have been always accused of aspiring to build up and head a party, while in truth we have always been forced to occupy the ground on which we now stand. I have for one or two years past labored to annul this impression, which I know is more secretly and generally bandied about than one in a hundred of our brethren suspect. On this account I consented the more readily to defend Protestantism; and I have, in ways more than I shall now state, endeavored to show the Protestant public that it is with the greatest reluctance we are compelled to stand aloof from them - that they are the cause of this great "schism," as they call it, and not we.[16]

Campbell also suggests that he was addressing John Thomas and his followers. This becomes even more clear in light of an "Extra" which Campbell produced in December 1837. This is a twelve-page refutation of Thomas and his ideas which is inscribed specifically to those who have addressed him on the subject of the "Lunenburg Letter." At the end of the article he states specifically: "The answer I gave to the sister of Lunenburg, I gave with a reference to this discussion [on the errors of Thomas]. I saw the hand of the *Advocate* [Thomas' publication] in those questions and answered accordingly: and for this reason have dedicated this Extra to all who were startled at said answer."[17]

Roper notes that Campbell, if anything, emphasized even more strongly the importance of baptism for the remission of sins in his subsequent writings.[18] Roper concludes his discussion with these words:

> Was Campbell right in using the word "Christian" in an accommodative sense? Was he right in speaking so strongly against one extreme that his words can be used to give aid to the other extreme? I believe that time has shown that Campbell was not right. The denominations did not give up their denominational ways even after he courted their favor. And his words, primarily directed against the errors of Thomas, have been used to foster positions that are, in their own way, just as deadly as any Thomas ever proposed.[19]

Upon reading all of the articles written by Alexander Campbell on the subject of Christians among the sects, it seems reasonable to conclude that he was both consistent and mainstream in his contentions. He was mainstream because he relied on that most influential of all disciples, Paul, for the basis of his argument:

> We have in Paul's style, the *inward* and the *outward* Jews; and may we not have the *inward* and the *outward* Christians? for true it is, that he is not always a Christian who is one outwardly: and one of my correspondents will say, 'Neither is he a Christian who is one inwardly? But all agree that he is, in the full sense of the word, a Christian who is one inwardly and outwardly. As the same Apostle reasons on circumcision, so we would reason on baptism: - "Circumcision," says the learned Apostle, "is not that which is outward in the flesh;" that is, as we apprehend the Apostle, it is not that which is outward in the flesh; but "circumcision is that of the heart, in the spirit, and not in the letter [only,] whose praise is of God, and not of man." So is baptism. It is not outward in the flesh only, but in the spirit also.[20]

Campbell was also consistent and took great pains in his December 1837 article to cite past statements to demonstrate this fact. None of these are more telling than the first, since it refers to one of the fundamental principles of the movement, that is, to the unity motive: "Let me ask, in the first place, what could mean all that we have written upon the union of Christians on apostolic grounds, had we taught that all Christians in the world were already united in our own community?"[21]

The consequences of the debate over the Lunenburg Letter are still apparent today. One popular conservative states flatly, for example, that "we simply are not on firm biblical ground to assume that one is forgiven, and hence a Christian, without having been immersed."[22] This conclusion has profound consequences, because it is based on biblical authority. In other words, if one accepts that the Bible teaches that baptism is immersion; that immersion is for the remission of sins; and that no one is to be considered a Christian without immersion, then it is impossible to violate the word of God and grant Christian status to the unimmersed. Of course some would also argue that God could grant clemency if God so chose. Nevertheless, most conservatives would reject modern ecumenism since it is based on erroneous principles. Denominationalism is itself an evil and to create, in effect, a super-denominational ecumenical structure is only to exacerbate the problem. That problem is that ecumenism is based on unity without shared beliefs and a genuine concern for truth. In the end the conservative in the Restoration Movement asks the question: How can we relate to other religious groups as Christians when they refuse to obey the explicit word of God which defines Christians as those who have been immersed for the remission of sins?[23]

Ultimately, the questions raised in the Lunenburg Letter are far-reaching because within them lie the definition of who is Christian and who is saved. Moreover, the debate which has proceeded from Campbell's response, reveals the kind of fissure which developed in the Restoration Movement. Here is how one conservative writer analyzed the implications of baptism:

> The liberal element in the movement sought to resolve this problem by removing baptism from its position of importance in the kingdom of God. While outwardly continuing to stand for immersion as the best expression of one's acceptance of Jesus, they played down the function of immersion that procures forgiveness through the blood of Christ. Thus in effect they were saying, "We differ on baptism, but this isn't really more important than other matters of disagreement. Let's work as fellow Christians for unity." Their continued stress on Christian union was at the expense of a fundamental teaching of God's word.[24]

To put it into familiar terms, it has been said that the liberals have sacrificed the truth motive for the unity motive. Of course the liberal would respond that conservatives have neglected the unity motive for the truth motive. In fact, such disagreements are rooted in varying perceptions of just what "truth" and "unity" mean.

The whole controversy about the Lunenburg Letter is crucial to the intellectual development of the Restoration Movement. It is difficult to avoid the conclusion, admittedly the opinion of an outsider, that the issue is less about the actual ideas contained in Campbell's articles than about ideological divisions within the movement. In other words, the actual function of the controversy has been to provide an ideological test to separate liberals from conservatives. Both sides have gone beyond the facts of the matter and have used their interpretation to justify their view of the Restoration Movement. But what is even more instructive for the purposes of this study is that as early as 1837, when the movement as an independent entity was barely five years old, serious ideological divisions were already manifest. Campbell was sincerely surprised by the controversy stimulated by his brief remarks because he felt he was applying principles which he had been advocating in print for years. What Campbell learned, perhaps, was that his carefully balanced ideas were being selectively received by his readers. The various components of Campbell's thought were being spun off into "liberal" and "conservative" interpretations, both of which invoked the authority of Alexander Campbell.

It is obvious that among some elements of the movement the idea of Christian unity had been seriously eroded. There seems to have been a strong predilection to find grounds for division between "Christians" and "Non-Christians" rather than on developing means to restore unity to the Church of Christ. It is ironic that Alexander Campbell, who had himself moved significantly in this same direction, especially in his series on the "Restoration of the Ancient Order of Things," was by 1837 being criticized as expounding an excessively "liberal" attitude towards the "sects." It is somewhat surprising that some within the movement were prepared to exclude all denominations from Christian status when just seven years before the movement was, at least technically, a part of one of those very denominations. I refer, of course, to the Reformers' Baptist connection. Above all, the Lunenburg Letter and the controversy it occasioned demonstrates that there were deep ideological divisions at the very inception of the Restoration Movement.

Roots of Division: Organizations

This period of restoration history reflects institutional growth and intellectual change. Not coincidentally, therefore, the two issues which produced the most passionate debate were organizations and instrumental music. Both issues challenged the movement to clarify its most basic principles. To state it so baldly is to oversimplify the matter. Certainly other issues were discussed and surely the issues themselves were rooted in other conditions which were political, social, or economic in origin. But it is not an overstatement to say that these two issues were and still are almost a means of identifying the three groups which have emerged from the Restoration Movement. In order to understand better the intellectual consequences of the Restoration Movement, it is necessary to examine the issues within which the great restoration principles, developed in the formative period, were being applied.

The controversy over organizations was rooted in the historical aversion of the Restoration Movement to denominationalism. To recall the genesis of the movement is to recall the rejection of presbyteries, creeds, and schisms, all of which had a non-scriptural and human basis. In the minds of many, to speak of almost any organization was to suggest the abandonment of one of the most cherished principles of restorationism and to become just like the "sects."

The debate can be best understood by keeping in mind that after 1840 the movement was entering into a new phase with different needs. In a very real sense the early movement, especially the part of it associated with Alexander Campbell had no need whatsoever to develop an organization. This was because both the Brush Run and Wellsburg congregations were members of Baptist associations. In other words they enjoyed the use of Baptist organizations. The Stone movement, which was independent, had developed by 1810 a system of conferences, although they had virtually no authority.[25] With the merger of the two groups and with the dynamic growth it experienced there was a new need, or at least a perceived need among many, for a new type of organization.

In the 1830's and 1840's "Cooperation Meetings" were common throughout the Restoration Movement. These were yearly meetings organized on a regional or later on a state level. Over time these organizations eventually came to elect officers. These Cooperation Meetings did not legislate but rather were opportunities for fellowship and edification. Typically, the meetings allowed several congregations to do what one could not. For example several congregations might pool their resources in order to support an evangelist. It was under similar circumstances that Walter Scott was engaged to evangelize in Ohio.

In 1845 the American Christian Bible Society was founded by D. S. Burnet in Cincinnati, Ohio. It was the first attempt to establish a movement-wide organization. Opposition to the society was widespread, including, significantly, Alexander Campbell himself. The society never enjoyed much support and after eleven years it ceased to exist.[26]

The real center of debate was the American Christian Missionary Society. Although the history of the Restoration Movement cannot be summed up solely by the thought of Alexander Campbell, it is obvious that his opinions had a profound impact on the direction of the movement. Perhaps the greatest difference then, between the Missionary Society and its Bible Society predecessor is that the former had the approval of Alexander Campbell.

In fact the relationship between Alexander Campbell and the Missionary Society goes well beyond mere approval. Campbell was the driving force behind the whole idea for such a society. It seems that Campbell had been paving the way, slowly and deliberately, during the 1840's through an occasional series of articles on church organization. In 1849, Campbell apparently decided that the time had come and he began an almost monthly series of articles in the *Mil-*

lennial Harbinger which sought to bring the issue to fruition. In one of those articles, Campbell set forth a principle which was a landmark in the history of the Restoration Movement, one which has been debated ever since:

> In all things pertaining to public interest, not of Christian faith, piety, or morality, the church of Jesus Christ in its aggregate character, is left free and unshackled by any apostolic authority. This is the great point which I assert as of capital importance in any great conventional movement or cooperation in advancing the public interests of a common Christianity and a common salvation. My strong proof for this conclusion is that, while faith, piety, and morality are all divinely established and enacted by special agents - apostles and prophets possessed of plenary inspiration; matters of prudential arrangements for the evangelizing of the world, for the better application of our means and resources, according to the exigencies of society and the ever-varying complexion of things around us - are left without a single law, statute, ordinance, or enactment in the New Testament.[27]

To simplify the matter a great deal, Campbell offers here a "liberal" interpretation of the motto adopted by the Christian Association of Washington back in 1809: "Where the Scriptures speak we speak; where the Scriptures are silent, we are silent." Campbell argues that when the scriptures are silent and when the matter lies outside of faith, piety, and morality, there exists the freedom to arrange things to best meet common needs. In this case, the common need is how to best evangelize the world. Since Jesus Christ gave no divine plan for conversion, the church is free to devise its own means to accomplish that end, based solely on the question of expediency. Conservatives have rejected this interpretation and have instead insisted that practices are prohibited unless they are specifically sanctioned by the New Testament.

Earl West has correctly understood the problem when he writes: "This is the heart of Campbell's reasoning on Church Organization. He insists upon beginning with the church in the aggregate or universal sense of the term. It is vital to his viewpoint to ignore, at least for the time being, the local character of the church. It is with the church universal that he begins."[28] West articulates the conservative position which tends toward a stricter interpretation of the motto adopted by Thomas Campbell. He disputes Campbell's argument based on expediency and rejects explicitly the notion of an aggregate or universal church:

> At the close of the apostolic age, when the last apostle died, the church was known only by the individual congregations scattered over the world. The work of Christ through the church to evangelize the world was carried on through the influence of the local church in its community. Even in apostolic times the churches

felt no need of an organization, devised by human planning, through which the church could cooperate to evangelize the world.[29]

Church organizations are rejected because the Scriptures are silent on the matter. There is no other position possible if one is to remain faithful to the truth motive.

The historiography of the Missionary Society controversy reads somewhat like: Did or did not Alexander Campbell change his mind about missionary societies? For example, Harold Lunger has written: "From about 1831 to the middle of the following decade Campbell's conception of the church underwent a gradual transformation from that of the radical sect form to that of the characteristic American church form - the denomination."[30] The assumption is, of course, that if Campbell underwent this transformation so did the Restoration Movement.

The Missionary Society controversy as it relates specifically to Alexander Campbell's thought has been discussed thoroughly by Earl West.[31] It is only necessary, therefore, to summarize West's observations.

Basically, there have been two schools of thought. The first, represented best by David Lipscomb, editor of the *Gospel Advocate* and a leader of the conservatives, has suggested that Alexander Campbell simply changed his mind on the subject. The argument put forward is that two events which occurred in 1847 seriously affected Campbell's mind so that it subsequently lost much of its vigor. These two events, which happened almost concurrently, were the imprisonment of Campbell while on a visit to Scotland as the result of a campaign against him by the local anti-slavery society, and the accidental death of his youngest son, Wickliffe, at age eleven. Lipscomb contended that Campbell's will was so weakened that he was persuaded by others that church organizations, which he heretofore had opposed, were harmless.

The second school of thought holds that Alexander Campbell did not change his mind about missionary societies. The members of this school – W. K. Pendleton, for example – suggest that Campbell was perfectly consistent and that he opposed not missionary societies but the abuse of such institutions. In attempting to resolve the discrepancies between these two schools, West draws several conclusions:

1. Alexander Campbell was active in the Society and defended its existence.

2. Alexander Campbell never himself believed that he had changed his conviction on the Missionary Society.

3. Alexander Campbell favored the principle of the missionary society before 1847.

4. Alexander Campbell did not criticize brotherhood organizations before 1847.

And finally: "As finally and honestly, as we can read Campbell's writings on the subject of human organizations, we are convinced that Campbell favored them even before 1847. His writings in the *Christian Baptist* are somewhat mystifying. Taken at their face value and for what they say on the surface they most certainly seem to oppose the missionary societies as unscriptural in their existence."[32]

These seem to be reasonable and fact-based conclusions. It is certainly true that Campbell pioneered the Missionary Society. But it is just as true that in 1823 he wrote: "Their [members of the apostolic church] churches were not fractured into missionary societies, bible societies, education societies; nor did they dream of organizing such in the world."[33] It is also true that Campbell lamented the dissolution of the Mahoning Association. What Robert Richardson has to say about Campbell's opinion of the matter is instructive:

> Mr. Campbell, who was present, entertained no doubt that churches had a right to appoint messengers to a general meeting, to bear intelligence to it and bring home intelligence from it, or transact any special business committed to them. He thought such meetings might be made very useful to promote the general advancement of the cause of unity and love of the brotherhood, and was in favor of continuing the Association, or something like it, which would, he thought, be needed. *He censured, indeed, the inconsistent conduct of which associations had been guilty in attempting to impose their decisions upon churches, but felt no apprehensions on this score in regard to the Mahoning Association, where the churches were so fully enlightened and so completely on their guard against encroachments on their rights.*[34]

This last sentence (my emphasis) begins to reveal how Campbell "changed his mind," and more importantly why the missionary society controversy is so important to the Restoration Movement. It is significant because it recognizes a distinction in the thought of Campbell between "associations," that is, sectarian associations and the Association, an association of the "enlightened." Placed within this context Campbell's "changes" make a great deal more sense. When writing in 1823 against missionary and other societies, Campbell is writing against sectarian societies. The passage quoted above, where Campbell denies that missionary societies had apostolic precedent, was written for the first volume of the *Christian Baptist* which was an organ devoted to exposing the sects and sectarianism. As such its purpose was to sound the opening blast in the campaign to restore the ancient order of things. On the other hand, in 1849, when he is promoting the idea of a missionary society, Campbell is addressing instead his "enlightened bretheren" who would not permit the encroachment of the rights of individual congregations by church organizations.

The point is not that Campbell changed his mind because he had become intellectually feeble, but rather that he recognized a new reality, a non-denominational reality, in which the movement now stood. Put another way, the thrust of Campbell's thought no longer lay in challenging sectarianism but in fostering the dissemination of the Restoration Movement and its ideals through worldwide evangelization. The transition from extirpator of the sects to guardian of a sacred movement represented a fundamental shift in the thought of Alexander Campbell, a shift which was not limited to the issue of organizations. It can also be detected, for example, in Campbell's attitude towards the most divisive public controversy of his time — slavery.

Campbell lived in what was then the slave state of Virginia. He had married the daughter of a prosperous farmer and through this marriage procured a large farm at Bethany. He was himself a slaveowner, though he eventually freed all of his slaves. In 1845 he devoted a series of articles in the *Harbinger* to the subject of "Our Position to American Slavery." At the close of these articles he presented the following summary:

> 1. That the relation of master and servant is not in itself sinful or immoral. 2. That, nevertheless, slavery as practiced in any part of the civilized world is *inexpedient*...3.That no Christian community governed by the Bible, Old Testament and New, can constitutionally and rightfully make the simple relation of master and slave a term of Christian fellowship or a subject of discipline...[35]

Where is the firebrand of the 1820's, the great debater who relished disputation and controversy? This Alexander Campbell had ceded to another whose principal concern was preserving the unity of the movement at a time in American history when unity was becoming rare:

> Every man who loves the American Union, as well as every man who desires a constitutional end of American slavery, is bound to prevent, as far as possible, any breach of communion between Christians at the South and at the North. No sensible abolitionist, who either loves the Union or who desires the amelioration of the condition of the slave, can look upon the disruption of the Methodist community...but with the most profound regret. Any one pleased with such a result, as to its bearings upon slavery, is a fanatic rather than a philanthropist or a Christian.[36]

It may be unfair to insist that an individual maintain a high level of consistency over a lifetime. This is especially true when that individual, Alexander Campbell, expressed himself, with a few exceptions, in debates and articles written over a period of more than forty years. The articles and certainly the debates, which were transcribed and published, were advocating particular points of view in an atmosphere of lively debate. Neither was meant to be combined into a coherent system of philosophy or theology. More importantly perhaps, because it addresses the intellectual origins of his "change of mind," is the fact that Campbell was more aware of historical change than were his critics. He recognized that the Restoration Movement had entered a new phase after the merger of Reformers and Christians, which required new emphases. He also understood that the United States was entering a new, more divisive phase in its history at precisely the same time. In both the issues of the Missionary Society and slavery Alexander Campbell shifted his attention to the preservation and nurturing of the movement he helped to define.

The early critics of Campbell's position on the Missionary Society, men such as Jacob Creath, Jr., Tolbert Fanning, and Benjamin Franklin, shared a mentality which was different from that of Campbell. These men opposed the Missionary Society because its membership was based upon the contribution of a sum of money, which gave it an elitist air they disliked. But probably more important in their minds were objections based on their conviction that human organizations were not authorized by Scripture. Consequently such organizations would infringe upon the rights of local congregations, which after all were the only kind of church organization found in the New Testament. These men have often been labeled "legalistic," and in a certain sense they were. To them, extra-congregational organizations were simply not scriptural and not permissible under any circumstances; something is either true or it is not. But they were also ahistorical, freezing truth in a biblical past. They were men of the frontier who saw a simpler truth. They did not share Campbell's philosphical and historical perspective, which enabled him to express a more complex reality.

The creation of the American Christian Missionary Society evoked such opposition that the leadership of the movement realized that some sort of amendment of the society was necessary. This was undoubtedly facilitated by the death of Alexander Campbell in 1866. Three years later these leaders met in Louisville and hammered out a new missionary entity called the General Christian Missionary Convention. The blueprint for this new convention is known as the Louisville Plan.

The Louisville Plan was a compromise. The old Society was really an organization of individuals. A scale of payments procured corresponding status within the Society. One of the most frequent objections to this arrangement was the fact that membership was made contingent upon the payment of specific sums of money. In response to this, the Louisville Plan made the Convention an organization of churches with a highly elaborate structure. Each congregation was to send "messengers" to district meetings which in turn sent delegates to the state meeting. Each state meeting was to be represented on the General Board of the Convention by its corresponding secretary, two delegates, and an additional delegate for each 5,000 members in the state. Congregations were urged to pledge offerings to the district treasurer which were divided in half between the district and the state society. The state society was to keep half of what it received and turn the other half over to the General Convention.[37]

The Louisville Plan was a failure. The new plan raised less than half the money raised under the old Society. The intransigents opposed any organization because it was a human invention. Those who were more moderate found the elaborate machinery to be cumbersome and alien to the simplicity that had always marked the movement. Though the Louisville Plan was abandoned in 1875, it was a real watershed in the development of the Movement. With its implementation, the division within the Movement began to take on the dimension of a choice between non-denominational Christianity and denominationalism. In the eyes of many the Louisville Plan created a structure which was a full-fledged denominational organization, that is, one in which an organization usurps the autonomy of the local church.[38] Henceforth, the division within the Restoration Movement was going to focus largely on whether the Movement was going to become another denomination or remain faithful to what some saw as non-denominational Christianity. Today, this question still frames the division among the three modern Restoration groups.

Instrumental Music

The second issue which tended to divide the Restoration Movement was the use of instrumental music in church services. To the outsider the issue may seem not very important; even to some within the movement the adoption of the organ or some other instrument was made with relative ease. The issue, though simple, involved principles fundamental to the Restoration Movement. How these principles were to be interpreted was going to determine the divergent paths which the movement was going to take.

Simply put, the principle involved was embodied in the question: 'What does scriptural silence mean?' All of the disputants agreed that the New Testament was silent on the use of musical instruments in churches; the dispute was over how to interpret that silence. The dispute first became public in the early 1850's. Alexander Campbell was quickly recruited to offer his influential opinion. In this case he came down squarely on the side of the conservatives in opposing instrumental music.[39] It is interesting to note that Robert Richardson, who is closely associated with Alexander Campbell, as a professor at Bethany College and later, as Campbell's biographer, followed Campbell both on this issue and that of church organizations. In both cases Richardson invokes the rationale of expediency, though on organizations he invokes the principle in *sup-*

port of mission societies while on the issue of instrumental music he argues strongly *against* expediency.[40] This kind of fluidity must have been typical during this phase of Restoration history.

By the 1860's and 1870's instrumental music was the subject of vigorous debate and growing alienation. Two of the most influential personalities of the time clashed over the issue and while doing so each articulated what was to become a classic interpretation of a basic restoration principle. Isaac Errett, editor of the *Christian Standard,* was actually quite conservative but argued upon a principle which was to be taken up by the liberals. After remaining silent on the subject for several years he finally wrote about it in 1870. While he personally counselled against the use of instruments, he argued on the basis of opinion and expediency. He wrote:

> Before proceeding to give our reasons against instrumental music
> in public worship, we desire to elaborate more fully the thought
> presented in our last article on this subject, namely, that the real
> difference among us is a difference of opinion as to the *expedien-
> cy* of instrumental worship in public worship, and therefore, *it is
> wrong to make this difference a test of fellowship,* on one hand, or
> an occasion of *stumbling,* on the other. [41]

Errett's judgment was based on the presupposition that when the Scriptures are silent the issue is then simply a matter of opinion and expediency. Presumably then, majority rule would apply. Ben Franklin, editor of the *American Christian Review,* understood well where Errett's reasoning would lead. He responded immediately and undoubtedly directly to Errett when he wrote:

> We put it on no ground of *opinion* or *expediency*. The acts of wor-
> ship are all prescribed in the law of God. If it is an act of wor-
> ship, or an element of worship, it may not be added to it. If it is
> not an act of worship, or an element in the worship, it is most
> wicked and sinful to impose it on the worshippers. It is useless
> to tell us, *It is not to be made a test.* If you impose it on the con-
> science of bretheren and, by a majority vote, force it into the wor-
> ship, are they bound to stifle their consciences? Have you a right
> to compel them to submit and worship with the instrument? They
> stand on the *old ground,* where the first Christians stood, as we
> all admit, and where we have all stood... *you cause division - You*
> are the *aggressor* - the *innovator* - you do this, too, for the accom-
> paniment of corruption and apostasy, admitting at the same time
> that you have no conscience in the matter.[42]

Franklin articulated a stricter (his critics would say a more legalistic) interpretation of the silence of the Scriptures. For him the acts of worship are clearly laid out in the New Testament and they do not include the use of instruments. To introduce them is to disregard the will of God. Attempts to cite the use of instruments in the Old Testament were generally dismissed as a "Jewish Practice," a point of view consistent with the opinion expressed by Alexander Campbell, years earlier, in his *Sermon on the Law*.

By 1875 the lines had been clearly drawn and the Restoration Movement was in the process of dividing into two separate groups, which became official in 1906. The instrumental music controversy was crucial to this process. Whereas congregations could in good conscience disagree over the Missionary Society and still worship together, instrumental music almost always made it inevitable that the congregation would split. In church after church majorities voted to allow the organ and those opposed were forced by their consciences to withdraw and establish another congregation.[43] By the end of the century the process of dividing congregations, members, and preachers was largely done.

The psychology behind the need to separate is best articulated by a spokesman for the Churches of Christ:

> Clearly, then, to Franklin instrumental music was no matter of opinion. Man had no right to add an element of human origin to the divine worship, for such inescapably had to be an innovation. The two views, championed by Errett on one side and Franklin on the other, were poles apart. Down to the present day they have been the fundamental reason why fellowship between the churches of Christ, on one side, and the Disciples of Christ denomination, on the other, is inconceivable. If the use of the instrument is purely a matter of opinion, then, admittedly, any dispute about it borders on the ridiculous. If, however, the instrument is a human innovation, an addition to the divine worship, then it is sinful to use it. This latter view being accepted, there is no possible, consistent ground for compromise with the former.[44]

Social Factors

This study has been designed as an intellectual history because the ideas embodied in the Restoration Movement are uniquely combined and can teach much about Christianity in the United States. However, one of the dangers in writing pure intellectual history is the tendency to portray whatever is being studied as a series of autonomous ideas which are isolated from material (that is social, economic, and political) considerations. I have suggested that the divisions in a movement which was so self-consciously dedicated to the concept of unity lay mostly in internal and intellectual factors. The thirty years between the merger of the Reformers and Christians and the Civil War saw two basic developments: large numerical growth and also a growing political, social, economic, and geographical diversity within an institution of now respectable size. I have also suggested that the division was inherent to the movement itself since it embodied two ideas — biblical primitivism and unification of the Church of Christ through that primitivism — which were not reconcilable, because they were not definable, at least not within the context of the time and place under study.

I would not suggest, however, that the divisions within the Restoration Movement were not influenced by events or trends found in American society as a whole. Obviously the nineteenth century witnessed the most grievous division of society in the history of the nation, a division which degenerated into the armed conflict of the Civil War. Furthermore, most of the largest Protestant denominations (Baptist, Methodist, and Presbyterian) all split along sectional lines, principally over the issue of slavery. While it is true that these trends in American society undoubtedly affected the movement, it must also be recalled, for example, that unlike those other religious groups, the Restoration Movement did not split before the Civil War but after it. In other words, while those general factors affected the Restoration Movement as they did the rest of American society, precisely how they operated was somewhat different because of certain factors within the movement. It must be kept in mind, therefore, that the history of the Restoration Movement is the confluence of both general American trends and also others which are unique to the movement.

David Harrell, Jr. concluded one of his articles with this sentence: "The twentieth-century Churches of Christ are the spirited offspring of the religious rednecks of the post bellum South."[45] With this striking sentence Harrell concludes that division within the Restoration Movement was also rooted in sectional origins. According to the 1906 religious census, 101,734 of the Churches of Christ's 159,658 members lived in the eleven states of the former Confederacy. Another 30,206 lived in the four border states of Kentucky, West Virginia, Missouri and Oklahoma.[46] At the same time there were more than a million members of the more liberal Disciples of Christ, but only 138,703 of that total lived in the old Confederacy. Obviously the large majority of those congregations that divided from the main group of Disciples were located in the South.

Once the Southern character of the future Churches of Christ is understood, the events and attitudes concerning the Missionary Society and other developments become more clear. By the 1850's it was not pro-slavery supporters but rather radical abolitionists who were in the process of breaking from the church. Although opinion certainly varied, the moderation of Alexander Campbell on the subject of slavery was typical of the movement. In 1859 the refusal of the American Christian Missionary Society to support an ardent abolitionist preacher in Kansas led to a rift.[47] The abolitionists created their own missionary society, produced their own periodical and won the sympathy of many congregations.

Times changed with the coming of the Civil War. Sentiment had shifted to the point that in fact the movement as a whole came around to the position of the abolitionists. The 1863 meeting of the American Christian Missionary Society saw the triumph of the northern radicals. Several resolutions were passed declaring allegiance to the government of the United States and sympathies with the union soldiers "who are defending us from the attempts of armed traitors to overthrow the Government."[48] Southern leaders were prevented by the war from participating in the convention held in Cincinnati and for the duration of the conflict.

After the war, sectional feelings were institutionalized in competing journals. The *Christian Standard* edited by Isaac Errett was funded by wealthy and influential northerners such as Representative James Garfield, a Republican, who became the first president with a restoration background. The *Gospel Advocate*, edited by Fanning and Lipscomb in Nashville was just as vocal in articulating the Southern point of view. As late as 1892 Thomas R. Burnett of Texas could express a point of view which was both Southern and biblical: "We know the doctrine advocated by them [writers in the *Christian Standard*] comes from the *North*. It is neither scriptural nor *Southern*, and is not suited to Southern people. But it is the determination of the *Stan- dard* and its *Northern* allies...to force the new things upon the churches of this section."[49]

Harrell also provides convincing evidence that the causes for division went beyond sectionalism and were social in character. For example, he cites statistics from the 1936 religious census which indicates that about 63 percent of the members of the northern-dominated Disciples of Christ were urban, while about 57 percent of the members of the more southern Churches of Christ were rural. The same census also reveals that value of church edifices for the Disciples was three, four, even six times the value of Churches of Christ edifices. In Memphis, Tennessee the average size of Disciples' congregations was more than four times larger than those of the Churches of Christ.[50]

David Harrell has convincingly demonstrated that there were social origins of division between the Disciples of Christ and the Churches of Christ. This is not to discount the intellectual origins already discussed, but rather to suggest that social, that is, sectional, economic, and political factors influenced the interpretation of certain principles. It can be generally stated that the Disciples of Christ were mostly northern, but also that they were urban; self consciously richer, they built large church edifices which were worth more money; they supported a college-educated clergy; and articulated an ideal which revolved around the businessman. On the other hand, the Churches of Christ were mostly southern and rural; they denounced elaborate church buildings and such practices as the wearing of fine, expensive clothing to church; built relatively more but smaller and more modest churches for smaller congregations; and articulated an ideal which remained the simple and austere yeoman farmer. They also tended to attack theological education because it created a professional clergy.[51]

Ideas and mentalities are never developed completely outside of material conditions. Therefore, the divisions within the Restoration Movement, which were quite obvious by the end of the nineteenth century, were the result of intellectual differences. But those differences were aggravated by specific social conditions which helps to explain why some Restoration principles came to be variously interpreted by those within the Movement.[52]

Chapter Seven

Epilogue

David Harrell has described the religious personality of the nineteenth-century Restoration Movement as having "decided schizophrenic tendencies." Most members of the movement possessed a perplexing mixture of traits: they were fanatics with a compulsive sense of mission, yet they were also nineteenth-century rationalists with an almost "psychotic" aversion to fanaticism.[1] This "schizophrenia" can be traced to the intellectual origins of the movement.

The Enlightenment

The first of these origins was the eighteenth-century intellectual movement known as the Enlightenment, which itself possessed certain schizophrenic tendencies. The Enlightenment was a radical movement which challenged the religious status quo, and even on occasion proclaimed some radical social and political ideas. But the Restoration Movement was most influenced by the less radical English and Scottish elements of the Enlightenment and even here it focused on the most conservative aspects of British thought. Much of this can be traced back to John Locke's principles of empiricism; religious toleration; political liberalism; modern ideas of education; and the function of philosophy as criticism, which were all adopted by the Enlightenment.[2]

Locke was in reality a pre-Enlightenment figure, the person who provided the "laws" upon which the Enlightenment was built. Despite his preeminent place in the Enlightenment pantheon, Locke's writings on Christianity were conspicuously ignored by the predominantly French group of intellectuals known as the *philosophes*, who propounded the ideas associated with the Enlightenment. His most famous work on religion, *The Reasonableness of Christianity*, seemed to them a contradiction in terms.

By following Locke and the more pious Reid, and not the skeptic Hume and the French *philosophes*, the Restoration Movement — especially regarding questions of religion — was thoroughly Anglo-Saxon and Protestant. For example, the *philosophes* were largely ambivalent towards the Reformation, seeing it as a dispute among Christians, though they also recognized that it had been useful in dissolving the moral monopoly of the Catholic Church. In contrast, Alexander Campbell saw the Protestant Reformation as the very salvation of Western civilization:

> Three full centuries, carrying with them the destinies of countless millions, have passed into eternity since the Lutheran effort to dethrone the *Man of Sin*. During this period many great and wonderful changes have taken place in the political, literary, moral, and religious conditions of society. That the nations composing the western half of the Roman empire have already been greatly benefited by that effort, scientifically, politically, and morally, no person acquainted with either political or ecclesiastical history can reasonably doubt. Time, that great arbiter of human actions, that great revealer of secrets, has long decided that all the reformers of the Papacy have been public benefactors. And thus the Protestant Reformation is proved to have been one of the most splendid eras in the history of the world, and must long be regarded by the philosopher and the philanthropist as one of the most gracious interpositions in behalf of the whole human race.[3]

The Separation of the Sources of Knowledge

As W. E. Garrison put it, Alexander Campbell accepted the principles of the Enlightenment but he rejected its results.[4] He accepted the Deists' Lockian principles but rejected their conclusion that we can know God through reason. He went back to an idea which was at least implicit in Locke and which the common sense philosophy also focused on: that all knowledge does not come from sensation and reflection, but only knowledge of the material world. This is the origin of the "schizophrenic" tendencies in the thought of Alexander Campbell.

One scholar has called Campbell a "rational supernaturalist."[5] Campbell's "supernaturalism" manifests itself in a rejection of natural religion: "...I have found learned men who have been unfortunately misled and mystified in their minds, by not knowing the radical difference between natural and revealed religion. Natural religion is pure Deism.... We wish to have the line of demarcation between natural and revealed religion clearly drawn."[6] Having established the difference between natural and supernatural religion, Campbell goes on to define what divine revelation is:

> To constitute a divine revelation, in our sense of the terms, it is not only necessary that God be the author of it, but that the things exhibited be supernatural, and beyond the reach of our five sen-

ses. For example; that God is a Spirit, is beyond the reach of our reasoning powers to discover, and could not be known by any human means. That a Spirit created matter, or that God made the earth, is a truth which no man could, from his five senses or his reasoning powers, discover. It is therefore a revealed truth.[7]

The source of divine revelation is the Bible:

> The Christian has two sources of original ideas: the unbeliever has but one. The Book of Nature and the Book of Revelation furnish the Christian with all his original simple conceptions. For the Book of Nature he is furnished with five senses: - the sense of seeing, hearing, tasting, smelling, feeling. His reflections on the objects of sense, and the impressions these objects make on him, furnish him with ideas compound and multiform; but every idea properly original and purely simple, is a *discovery*. Its model, or that which excites or originates it, is found in the volume of Nature, or in the volume of Revelation. Sense fits him for one, and faith for the other. Every supernatural idea found in the world, as well as the proper term which represents it, is directly or indirectly derived from the Bible.[8]

The "rationalist" side of Alexander Campbell is best seen through the rational way in which the Bible can be understood. As stated, we receive knowledge of the supernatural through the Bible only, or as Campbell puts it, we receive information about facts, which are not the immediate objects of our senses, through testimony. Testimony is the report of things said or done and faith is simply the acceptance of testimony as true. Since Campbell operates with Lockian principles, he conceives of revelation in intellectual terms, that is, it cannot be received through the emotions but is rather essentially a matter of knowledge, albeit of supernatural knowledge. Since knowledge comes only through the senses, God communicates the divine facts—truth—through only one medium: the written word, the Bible. Garrison writes: "Since revelation is essentially the deliverance of *ideas* to men, and since a word is the sensible body of an idea, it may be said that Lockian sensationalism gives the philosophical basis for the doctrine of verbal inspiration."[9] This reasoning seems then to provide the basis of a concept of objective truth or external authority "...lodged in the Bible, which is the repository for a deposit of divine revelation in the form of ideas and commands to be apprehended by the intellect."[10]

In this way the principles of Lockian philosophy can form the basis of a rational biblicism. Even though the Bible is conceived as being beyond reason, it can be understood rationally, as all knowledge can. The will of God is communi-

cated through the written word contained in the Bible, the source of all our
knowledge about spiritual things. Through our senses we can comprehend the
ideas contained in the Bible, or as Campbell stated it:

> The words of the Bible contain all the ideas in it. These words,
> then, [are] rightly understood, and the ideas are clearly per-
> ceived. The words and sentences of the Bible are to be trans-
> lated, interpreted, and understood according to the same code
> of laws and principles of interpretation by which other ancient
> writings are translated and understood; for, when God spoke to
> man in his own language, he spoke as one person converses with
> another - in the fair, stipulated, and well-established meaning of
> the terms. This is essential to its character as a revelation from
> God; otherwise it would be no revelation, but would always re-
> quire a class of inspired men to unfold and reveal its true sense
> to mankind.[11]

Campbell specifically rejects the need for specially trained individuals to interpret the Bible. Scripture can be understood by all because it communicates,
through the senses, in a way that all people can comprehend. This is, as
Campbell notes, why it is called revelation, the revealed word of God. It is
characteristic of Campbell's thought that he holds the Bible to be the sole
source of supernatural knowledge, that is of knowledge which is beyond the senses. Yet at the same time he also holds that the written word derived from that
supernatural knowledge is easily understood by the senses. He has almost no
realization that these two propositions are in any way paradoxical. He writes:
"...the fact that God has clothed his communications in human language, and
that he has spoken by men, to men, in their own language, is decisive evidence
that he is to be understood as one man conversing with another...[12]

Campbell expended a great deal of energy writing on the interpretation of
the Bible. Undoubtedly this is because the Bible functions as the means of uniting Christians:

> All the differences in religious faith, opinion, and sentiment,
> amongst those who acknowledge the Bible, are occasioned by
> false principles of interpretation, or by a misapplication of the
> true principles...Were all students of the Bible taught to apply
> the same rules of interpretation to its pages, there would be a
> greater uniformity in opinion and sentiment than ever resulted
> from a simple adoption of any written creed.[13]

Campbell goes on to list a series of principles for interpreting the Bible.
These are rooted in the common sense empirical method which Bacon applied
to science and Locke to philosophy.[14] In a very rational, scientific way the ul-

timate truths of religion are deduced from the particulars of Bible testimony. These truths thus deduced constitute a very clear source of authority for Christian truth:

> Great unanimity has obtained in most of the sciences in consequence of the adoption of certain rules of analysis and synthesis: for all who work by the same rules, come to the same conclusions. And may it not be possible, that in this divine science of religion, there may yet be a very great degree of unanimity of sentiment and uniformity of practice amongst all who acknowledge its divine authority? Is the school of Christ the only school in which there can be no unanimity - no proficiency in knowledge? Is the book of God the only volume which can never be understood alike by those who read and study it?[15]

The "schizophrenic" and paradoxical tendencies of the Restoration Movement were derived, in large part, from the thought of its greatest theologian, Alexander Campbell. He separated the supernatural from the natural, divine revelation from philosophy and metaphysics, but then bridged the chasm he had created with a Lockian epistemology. By reducing Christian authority to testimony, to the written Word, Campbell reintroduced a Lockian rationalism which asserted that the Bible could be understood clearly and directly by all readers through the senses, which everyone possessed. This led Campbell to a hermeneutic rooted in a rather extreme biblical positivism:

> ...men cannot think but by words or signs. Words are but embodied thought, the external images or representatives of ideas. And who is there that has paid any attention to what passes in his own mind, who has not perceived that he cannot think without something to think about, and that the something about which he thinks must either assume a name, or some sort of image in his mind, before his rational faculties can operate upon it; and moreover, that his powers of thinking while employed exercise themselves in every effort, either by terms, names, or symbols, expressive of their own acts and the results of their own acts? Now, as men think by means of symbols and terms, and cannot think without them, it must be obvious that speaking the same things and hearing the same things, though it might be alleged as the effect of thinking the same things, is more likely to become the cause of thinking the same things than any natural or mechanical effect can become the cause of a similar effect. This much we say

for the employment of the speculative reader; but for the practical mind it is enough to know that speaking the same things is both rationally and scripturally proposed as the most sure and certain means of thinking the same things....Perhaps in this one view might be found the only practicable and alone sufficient means of reconciling all the christian world, and of destroying all partyism and party feelings....But how shall we all speak the same things relating to the christian religion? Never, indeed, while we add to, or subtract from the words which the Holy Spirit teaches. Never, indeed, while we take those terms out of their scriptural connexions, and either transpose them in place, or confound them with terms not in the book. If I am not greatly mistaken,...the adding to, subtracting from, the transposition of, and mingling the terms of the Holy Spirit with those of human contrivance, is the only cause why all who love the same saviour are disunited.[16]

Although he is rather sophisticated, theologically and philosophically, Campbell exhibits a surprising confidence in thinking that if everyone speaks and hears the same things — that is, if everybody reads the Bible and hears it preached and interpreted according to scientific principles — then they will all think the same thing and will restore the unity of the Church of Christ. He underestimates the proclivity of each person to filter experience through the diversity of his or her own mind. In an attempt to preserve individual freedom of interpretation Campbell overestimates the objectivity of supernatural knowledge and its ability to neutralize human difference of opinion. It can only be concluded that Campbell's faith and earnest desire for the unity of Christ's Church led him down a path which his intellect alone would never have allowed him to tread.

Authority

There was an acute need for authority within the Restoration Movement. This was true for all Protestants once the moral, disciplinary, and teaching authority of the Catholic Church had been rejected. This was particularly true for the Restoration Movement because it also rejected the authority of the organizational structures, creeds, and complex doctrines of magisterial Protestantism. In the early stages of the movement, a purely scriptural form of authority must have been particularly appealing to the great mass of less sophisticated believers on the American frontier, who did not have Campbell's philosophical training. The self-confident American frontiersman, who disdained human authority, was in this case accepting only the authority of God as contained in the Gospel facts which were received by the senses and subject to individual interpretation. In this way the epistemology of the Enlightenment became the progenitor of a rational but strict biblical literalism among certain segments of the Restoration Movement.

Did the Enlightenment affect the Restoration Movement in other ways? The answer quite clearly is yes. To examine the Restoration Movement in relation to some of the principle ideas of the Enlightenment is to understand better its origins. A note of caution: to suggest influences is not to imply a relationship of cause and effect. The Restoration Movement is not an offshoot of the Enlightenment in a strict sense. The first is of course a religious movement, the latter was largely anti-Christian and at times even anti-religious. Nonetheless, the decades before the French Revolution were the high point of the influence of the Enlightenment. Thomas Campbell, born in 1763, was educated precisely during this time. His son Alexander, in large part educated by his father in the philosophy of Locke and others, would have imbibed many of the same ideas a generation later, as would have Barton Stone, Walter Scott and many of the other leaders of the movement who had received good educations. The very age from which the Restoration Movement emerged was imbued with Enlightenment ideas.

Reason

No term has been more frequently associated with the Age of Enlightenment and with the eighteenth century than "reason." Consider Peter Gay's comparison of Thomas Aquinas and Voltaire on "reason":

> Aquinas and Voltaire both believed that the powers of reason are limited, but they drew sharply different conclusions from this: for Aquinas, that which is inaccessible to human reason concerns the foundations of Christian theology. Where the light of reason does not shine, the lamp of faith supplies illumination. For Voltaire, on the contrary, that which is inaccessible to reason is chimerical. What can never be found ought not to be sought; it is the realm not of the most sacred, but of the most nonsensical - that is, of "metaphysical" speculation. Where the light of reason does not shine, man must console himself with that philosophical modesty so characteristic of Voltaire's heroes, Newton and Locke. While Aquinas could make categorical statements about the nature of the soul, Voltaire proudly proclaimed his ignorance in such matters.[17]

The Restoration Movement was based on a notion of reason which was essentially the same as that attributed above to Voltaire. The very basis of the movement was rooted in the conviction that the Bible alone was sufficient, that all creeds, and other formulations were simply human deductions, what individuals *thought* that the Bible said. As Thomas Campbell wrote: "...there is a manifest distinction between an express Scripture declaration, and the conclusion or inference which may be deduced from it; and that the former may be clearly understood, even where the latter is but imperfectly if at all perceived."[18] To put it into both Lockian and Voltairian terminology: The Bible is fact; creeds and other formulations are metaphysical speculations.

It is not of course that either the *philosophes* or the Restoration leaders relished ignorance. Quite the contrary, it was a question of being able to distinguish between true and false knowledge. Neither group was naive, neither was convinced about the inevitablity of progress (another idea attributed to the Enlightenment) though both felt that if their proposals were adopted progress would result.[19] In a Restoration context, the conviction that by restoring Biblical primitivism Christian unity could be achieved was fueled less by naiveté than by a confidence in the truth of the Bible.

History

The historical perspective of Alexander Campbell had many dimensions. Certainly he was very well acquainted with the past and when the opportunity presented itself, as in the debate with Archbishop John Purcell of Cincinnati, he could delve into history and utilize it as a formidable rhetorical arsenal. Of course he would often find in the past justification for his own personal convictions, but in this practice he was far from being alone. One aspect of Campbell's thought which pervaded the whole Restoration Movement was a determination to escape the past. In this, the whole movement was deeply rooted in eighteenth-century thought.

The Enlightenment adapted the Renaissance historical perspective for its own purpose. The Renaissance admired classical antiquity. This admiration led individual thinkers to focus on various classical writers. Some were led to Plato, others to Cicero, still others to Augustine. There was nothing particularly anti-Christian about this rediscovery of antiquity, at least not in the eyes of those who lived during this time. Nearly all writers sought out authority from antiquity. Even Machiavelli, who relied more than most on his own experience, almost always also relied on the example of the Greek and Roman past to justify his observations and conclusions.

The attitude of the *philosophes* was related but somewhat different. They tended to see the age of Lorenzo dé Medici as the beginning of their own movement, when humanity first attempted to peel away the incrustations of the past.

Although they disapproved of much associated with the comtemporaneous Protestant and Catholic Reformations—religious intolerance, for example— they generally looked favorably on the Renaissance and unfavorably on the Middle Ages. Both the Renaissance and the Enlightenment, therefore, looked approvingly on classical antiquity, while they disparaged the Middle Ages.

There was one crucial difference between Renaissance and Enlightenment attitudes toward the past. Largely because of the Scientific Revolution, al- though there are also parallels with "modern" artistic accomplishments as well,[20] eighteenth century thinkers developed a more critical attitude toward the classical past. It was obvious to them that since the time of Copernicus, modern scientific thought had progressed well beyond the knowledge of the an- cient Greeks and Romans. The Enlightenment, therefore, continued to admire classical antiquity and in some regards continued to accept it as authoritative, but not completely so. Modern times, beginning with the Renaissance, became the latest and at least potentially the greatest age of rationality, science and en- lightenment. Ancient Greece and Rome were inspirations, indications of what the human spirit could achieve through the arts and sciences when unfettered by superstition. In between lay the Christian epoch, an age of myth, belief, religion, ignorance and decay, an age of darkness. In essence this was and still is the his- torical scheme of the Restoration Movement. As will be discussed below, the Restoration Movement depended on a notion of a golden age—New Testament Christianity—a restoration of the beliefs and practices of that age, and a "dark age" in between.

Freedom

The historical perspectives of both the Enlightenment and the Restoration Movement were closely related to a very important eighteenth-century idea: freedom. In one sense the Enlightenment was all about freedom—freedom from superstition; freedom from intolerance; freedom from privileged aris- tocracies and a privileged Church; and freedom from an arbitrary government, to name just a few. One of the most important freedoms in enlightened thought was freedom from the past. One of the manifestations of this idea of freedom was a fascination with primitivism.

The Enlightenment was deeply interested in all sorts of primitive cultures: Indians, Persians, Tahitians, aborigines, even some who were not very primitive such as the Chinese but who seemed more "natural" to Western eyes. One of the popular notions often associated with Rousseau was the "noble savage." But as Peter Gay has pointed out, Rousseau's prepolitical humans may have been noble but they were not savages.[21] They did not run wild, they lived by rules and restrained their impulses. What Rousseau and others were advocating was not savagery but a better civilization. Primitivism was the *philosophes'* method for calling for reform.

"Reform" and "Reformers" were terms traditionally associated with the followers of Alexander Campbell. They advocated the reform of Christianity, but the method of this reform was not to devise anything new but rather to restore the old — primitive Christianity. The Restoration Movement was deeply rooted in an Enlightenment idea of the primitive as an ideal, natural, and pristine state before "civilization" (sometimes personified by Constantine) had polluted Christianity.

In another context I have suggested a schema for understanding Southern Religion.[22] It focused on four centers of influence: 1)The Lutheran Reformation, 2)The Calvinist Reformation, 3)The English Reformation, and 4)The American Frontier. I have to admit that this schema applies only imperfectly to the Restoration Movement. One reason it may not apply well is that the Restoration Movement is not particularly Southern. Certainly, this is true geographically. While there were important concentrations in Tennessee and in others parts of the old Confederacy, the bulk of the movement was centered in the border states and in the North. More important, although part of the movement was in the South, it was not of the South.[23] Since the movement was so fundamentally wedded to a non-sectional, even a non-national vision of a united Church of Christ, without a denominational structure, it could not easily belong to a Southern Christendom.

There is another difference between Southern religion and the Restoration Movement. All elements of American Protestantism have been affected by the Protestant Reformation. But the Reformation was not monolithic and different Reformation traditions have affected various parts of American Protestantism. Moreover, since the Restoration Movement is a nineteenth-century phenomemon it was removed from the direct influence of the sixteenth-century Reformation. Nevertheless, it can be fairly stated that the movement is the spiritual heir of the most radical part of the Protestant Reformation. True, the Baptists were also heirs of the Radical Reformation. It is no accident that the Campbells associated themselves with the Baptists for almost twenty years. But the Baptists had been acculturated to the Southern ethos and had become more and more "denominational."

Primitivism and the Radical Reformation

The Restoration Movement was deeply affected by Enlightenment ideas of *history, freedom* and *primitivism*. Primitivism exerted an especially powerful influence on the intellectual origins of the Restoration Movement. It was such a congenial notion because it reinforced an idea which was basic to the movement — the restoration of primitive Christianity. But the Restoration Movement was in essence a religious movement. It interpreted these Enlightenment ideas through a religious, and in particular, Protestant filter. Therefore, from the most radical elements of the Protestant Reformation came restorationism, in a broader sense. Thus the other principal source of the intellectual origins of the Restoration Movement was the radical Reformation.

George H. Williams has written that: "So widespread was restorationism (or restitutionism) as the sixteenth-century version of *primitivism* [my emphasis] that it may be said to be one of the marks of the Radical Reformation, over against the (institutional, ethical, and partly dogmatic) Reformation on the Magisterial side."[24] Interestingly, Williams observes that of all the major Protestant Reformers the one who most often came close to the "radical spirit" was John Calvin. Perhaps, then, there is an intellectual link between the Scottish and American Presbyterianism of the Campbells, Scott and Stone on the one hand and the Restoration Movement on the other, through Calvin and his theology.

Franklin H. Littell has noted that the

> Reformers were not willing to make so radical a break from the
> past, but those whose key concept was *restitutio* rather than *reformatio* were determined to erase what they considered the shame
> of centuries and to recapitulate the purified church life of the
> Golden Age of the faith. In reviewing the records, the reader is
> struck with the Anabaptists' acute consciousness of separation
> from the 'fallen' church — in which they included the Reformers
> as well as the Roman institution.[25]

Littell in fact speaks of a "Third Type" of church, and this hypothesis has a direct relevance to the Restoration Movement.

The Restoration Movement has something of an identity crisis. Historically, the movement has sometimes considered itself to be part of Protestantism and sometimes not. In some instances, such as the debate with Archbishop Purcell, the movement and Alexander Campbell in particular, posed as the defender of Protestantism. But it must be kept in mind that Campbell also debated Protestants, (and he did it many more times) especially Presbyterians. Restorationism, which has a tendency towards exclusivism and towards the notion of one true church, while rejecting other Christian bodies as false, has imprinted a peculiar character on the modern Restoration Movement. In this context then, the Protestant Reformation becomes a sympathetic and wellmeaning movement but one which was fatally flawed by failing to break the bond between church and state, and which settled for trying to reform medieval Christianity instead of restoring the primitive church. The modern Restoration Movement in this way has often viewed itself as a third force in American Christianity along with sectarian Protestantism and Catholicism.

It is fair to say that the movement has split along ideological lines. Members of the more liberal group tend to think of themselves as Protestants and are active in Protestant ecumenical movements. Conservatives tend to speak of the Protestant Reformation as a well-meaning but half-hearted attempt to reform, and reject the denominationalism it spawned. The more conservative approach brings with it an interesting historical perspective. For example, James De-Forest Murch has formulated a cycle of purity, power, apostasy and restoration in the church of Christ.[26] The first apostasies occurred as early as apostolic times. They included the Judaizers, the Greek philosophers and the devotees of worldly lust. The last threat was manifested in the assumption of authority over individual churches by the bishops and the baptism of infants. By the time of Constantine a humanly devised church institution, with humanly crafted creeds, which was authoritarian, and which was in union with the state had been created. The primitive New Testament church had apostatized.

Many of the most radical sixteenth-century Anabaptists spoke as if the church had ceased to exist and needed to be literally restored. Murch, however, speaks in terms of "true Christians," a faithful remnant who preserved the primitive practice. A list of these "true Christians" includes Montanus, Tertullian, Priscillian, the Bogomils, the Albigensians, the Waldenses, John Wycliffe, John Huss, Jan Zizka of Tabor, Luther, Calvin, and Zwingli, Anabaptists, Puritans such as Robert Browne, and Baptists such as John Smyth and Roger Williams. The next name on Murch's list are the Haldane brothers, which brings us to the immediate predecessors of Thomas Campbell. It is obvious that a "Restorationist" like Murch has a view of church which is somewhat different from, say, the Catholic perspective.

The American version of Restorationism can trace its origins to several sources. Its emphasis on primitivism was philosophically justified by Enlightenment thought and inspired by the *philosophes'* view of history and by their sociology. However, the antecedents of the movement can be traced back to the very early Church which was the particular focus of the radical Reformation. Little wonder, then, that a movement which has drawn so heavily on intellectual trends as diverse as the Enlightenment and the radical Reformation has certain "schizophrenic" tendencies.

Relativism, Eclecticism and Toleration

In his biography of Barton Stone, William Garrett West devoted an entire chapter to the argument that Stone was "an American left-wing Protestant."[27] H. Leon McBeth, a Southern Baptist, has called Campbellism "an ultraconservative movement."[28] David Harrell has described the Restoration Movement as having a "schizoid middle-of-the-road psychology."[29] Left-wing, right-wing, middle-of-the-road, which of these labels best describes the Restoration Movement? Certainly the opinions of these and other writers have influenced their perspectives. But this begs the question. In truth, the Restoration Movement is all of the above. It can be all of these things because of the complexity of its intellectual origins and of the social environment in which it developed.

The origin of the Protestant Reformation lay in the excessive objectivity of late medieval Catholicism. This is most easily and infamously demonstrated by the example of Tetzel and his abuse of the doctrine of indulgences. The reaction was a natural one, to individualize and subjectivize. The path of salvation was shorn of intermediaries. Indulgences and other devotions that the church had developed to aid the faithful were expunged. In their place was inserted a one-to-one relationship between God and sinner, where God offered grace and the sinner accepted or rejected the gift depending on sufficient faith. If Luther's question — 'How does a person gain salvation?' — demanded an individual response that ultimately depended on the strength of personal faith, the ruling members of society were less willing to grant the lower classes means of demonstrating the answer. In other words, late medieval society, which had been raised on the notion of the oneness of the church, which may have experienced the dispute between ecclesiastical and secular authority, but which nonetheless recognized the necessity for authority, was not willing to allow the free exercise of individual choice when it came to the sureties of religion. Dissent of a sufficently grave nature was not perceived as a right but as an infection which contaminated the body politic as well as the body of Christ. This view was equally held by magisterial Protestants, the Catholic Church and secular rulers.

It took two hundred years to alter this attitude, but not for want of trying. Sebastian Castellio published in 1554 his famous *On Heretics, Whether They Ought to Be Persecuted* in which he argued for love and understanding, stressing that nobody had a monopoly on truth.[30] I suspect it was this latter point which explains the very slow and painful acceptance of the idea of toleration. There must be something very deep in the human pysche which craves an absolute notion of truth, especially regarding religion. It required a new attitude, a new philosophy to break down this desire for absolute truth.

By virtue of his popularity, it was John Locke who introduced this new attitude and new philosophy by articulating a theory of knowledge which was based on individual experience and reflection. In Locke's epistemology, his views of religion and politics were interrelated. For example, his famous definition of church as a voluntary society betrays many of his ideas on knowledge, truth, religion, and political liberty. Peter Gay has summed up the essence of these new attitudes:

> Relativism, Eclecticism, and toleration are so intimately related
> that they cannot be strictly separated even in thought. Relativism
> is a way of looking at the world, the recognition that no single set
> of convictions has absolute validity; Eclecticism is the philosophi-

cal method consequent on relativism - since no system has the whole truth, and most systems have some truth, discriminating selection among systems is the only valid procedure. Toleration, finally, is the political counterpart of this world view and this method: it is a policy for a large and varied society.[31]/

Gay is referring here to the world view of the *philosophes*. It is a world view which can be discerned in modern religious thought as well. It need not concern us here whether there is a relationship between the philosophes and modern religious thought and whether it is a question of cause and effect or simply of parallel developments during the same period of time. Neverthless, certain affinities between the Enlightenment and contemporary religious movements can be observed.

The mystical movements of the eighteenth century, Pietism, Moravianism, Methodism, while not rationalistic, all reflected a certain spirit of the age. They reduced the importance of church dogma and stressed personal experience. Methodism, of course, was in origin not a church but a reform. It stressed true feeling (love), not true knowledge. It is not that Wesley was exactly a *philosophe,* but then neither did the Enlightenment precisely exalt reason and abandon the passions. The heroes of the Enlightenment were men such as Locke who while praising reason were nonetheless dubious about just how much humanity could know. If one could penetrate the *philosophes'* hostile attitude towards religion, one would detect a certain congeniality with the mystics based on a shared hostility to dogmatism and a shared hospitality for simplicity, naturalness, and feeling. Ultimately both the *philosophes* and the mystics were certain that "no single set of convictions had absolute validity."[32]

On the American frontier, through the Great Awakening and Great Revival, a certain relativism, at least in a doctrinal sense, became dominant in American religion. As John Boles has noted, frontier religion was characterized by a pietistic theology, a homogenization of beliefs, and an emphasis on private perfectionism: "Abstruse theological doctrines, in the final analysis, were less important than the individual sinner's coming to grips with his depraved position in relation to God and recognizing the escape provided by faith in Jesus Christ. Here was the central matter in the whole concept of individual conversion."[33]

Camp meetings were themselves means of bringing different religious groups together. For a time at least, Baptists, Methodists, and Presbyterians preached together without discord. The context in which the camp meetings flourished was the American frontier. In a religious sense it was a situation in which the vast majority of the population was outside of the Church. For practical reasons, it was necessary that all religious groups cooperate in freedom and mutual respect to convert the rest of society to the Christian faith. The concept which served this end was denominationalism.

Denominationalism

Winthrop Hudson has defined denominationalism as the opposite of sect. Whereas a sect is exclusive and separate, "denomination" is an inclusive term, an ecumenical term which connotes membership in a larger group, the catholic Church:

> The basic contention of the denominational theory of the Church is that the true Church is not to be identified exclusively with any single ecclesiastical structure. No denomination claims to represent the whole Church of Christ. No denomination claims that all other churches are false churches. Each denomination is regarded as constituting a different "mode" of expressing in the outward forms of worship and organization that larger life of the Church in which they all share.[34]

The origin of denominationalism can be traced to the insights of the sixteenth century reformers and especially to the seventeenth-century Puritan divines. It was an idea easily transferable to the English colonies and especially to the United States after independence and disestablishment.[35] The world view contained in denominationalism was essentially the same as that of the *philosophes*. This gives reason to consider that perhaps there is a closer connection between the Reformation and the Enlightenment than is commonly supposed. Of course the relativism, eclecticism, and toleration of American frontier religion had its peculiar context. This has been summed up by Boles for the South (especially Kentucky) but applies as well to the greater area in which the Restoration Movement developed: "The central thrust and goals of all three popular denominations [Methodists, Baptists, and Presbyterians] were identical. Each contributed to the peculiarly nonabstract religious frame of mind that prevailed in the South: a personal, provincial, pietistic emphasis on the work of God in the hearts of individuals."[36]

The Great Revival

The Great Revival exerted a strong influence on the Restoration Movement. The cooperation of the Camp meetings and their ability to attract large numbers of people certainly helped to impress Barton Stone with the need to overcome doctrinal division in order to unite the Church of Christ. The "Enlightenment-Denominational" nexus of relativism, eclecticism, and toleration helped to form American frontier religion. The Restoration Movement was not untouched by it, although it came to reject many of the ideas it contained.

Generally, the left-wing of the movement tended to accept the "Enlightenment-Denominational" world view, while the right-wing tended to reject it. This can best be seen in attitudes and differences regarding the concept of church.

Conclusion

Robert H. Nichols has quoted a definition of church which he describes as "Baptist," but which certainly can be applied to Methodists and Presbyterians as well, at least, during the time of the Great Awakening and Great Revival: "that the true Church was composed by the voluntary association of men who had experienced personal regeneration."[37] This definition is both a paraphrase of Locke coupled with an evangelical definition of church which accepts individual "experience" as crucial. For the most part it was a definition rejected by the Restoration Movement.

Batsell Barrett Baxter, one of the most influential voices within the Churches of Christ for the past thirty years, has written a study of the New Testament Church. In it he speaks of the Church in several different senses. One of these is the "Church Universal" which includes all of the saved in the world. Another is the "Local Church" which "...refers to a voluntary association of Christians who band themselves together to carry out God's plans."[38] This is a most Lockian definition of church. It is certainly true that the Restoration Movement as a whole has always been strongly in favor of the autonomy of the local church. But to leave it at that is to omit much of the message of the movement.

The diversity and independence of local congregations is one thing, the diversity of churches, that is of sects or denominations, is quite another. Here is what Baxter has to say immediately following a subsection of his book entitled "Too Many Churches":

> However, when we move into the realm of religion, modern man hauls down the flag of truth and raises in its stead the flag of sincerity, honesty of purpose, and depth of feeling. No matter what faith one may hold, if a man is honest and sincere in his religion, he is judged to be all right. No matter how divergent the doctrines, modern man feels that everyone is on his way to heaven, simply traveling by a different road from that of his neighbor. In other fields the facts count. In the field of religion the facts are no longer sought, but are buried under an avalanche of *tolerance* and generosity of feeling toward one's fellowmen. The motive behind this generosity is admirable and fine, but the disregard of truth is tragic...Truth does not lie on opposite sides of the same fence. Truth is narrow and cannot be described in terms of anything that man might wish.[39]

The italics are mine but the rejection of "tolerance" is at the heart of the Restoration Movement. This is not to say that the movement condones bigotry and persecution, but it does reject the "Relativism" and the "Eclecticism" of the Enlightenment. If the Restoration Movement is "left-wing" it is because it has accepted the rationalism and individualism of Lockian epistemology. If the movement is "right-wing" it is because it has rejected Enlightenment Relativism, Eclecticism and tolerance by attempting to restore the notion of "absolute authority." This authority is, of course, the Bible, though in the passage just cited Baxter refers to it as "fact" (a very Lockian and Campbellian term) or "truth." The Radical Reformation certainly plays a role here. If the Restoration Movement is middle-of-the-road it is because it has been pulled in these two different directions. I have also referred to these as the unity and truth motives respectively. The schema of a dialect between Enlightenment individualism, relativism, and rationalism; and a search for absolute authority could also apply. All of these constructions are useful, though no one of them contains the whole truth. In this sense, the Restoration Movement is a synthesis, an attempt to unite absolute truth with individual opinion. In this synthesis can be found the genius and the fatal flaw of the movement. Has the Restoration Movement succeeded? Is it a failure?

Rubel Shelly, who would not classify the movement as a failure, nonetheless does have some candid and critical things to say:

> Churches of Christ are not growing generally, our image in parts of the United States where we are best known is quite poor (i.e., usually known for what we are against and accused of thinking everyone but us is going to hell), and we are so splintered over so many issues - from instrumental music to church cooperation to translations of Scripture - that no one takes us seriously as a "unity movement." Much less do they see us as the embodiment of the church described in the New Testament.[40]

In this sense, the Restoration Movement has been a failure. It is easy to repeat the trite judgment that the Restoration Movement intended to unite the Church of Christ but ended up adding three more denominations. It is easy, but simplistic and superficial. This is not to suggest that one cannot challenge the presuppositions of the movement. For example, I would respond to Shelley's observation that it is not realistic nor even desirable that the Church at the end of the twentieth century be the embodiment of the Church in the first century. But how much more fruitful it is to focus on the success of the movement.

The words of Lucien Febvre written almost sixty years ago regarding the origins of the French Reformation still ring true:

It was not the purpose or the desire of men to separate from the church; quite the contrary, the men in question claimed in all sincerity to be motivated simply by the desire to 'restore' it on the pattern of a primitive church which, acting as a kind of myth, had captured their imagination. 'Restoration','primitive church' - these were comfortable expressions with which to cover up their own eyes the very temerity of their secret desires. What they really ly wanted was not restoration but a complete renewal. The ultimate achievement of the Reformation was that it gave the men of the sixteenth century what they were looking for - some confusedly, others entirely lucidly - a religion more suited to their needs, more in agreement with the changed conditions of their social life. If we set aside rivalries between churches and controversies between scholars, the essential feature of the Reformation is that it was able to find a remedy for the disturbed consciences of a good number of Christians; it was able to propose to men, who seemed to have been waiting for it for years and who adopted it with a sort of haste and greed that is very revealing, a solution that really took account of their needs and spiritual conditions; it offered the masses what they had anxiously been searching for: a simple, clear and fully effective religion.[41]

Febvre's essential point here is that the Reformation above all satisfied a social need. Although Febvre is referring to the needs of the bourgeoisie in sixteenth-century France, his argument can be redirected towards the Restoration Movement and American Christianity. To ask if the Restoration Movement has been a failure is, to borrow from Febvre, "a badly-put question," although it is valid to draw the obvious conclusion that unity based on the authority and practices of the New Testament alone has proved inadequate. A more pertinent question is: What were the needs which the Restoration Movement attempted to address?

American Christianity has flourished in a political and social environment which is probably the freest in the history of Western civilization. Human imagination, private opinion, socioeconomic factors, and ethnic, regional, and linguistic differences have helped to produce a plethora of Christian groups. None of these elements is scriptural, but all of them are deeply rooted in the American experience. The need which the Restoration Movement perceived was how to balance the human liberty which Americans cherish, with the message of the Gospel, which after all is not about the diversity but the unity of humanity. How can we balance the human need for pluralism and authority, individual conscience and community, toleration and religious certitude? These are questions for our own age. In these questions, in these perceived needs, rests the genius of the Restoration Movement.

NOTES

Introduction

1. James Deforest Murch, *Christians Only* (Cincinnati: Standard Publishing, 1962), p. 238.

2. Bernard Quinn et al. (Atlanta: Glenmary Research Center, 1982). All subsequent statistics are also derived from this source.

3. David E. Harrell, Jr., "The Sectional Origins of the Churches of Christ," *Journal of Social History* 30 (1964), n. 37.

4. Suggested readings are discussed at the end of this study.

5. Winfred Ernest Garrison, *Alexander Campbell's Theology* (St. Louis: Christian Publishing, 1900), pp. 9-10.

6. Royal Humbert, ed. *A Compend of Alexander Campbell's Theology* (St. Louis: Bethany Press, 1961), p. 196.

7. Gerald A. McCool, *Catholic Theology in the Nineteenth Century* (New York: Seabury, 1977), p. 14.

8. Ibid., p. 19.

9. Ibid., pp. 186-7.

Chapter One

1. Quoted in Roland H. Bainton, *Here I Stand: A Life of Martin Luther* (New York: Mentor, 1950), p. 109.

2. Winfred E. Garrison, *Alexander Campbell's Theology* (St. Louis: Christian Publishing Co., 1900), pp. 78-80.

3. *The Works of John Locke* (12th ed.) 9 vols. (London, 1824), 5:13. All subsequent references to Locke refer to this edition.

4. *Toleration*, 5: 15.

5. In the influence of Locke on Campbell, see Robert Richardson, *Memoirs of Alexander Campbell* 2 vols. (Philadelphia: J.B. Lippincott, 1868-70) reprint ed., Indianapolis: Religious Book Service, n.d., 1:33. "As he advanced in age, he learned greatly to admire the character and the works of Locke, whose 'Letters on Toleration' seem to have made a lasting impression upon him, and to have fixed his ideas of religious and civil liberty. The 'Essay of the Human Understanding' he appears to have thoroughly studied under the direction of his father..."

6. *Toleration*, 5: 27.

7. *Reasonableness*, 6: 3.

8. *Reasonableness*, 6: 5. Compare Alexander Campbell's remarks in *The Christian System* (Cincinnati: Standard Publishing Co., n.d.), pp. 16-17. First pub. 1835, subsequently revised.

9. *Reasonableness*, 6: 17.

10. Ibid., 6: 20 and 6: 103-5 respectively.

11. *Mr. Locke's Reply to the Right Reverend the Bishop of Worcester's Answer to His Second Letter* (London, 1699), 3: 345.

12. See, for example, *Essay*, 4.3.22. I use the edition in *Works*, vols. 1 and 2.

13. *Essay*, 4.17.2.

14. "... I mean enthusiasm: which laying by reason, would set up revelation without it. Whereby in effect it takes away both reason and revelation, and substitutes in the room of it the ungrounded fancies of man's own brain, and assumes them for a foundation both of opinion and conduct." (4.19.3)

15. John. W. Yolton, *Locke: An Introduction* (Oxford: Basil Blackwell, 1985), p. 91.

16. Bertrand Russell, *A History of Western Philosophy* (New York: Simon and Schuster, 1945), p. 672.

17. Frederick Copleston, *A History of Philosophy* (Garden City, New York: Image Books, 1964), vol. 5, pt. II, pp. 114-15.

18. *Lettres philosophiques*, Letter Seven.

19. Much of this section is derived from the discussion found in Copleston, vol. 5, pt. II, pp. 167-76.

20. *Inquiry into the Human Mind,* I use the edition which is part of the *Series of Modern Philosophers,* Introduction and notes by E. Hershey Sneath (New York: Henry Holt and Co., 1892), 7.4. p. 357.

21. Ibid., 357-8.

22. *Essays on the Intellectual Powers of Man,* I used the edition edited by James Walker (Cambridge, Massachusetts: John Bartlett, 1850), 6.2.3, p. 342.

23. Ibid., 6.3.2, p. 355.

24. Reid writes about "first principles" as follows: "But there are other propositions which are no sooner understood than they are believed. The judgment follows the apprehension of them necessarily, and both are equally the work of nature, and the result of our original powers. There is no searching for evidence, no weighing of arguments; the proposition is not deduced or inferred from another; it has the light of truth in itself, and has no occasion to borrow it from another ... Propositions of the last kind, when they are used in matters of science, have common-ly been called axioms; and on whatever occasion they are used, are called first principles, prin-ciples of common sense, common notions, self-evident truths ... I hold it to be certain, and even demonstrable, that all knowledge got by reasoning must be built upon first principles." *Powers,* 6.3.1, p. 345-6.

25. Ibid., 6.3.5., p. 392.

26. Ibid., p. 393.

27. Ibid., p. 397.

28. Ibid.

29. Theodore Bozeman, *Protestants in an Age of Science* (Chapel Hill, North Carolina: University of North Carolina Press, 1972), p.21.

30. Sydney Ahlstrom, "The Scottish Philosophy and American Theology," *Church History* 24 (1955): 267-68.

31. D.S. Robinson, *The Story of Scottish Philosophy* (New York: Exposition Press, 1961), p.8. (Forward by Perry Gresham.)

32. Richardson, 2: 226.

33. Quoted by Richardson, 2: 236-7.

34. Ibid. In his 1829 debate, Campbell personally put this same question to Robert Owen, who responded that the idea of God came into the world "by imagination." Campbell responded with a consistent Lockean reply that imagination could originate nothing but could merely com-bine or rearrange in new forms ideas previously derived through the senses and reflection. Ibid, 2: 273.

35. See Appendix A.

36. Campbell, *The Christian System,* p. 15.

37. Ibid.

38. Quoted by Garrison, p. 111-12.

39. Ibid., pp.108-11.

40. Ibid., p.111.

Chapter Two

1. H. Richard Niebuhr, *The Social Sources of Denominationalism* (New York: Henry Holt and Co., 1929), passim and especially pp. 15-17.

2. Niebuhr, pp. 136-43.

3. Richard Tristano, *What Southern Catholics Need to Know about Evangelical Religion* (At-lanta: Glenmary Research Center, 1984), pp. 30-31.

4. Robert E. Thompson, *A History of the Presbyterian Church in the United States. The American Church History Series Vol.6* (New York: The Christian Literature Co., 1893), p. 87.

5. Sydney Ahlstrom, *A Religious History of the American People* (New Haven: Yale Univer-sity Press, 1972), p. 323.

6. William L. Lumpkin, *Baptist Foundations in the South* (Nashville: Broadman, 1961), pp. 28-32.

157   The Origins of the Restoration Movement

7. Ahlstrom, pp. 328-9.

8. Asbury, *Journals and Letters*, March 26, 1797, 2: 125, quoted by John B. Boles, *The Great Revival, 1787-1805* (Lexington, Kentucky: The University Press of Kentucky, 1972), p. 17.

9. The following section is largely derived from Boles, pp. 25-31.

10. Bethel [S.C.] Baptist Association, *Circular Letter*, 1802 ([n.p., n.d.]), p. 6 in South Carolina Baptist Historical Collection, Furman University. Quoted by Boles, pp. 30-31.

11. Thompson, p. 88.

12. Boles, pp. 37-8.

13. James McGready, *The Posthumous Works of the Reverend and Pious James M'Gready, Late Minister of the Gospel in Henderson, Kentucky*, ed. James Smith. 2 vols. (Louisville, Kentucky, 1831 and Nashville, Tennessee, 1833), 1: 54.

14. *The Biography of Elder Barton Warren Stone, Written by Himself: with Additions and Reflections by Elder John Rogers* (Cincinnati: J.A. and U.P. James, 1847 reprint ed., Joplin, Missouri: College Press, 1986), p. 8.

15. John Opie, Jr., "James McGready: Theologian of Frontier Revivalism," *Church History* 34 (December 1965): 453-54.

16. McGready, 1: 316-17.

17. Ibid., 1:73.

18. Ibid., 2:71.

19. William Garrett West, *Barton Warren Stone: Early American Advocate of Christian Unity* (Nashville: The Disciples of Christ Historical Society, 1954), p. 9.

20. Boles, p. 42.

21. For a full description of events leading to the Revival, see Boles, pp. 48-50.

22. McGready, "A Short Narrative of the Revival of Religion in Logan County, in the State of Kentucky, and the adjacent Settlements in the State of Tennessee, from May 1797, until September 1800." *New York Missionary Magazine* 3 (1802): 193. Quoted by Boles, p. 56-7 who also gives a good summary of the Red River and Gasper River meeting, see pp. 51-57.

23. Stone, *Biography*, p. 10.

24. Ibid., p. 11.

25. Winfred E. Garrison and Alfred T. De Groot, *The Disciples of Christ, A History* (St. Louis: Bethany Press, 1948 revised 1958), pp. 82-87.

26. Quoted by Garrison and De Groot, p. 90.

27. W.G. West, *Stone*, p. 41. See also Stone's remarks in *The Christian Messenger*, 7, no. 7 (July 1833) pp. 210-12, reprinted in Max Randall, *The Great Awakenings and the Restoration Movement* (Joplin, Missouri: College Press, 1983), p. 391.

28. W.G. West, *Stone*, p. 44.

29. The following section is based on W.G. West, *Stone*, pp. 94-96, which is amply documented with references to Stone's works.

30. Stone, *The Christian Messenger* 5 (Juy 1831): 164-67, quoted by Randall, p. 388.

31. Boles, pp. 162-3.

32. Stone, *An Address to the Christian Church in Kentucky, Tennessee, and Ohio on General Important Doctrines of Religion* 2nd ed. (Lexington, Kentucky: I. T. Covins, 1821), p. 13-14, Quoted by W.G. West, *Stone*, p. 71.

33. W.G. West, *Stone*, p. 55.

34. The document is reproduced in W.G. West, *Stone*, pp. 57-8.

35. *The Confession of Faith of the Presbyterian Church in the United States* rev. ed. (Richmond: John Knox Press, 1961), pp. 74-77.

36. *An Apology for Renouncing the Jurisdiction of the Synod of Kentucky, to which is added a compendious View of the Gospel, and a few remarks on the Confession of Faith* (Lexington, Kentucky: 1804). The *Apology* was reprinted in *The Biography of Elder Barton Warren Stone, Written by Himself: With Additions and Reflections* by John Rogers (Cincinnati: J.A. and U.P. James, 1847). This title in turn has been reprinted by College Press, Joplin. Missouri, 1986, p. 231.

37. Ibid., p. 232.

38. Ibid., pp. 232-33.

39. Ibid., p. 234.

40. *The Last Will and Testament* is rather brief and has been reproduced many times. See, for example, *Historical Documents Advocating Christian Union*, introduction by Charles A. Young, reprinted (Joplin, Missouri: College Press, 1985); Garrison and De Groot, pp. 109-110; and James DeForest Murch, *Christians Only* (Cincinnati: Standard Publishing, 1962), pp. 88- 9.

41. Max Randall, pp. 72-98, has traced, at great length, the fascinating influences of Haggard's use of the term "Christian."

42. Garrison and De Groot, p.115.

43. W.G. West, *Stone*, p.88.

44. Ibid., pp. 84-88.

45. *Christian Messenger*, III (1829), 65, quoted by Garrison and De Groot, p.120.

46. W.G. West, *Stone*, pp. 121-27.

47. *Christian Messenger*, XI (1841), 334, quoted in W.G, West, *Stone*, p.129.

48. Quoted in W.G. West, *Stone*, p.97.

Chapter Three

1. Lynn A. McMillon, *Restoration Roots* (Dallas: Gospel Teachers Publications; 1983), p.1.

2. The argument that it was Presbyterianism rather than Scotland, as a geographic and cultural entity, which was the crucial factor in the development of the Restoration Movement can be further demonstrated by the fact that while John Glas was expelled by the main body of Presbyterianism in Scotland, Barton Stone was expelled by mainstream Presbyterianism, not in Scotland, but in the United States. Finally, Thomas Campbell was expelled by the Seceder branch of Presbyterianism in the United States. In other words, their common experience is not residence in Scotland but rather membership in the Presbyterian Church.

3. Richardson, 1:67.

4. Ibid., 1:69-70.

5. Question 45. *The Confession of Faith of the Presbyterian Church in the United States* eleventh ed. (Richmond: John Knox Press, 1961).

6. Ibid., p. xv.

7. Quoted in McMillon, p. 24.

8. Ibid.

9. L. Tyerman, *The Oxford Methodists* (London: Hodder and Stoughton, 1873), pp. 201-333.

10. Garrison and De Groot, p. 49

11. [Robert Sandeman], *Letters on Theron and Aspasio* (1st pub. 1757) 2 vols. 3rd ed. (Edinburgh: A. Donaldson and J. Reid, 1762), pp. 15-17.

12. Ibid., p.44.

13. Sandeman's attack on the "popular preachers" is probably not to be interpreted as an attack on Methodists only, but rather on all preachers in England, Scotland and Wales who shared the importance of "conversion" to justification.

14. Ibid., pp. 89-90.

15. Ibid., p. 60.

16. Ibid., p. 64.

17. Ibid., p. 23.

18. The following section is based on Ibid., pp. 29-31.

19. Ibid., pp. 30-31.

20. Ibid., p. 137.

21. Ibid., p. 29 and p. 136.

22. Ibid., p. 31.

23. Ibid., p. 68.

24. It is interesting to note that Wesley responded to Sandeman's anonymously published book. Wesley accused the author of lacking charity and expressed his suspicion that he would be prone to persecution. He quipped: "You would make more bonfires in Smithfield than Bonner

and Gardner put together." "A Sufficient Answer to 'Letters to the Author of Theron and Aspasio,'" *The Works of John Wesley*, vol.10 (Peabody, Massachusetts: Hendrickson Publishers, 1984), pp. 298-306.

25. Richardson, 1:150-65. p. 39.

26. Richardson, 1:161.

27. Ibid, 1:178-79.

28. *The Christian Baptist*, (1827): 399, quoted by Randall, p. 136.

29. Richardson, I:149.

30. McMillon, p. 59-61.

31. Garrison and De Groot, p. 180.

32. Murch, pp. 165-178.

33. McMillon, pp. 90-93.

34. Richardson, I:149.

35. Richardson, I:53.

36. Garrison, pp. 147-48.

37. Richardson, I:56-8.

38. Most of the information we know about the early lives of both Thomas and Alexander Campbell can be found in Richardson. Most subsequent authors have reworked material found there.

39. Richardson, I:224.

40. Ibid.

41. William Hanna, *Thomas Campbell, Seceder and Christian Union Advocate* (Cincinnati: The Standard Publishing Company, 1935 reprinted by College Press, Joplin, Missouri, n.d.), pp. 37-38.

42. These are quoted and condensed from Hanna, pp. 39-42.

43. Hanna, pp. 46-7.

44. The citation in the Libel can be found in Hanna, p. 40. The *Larger Catechism* can be found in *Confession of Faith*, p. 234.

45. Hanna, pp. 47-8.

46. On the opinions of Glas and Sandeman, respectively, see McMillon, p. 31 and p. 62.

47. Hanna, p. 48.

48. Hanna, p. 50.

49. Hanna, p. 80.

50. Hanna, pp. 90-91.

51. Richardson, I:236.

52. Richardson, I:237.

53. Thomas Campbell, *Declaration and Address of the Christian Association of Washington* (Washington, Pennsylvania: Brown and Sample, 1809) is the original edition. I use the edition printed in Charles A. Young, *Historical Documents Advocating Christian Union* (Chicago: The Christian Century Co., 1904) reprinted by College Press, Joplin, Missouri, 1985, pp. 71-209. The passage quoted can be found on p. 72.

54. Ibid.

55. Ibid., pp. 72-3.

56. Ibid., pp. 73-4.

57. Ibid., p. 75.

58. The thirteen propositions can be found on pp. 107-114.

59. This latter suggestion, which seems plausible, is made by Lester G. McAllister, *Thomas Campbell: Man of the Book* (St. Louis: Bethany Press, 1954), p. 120.

60. *Declaration and Address*, pp. 113-14.

61. See Young's "Introduction to the Declaration and Address" in *Historical Documents*, p. 42.

62. *Declaration and Address*, p. 171 and p. 122 respectively.

63. Ibid., p. 133.

64. Ibid., p. 165.

65. Ibid., p. 95.
66. This section is based on *Declaration and Address*, pp. 170-75.
67. Ibid., pp. 189-90.
68. *Toleration*, p. 13.
69. *Reasonableness*, p.5.
70. *Toleration*, p. 57.
71. *Reasonableness*, p. 101.
72. *Toleration*, p. 56.
73. *Toleration*, p. 15.

Chapter Four

1. Richardson, *Memoirs of Alexander Campbell*, 1:188.
2. Ibid., 1:190.
3. Ibid., 1:325.
4. Ibid., 1:327.
5. Ibid., 1:441.
6. The sermon was delivered extemporaneously, but when it began to create controversy Campbell reconstructed and published it as a pamphlet. It was subsequently reprinted in the *Millennial Harbinger* (1846) p. 493ff. A modern edition is readily accessible in C. A. Young, *Historical Documents Advocating Christian Union* reprinted by College Press, Joplin, Missouri, 1985, pp. 217-282.
7. See, for example, Locke's *An Essay Concerning Human Understanding* III, Chapter 2, "Of the Signification of Words."
8. "Sermon on the Law," in Young, *Historical Documents*, p. 234.
9. "Sermon on the Law," p. 279.
10. William L. Lumpkin, *Baptist Confessions of Faith* (Chicago: Judson Press, 1959), p. 349.
11. Ibid., p. 277.
12. Alexander Campbell, *The Christian System*, (Cincinnati: Standard Publishing Co., n.d.), p. 111.
13. Ibid., p. 113-14.
14. Ibid., p. 115.
15. Ibid., p. 122.
16. I am not at all certain that Campbell would have used the term "conversion." He is meticulous in separating and defining terms. For example, in *The Christian System*, Chapter XVIII, entitled "Conversion, Regeneration," he identifies four things which constitute the change effected by baptism: a change of views; a change of affections; a change of state; and a change of life. He associates the last with "conversion." I use the term in a much more general sense here, and within the context of American frontier theology, to describe the process of how the sinner was made right with God.
17. *Christian System*, p. 53
18. Ibid., p. 53-4
19. All of the standard sources discuss Campbell's famous debates. But for a specific book-length study, see Bill J. Humble, *Campbell and Controversy*, 1952, reprinted by College Press, Joplin, Missouri, 1986.
20. Although Alexander Campbell debated with a good many Presbyterian ministers, they were not the only opponents with whom he sparred. Among his most famous debates was one with the socialist and atheist, Robert Owen and another with John Purcell, Catholic bishop of Cincinnati.
21. W.E. Garrison, *Alexander Campbell's Theology* (St. Louis: Christian Publishing Company, 1900), p. 246.
22. *Christian System*, pp. 204-6.
23. Ibid., p. 58.
24. William Philips, *Campbellism Exposed* (Cincinnati: Swormstedt and Poe, 1854 but based on chapters originally published in 1835-6), p. 77 and p. 21 respectively.

161   The Origins of the Restoration Movement

25. T. McK. Stuart, *Errors of Campbellism* (Cincinnati: Cranston and Stowe, 1890), pp. 73-74.

26. Ibid., p. 75; p. 23.
27. Ibid., p. 25.
28. Ibid., pp. 25-34.
29. Richardson, 2:68.
30. Earl Irvin West, *The Search for the Ancient Order*, 4 vols. (Nashville: Gospel Advocate Co., 1974-1987), 1:66.
31. *Christian Baptist*, 3 (January 1826): 320, quoted by Richardson, 2:134-5.
32. Quoted in Richardson, 2:50.
33. Ibid., 2:56.
34. Ibid., 2:57-8.
35. Ibid., 2:125.
36. Alexander Campbell, "A Restoration of the Ancient Order of Things - No. III," *Christian Baptist* 2, no. 9 (April 4, 1825), p. 140 quoted in Earl West, *The Search for the Ancient Order*, 1:70.

Chapter Five

1. The standard biography of Walter Scott is William Baxter, *Life of Walter Scott* (Cincinnati: Bosworth, Chase, and Hall, 1874). I use the edition published by the Gospel Advocate Company, Nashville, Tennessee, n.d.
2. Ibid., p. 61.
3. Ibid., p. 46, and Garrison and De Groot, p.18.
4. Richardson, 1:504.
5. Baxter, p. 66.
6. Richardson, 1:509-10.
7. Baxter, p. 73.
8. Quoted by Garrison and De Groot, pp. 183-4.
9. Richardson, 1:510-11.
10. Baxter, p. 89.
11. Ibid., pp. 89-90.
12. Richardson, 2:207.
13. Most of the following section is based on Garrison and De Groot, pp. 187-88, which offers the best account of Scott's method of evangelism.
14. So says Alexander Campbell. See Richardson, 2: 357.
15. Murch, p. 102-3.
16. Richardson, 2:209-10.
17. Richardson, 2:210-12, and Baxter, pp. 103-13.
18. Richardson, 2:212.
19. Quoted by Richardson, 2:219.
20. Ibid., 2:327-28.
21. This list is based on the one found in L. McAllister and W. Tucker, *Journey in Faith* (St. Louis: Bethany Press, 1975), pp. 139-41. Other, similar lists can be found in Garrison and De Groot, p.194 and Randall, *The Great Awakenings*, p. 267.
22. There is a certain implication among some Restoration writers that on the whole Baptists and Reformers shared an overwhelming unity of mind. The differences, they say, lay in degree or perhaps in a greater consistency and logic among the Reformers. See, for example, Garrison and De Groot, p. 202, who say: "So far as it [a particular ecclesiastical order] stressed the autonomy of the local congregation, it agreed with Baptist polity; but it went further than Baptists went in applying it, for it ruled out the associations, which - in Baptist practice but contrary to Baptist principles - were judging and legislating for the churches."
23. H. Leon McBeth, *The Baptist Heritage* (Nashville: Broadman, 1987), p. 377.
24. Ibid., p. 379.
25. Richardson, 2:302.

26. Ibid., 2:108-112.

27. Most of this section is based on Earl West, *The Search for the Ancient Order,* 1:242-50.

28. John Rogers, *The Biography of Elder J.T. Johnson,* (Cincinnati, 1861), p. 21 quoted by Richardson, 2:381.

29. Richardson, 2:383.

30. Garrison and De Groot, p. 215.

31. Richardson, 2:373-74.

32. *Christian Messenger* 5 (1831): 180 quoted in W.G. West, *Barton Warren Stone,* pp. 141-42.

33. *Millennial Harbinger* (1832): 195 quoted in Randall, *The Great Awakening and the Restoration Movement,* p. 281.

34. W. G. West, *Barton Warren Stone,* p. 155.

35. Ibid., pp. 157-62.

36. As we shall see, Campbell did soften his stand in the famous Lunenberg Letter of 1837.

37. *Millennial Harbinger,* 2 (1831):212 and 215, respectively.

38. W.G. West, *Barton Warren Stone,* p. 176.

39. Ibid., pp. 180-82.

40. Ibid., p. 183.

41. Ibid., pp. 183-86.

42. Randall, p. 320.

Chapter Six

1. Garrison and De Groot, p. 325.

2. Ibid., p. 329.

3. Ibid., p. 394.

4. For example, in 1900 there were 983,000 Presbyterians, 4,226,000 Methodists, and 1,658,000 Southern Baptists. *Historical Statistics of the United States, Colonial Times to 1970* (Washington, D.C.: U.S. Bureau of the Census, 1975), Part 1, Series H. 800-805, p. 392. See the appropriate notes for explanations.

5. Much of the following section is based on David Harrell, Jr., *The Social Sources of Division in the Disciples of Christ 1865-1900* (Atlanta: Publishing Systems, Inc., 1973), pp. 16-22.

6. Lester G. McAllister and William Tucker, *Journey in Faith* (St. Louis: Bethany Press, 1975.), pp. 162-3.

7. Richardson, 2:463-70.

8. Alexander Campbell, *The Christian System,* pp. 10-11.

9. Dated, "Bethany, Va., June 13, 1839."

10. On Thomas, see Monroe E. Hawley, *Redigging the Wells* (Abilene, Texas: Quality Publications, 1976), pp. 105-6.

11. *Millennial Harbinger* (September 1837): 411-14.

12. McAllister and Tucker, p. 158.

13. I have been unable to find, for example, mention of the Lunenberg Letter in Volume One of Earl West's *The Search for the Ancient Order.*

14. David Roper, *Voices Crying in the Wilderness* (Salisbury, South Australia: Restoration Publications, 1979). I gratefully acknowledge that Dr. Robert Hooper of David Lipscomb University brought this source to my attention.

15. Roper, pp. 77-8.

16. *Millennial Harbinger* (1837): 565.

17. Ibid., 588.

18. Roper, pp. 86-7.

19. Ibid., pp. 87-8.

20. *Millennial Harbinger* (1837): 507.

21. Ibid., p. 561.

22. Hawley, p. 101.

23. See, for example, Rubel Shelley, *I Just Want to be a Christian* (Nashville: 20th Century Christian, 1984), pp. 115-116 and Batsell Barrett Baxter, *Family of God* (Nashville: Gospel Advocate Company, 1981), pp. 154-59.

24. Hawley, p. 103.

25. Hawley, p. 113.

26. Earl West, *The Search for the Ancient Order*, 1: 164-65.

27. Alexander Campbell, "Church Organization — No. III, " *Millennial Harbinger*, ser. 3, vol. 6, no. 5 (May, 1849): 270, quoted by Earl West, *The Search for the Ancient Order*, 1:168-9.

28. Earl West, *The Search for the Ancient Order*, 1: 169.

29. Ibid.

30. Harold Lunger, *The Political Ethics of Alexander Campbell* (St. Louis: Bethany Press, 1954), p. 115.

31. Earl West, *The Search for the Ancient Order*, 1: 181-95.

32. Ibid., 1: 192- 95.

33. "The Christian Religion," *Christian Baptist* 1 (August, 1823)1: 6.

34. Richardson, 2: 327-8.

35. *Millennial Harbinger* (1845): 263, quoted by Richardson, 2: 531-32.

36. *Millennial Harbinger* (1845): 195-96.

37. McAllister and Tucker, p. 257.

38. Hawley, pp. 116-19.

39. Alexander Campbell, "Instrumental Music," *Millennial Harbinger*, ser. 4, 1 (October, 1851): 581-82.

40. Compare, for example, Richardson's remarks quoted by Earl West, *The Search for the Ancient Order* 2: 91 with Ibid., p. 110.

41. Isaac Errett, "Instrumental Music in our Churches," *Christian Standard* 5 (May 14, 1870), p. 156, quoted by Earl West, *The Search for the Ancient Order*, 2: 88.

42. Ben Franklin, "Two Standards," *American Christian Review* 13 (June 14, 1870), p. 188, quoted by Earl West, *The Search for the Ancient Order*, 2: 88.

43. The experience of a church in St. Louis must have been typical. See Earl West, *The Search for the Ancient Order*, 2:81.

44. Ibid., 2: 89.

45. David E. Harrell, Jr., "The Sectional Origins of the Churches of Christ," *Journal of Southern History*. 30 (1964), p. 277.

46. Ibid., p. 263.

47. Ibid., p. 266.

48. Quoted in Ibid., p. 268.

49. Quoted in Ibid., p. 271.

50. For all of these statistics see Harrell, *The Social Sources of Division in the Disciples of Christ, 1865-1900, A Social History of the Disciples of Christ*, 2 vols. (Atlanta: Publishing Systems, Inc. 1973), 2: 334-35.

51. Ibid., pp. 334-50.

52. Upon reading this section, Dr. Mac Lynn of David Lipscomb University commented: "It is interesting that intellectual enquiry led many Disciples into theological liberalism that was growing among the Protestants in the late nineteenth century. I suppose you could observe that the more conservative could appreciate the logical process involved in discovering the New Testament message, the church organization, worship, etc. but could not accept the newer methods of intellectual pursuit."

It seems to me that Lynn has quite perceptively indentified a crucial factor in Restoration history. Is the Movement part of Protestantism or opposed to it? To put it in the context of his observation, the question might read: Is it permissible to use the "methods of [Protestant] intellectual pursuit," or to repudiate them as unscriptural and illogical?

Chapter Seven

1. *Quest for a Christian America - A Social History of the Disciples of Christ*, Volume I (Nashville: Disciples of Christ Historical Society, 1966), p. 39.

2. Peter Gay, *The Enlightenment: An Interpretation.* 2 vols.(New York: Norton, 1966), 1: 320-21.

3. *Christian Systems*, p. 3.

4. Garrison, *Alexander Campbell's Theology*, p. 108.

5.Royal Humbert, ed. *A Compend of Alexander Campbell's Theology* (St. Louis: Bethany Press, 1961), p.62n. Humbert goes on to perceptively observe that, "this combination is an expression of Campbell's role as an apologist with one foot in the Enlightenment and the other in Protestant orthodoxy."

6. Ibid., p. 37. This is an excerpt from the *Lectures on the Pentateuch, 1859*. All subsequent references to Humbert's *Compend* will list the page(s) first and then the original source in parentheses.

7. Ibid., p. 63, (*Christian Baptist*, 1827, pp. 344-345).

8. Ibid., p. 75, (*Millennial Harbinger*, 1835, pp. 200- 201).

9. Garrison, pp. 197-98.

10. Ibid., p. 210.

11. *Christian System*, pp. 15-16.

12. Humbert, p.51, (*Millennial Harbinger*, 1846, pp.13- 24).

13. Ibid., p.50.

14. Garrison, p. 204-5.

15. Humbert, p.51.

16.Humbert, pp. 34-35, (*Christian Baptist*, 1827, p.312).

17. Peter Gay, *The Party of Humanity* (New York: Norton, 1959), p. 193.

18. *Declaration and Address*, p. 133.

19. Gay, *The Party of Humanity*, p. 270-1.

20. I refer here to the notion that by the sixteenth century many felt that artistic accomplishments had already surpassed the ancients. For example on Michelangelo, Vasari says: "He surpasses not only all those whose work can be said to be superior to nature but also the artists of the ancient world...He has so enhanced the art of sculpture that we can say without fear of contradiction that his statues are in every aspect far superior to those of the ancient world." Giorgio Vasari, *Lives of the Artists* trans. George Bull (Baltimore: Penguin, 1965), pp. 253-54.

21. Gay, *The Enlightenment*, 2: 96.

22. Richard Tristano, "Catholic Research into Southern Protestantism," (Paper delivered at "Table Talk," Oglethorpe University, Atlanta, Georgia, September 12, 1986), p. 5. To be published by the Glenmary Research Center in 1989.

23. Richard T. Hughes, "Churches of Christ" in *Encyclopedia of Religion in the South*, ed. Samuel S. Hill (Macon: Mercer University Press, 1984), p. 170.

24.George H. Williams, *The Radical Reformation* (Philadelphia: Westminister Press, 1962), p. 375.

25. Franklin H. Littell, *The Origins of Sectarian Protestantism* (New York: McMillan, 1958), p. 79. This title was previously published as *The Anabaptist View of the Church* in 1952.

26. Murch, *Christians Only*, pp. 9-18.

27. W. G. Garrett, *Barton Warren Stone*, pp. 203-15.

28. McBeth, *The Baptist Heritage*, p. 380.

29. Harrell, *A Social History*, 1:39.

30. Lewis Spitz , *The Protestant Reformation* (New York: Harper and Row, 1985), p. 180.

31. Peter Gay, *The Enlightenment* 1: 163.

32. I am thinking of the words of John Wesley: "I...refuse to be distinguished from other men by any but the common principles of Christianity....I renounce and detest all other marks of distinction. But from real Christians, of whatever denomination, I earnestly desire not to be dis-

tinguished at all....Dost thou love and fear God? It is enough! I give thee the right hand of fellowship." Quoted by Winthrop Hudson, *American Protestantism* (Chicago: University of Chicago Press, 1961), p. 33.

33. Boles, *The Great Revival*, p.138.

34. Hudson, p. 34.

35. Ibid., pp.35-44.

36. Boles, p.142.

37. Robert H. Nichols, "The Influence of the American Environment on the Conception of Church in American Protestantism," *Church History* 11 (September, 1942) :190.

38. Batsell Barrett Baxter, *Family of God* (Nashville: Gospel Advocate Co., 1980), pp. 7-8.

39. Ibid., pp. 157-8.

40. Shelley, xvii.

41. Lucien Febvre, "The Origin of the French Reformation: A Badly-Put Question?" *Revue Historique*, 161 (1929). Translated and reprinted in *A New Kind of History,* ed. Peter Burke (New York: Harper and Row, 1973), pp. 59-60.

Appendix A

Campbell and Locke: Theories
of the Knowledge of God

It seems to me that Locke's concept of the idea of God is somewhat inconsistent and lacking clarity. Locke identifies a threefold knowledge of existence. We have knowledge of our own existence by intuition, of the existence of God by demonstration, and other things by sensation. After demonstrating that man knows he exists by intuition, Locke proves the existence of God with the following argument: We are perceiving and knowing beings. It is impossible that a being wholly devoid of knowledge and without any perception should produce a knowing being. Therefore, there must exist a knowing being from eternity which we call God. He concludes: "From what has been said, it is plain to me, we have a more certain knowledge of the existence of a God, than of anything our senses have not immediately discovered to us. Nay, I presume I may say, that we more certainly know that there is a God, than that there is any thing else without us. When I say we know, I mean there is such a knowledge within our reach which we cannot miss, if we will but apply our minds to that, as we do to several other inquiries." (*Essay,* 4.10.6) I read this as saying that the only knowledge more certain than the existence of God is that which is directly discovered by our senses.

On the other hand, Locke seems to also state that we can know of the existence of God through experience. "Though God has given us no innate ideas of himself; though he has stamped no original characters on our minds, wherein we may read his being; yet having furnished us with those faculties our minds are endowed with, he hath not left himself without witness: since we have sense, perception, and reason, and cannot want a clear proof of him, as long as we carry ourselves about us." (4.10.1)

In an earlier section of the *Essay* Locke shows that we have no knowledge beyond our simple ideas which we have from sensation and reflection. This applies to our knowledge of God himself: "But whichever of these complex ideas be clearest, that of body, or immaterial spirit, this is evident, that the simple ideas that make them up are no other than what we have received from sensation or reflection: and so is it of all our ideas of substances, even of God himself... For if we examine the idea we have of the incomprehensible supreme being, we shall find, that we come by it the same way; and that the complex of ideas we have both of God and separate spirits are made up of the simple ideas we receive from reflection." (2.23.32-33) Locke suggests that our complex ideas about God are simply the result of combining simple ideas. Moreover, we form our knowledge of God by enlarging and perfecting our simple ideas to infinity: "...we frame the best idea of him [God] our minds are capable of: all which is done, I say, by enlarging those simple ideas we have taken from the operations of our own minds, by reflection; or by our senses, from exterior things; to that vastness to which infinity can extend them." (2.23.34)

Finally, Locke seems to state quite clearly that although we do not know the essence of God, what we do know of him is ultimately based on sensation and reflection, the source of all knowledge. "For it is infinity, which joined to our ideas of existence, power, knowledge, &c. makes that complex idea, whereby we represent to ourselves, the best we can, the supreme being. For though in his own essence (which certainly we do not know, not knowing the real essence of a pebble, or a fly, or of our own selves) God be simple and uncompounded; yet, I think I may say we have no other idea of him but a complex one of existence, knowledge, power, happiness, &c. infinite and eternal: which are all distinct ideas, and some of them, being relative, are again compounded of others; all which being, as has been shown, originally got from sensation and reflection, go to make up the idea or notion we have of God." (2.23.35) The distinction which Locke makes about how we come by knowledge (4.9.2) seems here less than consistently and clearly applied.

Campbell offers a direct criticism of Locke's ideas. His argument is basically that Locke has not been sufficiently consistent to his own epistemology and has confounded the origins of our knowledge of the natural and supernatural things which ought to be separate: "You leap over the distance from earth to heaven in your reasoning, or rather, you fledge yourself with the wings of faith, and find in the bible the idea of all things being dependent on a Being unlike any other, who produces no being like himself, contrary to your analogy from the book of nature, and who produces all beings both unlike himself and one another. You flew so nimbly and so easily over this mighty gulf, that you were not conscious that you had got out of the region of earth-born ideas altogether, and were farther than all space from the volume of nature which you sat down to read. Ask Locke and Hume, and they will tell you that you cannot have a single idea – a simple uncompounded idea, the pattern of which or the thing of which it is the idea, [sic] is not first presented to some one of your senses. Ideas are images, and before the image is seen in the glass, or exists in the mind, an object must be presented... Locke and other philosophers who have rejected the doctrine of innate ideas and who have traced all our simple ideas to sensation and reflection, have departed from their own reasonings when they attempted to show that, independent of supernatural revelation, a man could know that there is an eternal first cause uncaused." (*Christian Baptist* 1827, p. 376 quoted in Humbert, p. 76-7.) It is rather typical of both men that Locke has sacrificed clarity and consistency for a more complex and nuanced theory of knowledge while Campbell has emphasized a strictly logical, clearly defined, but somewhat simplistic notion that knowledge can be strictly and easily compartmentalized.

Appendix B

A Note on Recent Research
on Alexander Campbell and Catholicism

What follows is in essence a footnote based on information which came my way too late to be included in the body of this study. It concerns a new direction of research — an evaluation of the effects of Catholicism on the Restoration Movement — which may interest the reader.

Quite literally as this study was heading toward the printer's office, I returned from the American Historical Association Meeting in Cincinnati, Ohio. At that meeting there was a session sponsored by the American Society of Church History on the topic of Alexander Campbell. One of the papers, entitled, "The Two Faces of Alexander Campbell and the Singular Campbell of Myth," was delivered by Richard Hughes of Pepperdine University.

Professor Hughes suggested that Alexander Campbell had indeed changed much of his thinking, a major historiographical question within the Restoration Movement. Furthermore, Hughes categorized the modern-day Churches of Christ as inheritors of the "early Campbell" of the *Christian Baptist* and early *Millennial Harbinger* period. Hughes described The Christian Church (Disciples of Christ) as the followers of the "later Campbell." I find this construction to be very useful.

Particularly intriguing was that Hughes located Campbell's epiphany quite precisely in 1837 and ascribed anti-Catholicism as the cause. This is, of course, the year of the great debate between Campbell and Archbishop John B. Purcell of Cincinnati. Upon questioning Professor Hughes at the end of the session about this point, he referred me to a paper written by Don Haymes of the Library of the School of Theology at the University of the South at Sewanee, Tennessee.

Mr. Haymes has confirmed to me that he is engaged in a work in progress entitled, *A Battle of Giants*, which focuses on the Campbell-Purcell debate. He identified 1837 as a "crucial demarcation" for Campbell. During this year he moved from being a "radical sectarian," who criticized the leaders of American Protestantism (he called them "Protestant Popes"), to a defender of Protestantism against the Catholic Church. Mr. Haymes sees the famous "Lunenburg Letter" as Campbell's direct response to his debate with Purcell and Catholicism.

While the idea of Alexander Campbell as defender of Protestantism in the Purcell debate is not a new one, particularly among Disciples, (see, for example Garrison and De Groot, p. 228) the emphasis that Mr. Haymes places on the influence of the debate and on the influence of Catholicism as a whole on

Campbell's thought is new and intriguing. Traditionally, Churches of Christ historians have tended to virtually ignore the debate with Purcell (see, for example, Earl West, I: 75).

I also had the opportunity to meet Mr. Ed Hicks of Memphis State University at the Cincinnati meeting, who has informed me of an unpublished paper he has written entitled, "Republican Religion and Republican Institutions: Alexander Campbell and the Anti-Catholic Movement." Hicks also sees Catholicism as exerting an important influence on Alexander Campbell. Mr. Hicks describes Campbell's fears as centering on the conviction that the Catholic Movement would destroy republican (Protestant) institutions in the United States.

All three scholars cited here are in agreement that Alexander Campbell's anti-Catholicism was not vitriolic and was not personal in nature. They suggest instead that American Protestantism and American Catholicism, while largely hostile in the nineteenth century, were not isolated from each other. While it has long been recognized that Catholicism has been influenced by its American context, I find it a new and interesting idea that American Restorationism was influenced by Catholicism, even if that influence may have been largely negative.

I hope that these scholars will forgive me if I use their research to benefit my own ends. Upon pondering Campbell's fear that the Catholic Church threatened American (and Protestant) institutions, I could not help but think once again of John Locke. I refer to that section toward the end of A Letter Concerning Toleration where Locke discusses those who should not be tolerated. In a section quite clearly aimed at Roman Catholics he wrote: "That church can have no right to be tolerated by the magistrate which is constituted upon such a bottom that all who enter into it do thereby ipso facto deliver themselves up to the protection and service of another prince."

If I could reduce this all to two essential points it would be that Alexander Campbell was influenced in a crucial way by Catholicism, and that his own reaction to the Catholic Church was in turn influenced by Locke and by Enlightened thought, which had seen, after all, the Catholic Church as perhaps the greatest threat to civilization.

I wish to thank Professors Hughes, Haymes, and Hicks for their generosity in granting me permission to cite their research based solely on hearing a paper read and on two telephone conversations respectively. I do, of course, accept responsibility for summarizing their ideas and apologize if I have not accurately reflected their thoughts. I have no doubt that in all three cases I have grossly simplified their research.

Appendix C

Suggested Readings

There is only a limited need for a bibliography here because there are already several sources readily available with excellent bibliographies. These will be noted below. I have limited myself to a more general list of suggested readings that I found particularly useful. I have also concentrated almost exclusively on books, excluding articles. I have confined myself to suggestions regarding the Restoration Movement proper and not to related subjects such as the philosophy of John Locke or the Enlightenment.

There are a number of general histories which are excellent. *The Disciples of Christ: A History* (St. Louis: Bethany Press, 1948, rev. ed. 1958) by Winfred Ernest Garrison and Alfred T. DeGroot is a modern classic, written from the Disciples' point of view. It reflects the many strengths of its authors (including Garrison's interest in the philosophical background of the movement) and a few of their weaknesses. It contains a good bibliography, though it is now somewhat dated. In 1975 the Bethany Press decided to update Garrison's and DeGroot's book. The result is Lester G. McAllister and William E. Tucker, *Journey in Faith: A History of the Christian Church (Disciples of Christ)*. This is a denominational history, valuable mainly for its information on Disciples' history since 1958 and for its bibliography which is certainly one of the most extensive.

James DeForest Murch, *Christians Only: A History of the Restoration Movement* (Cincinnati: Standard Publishing, 1962) is another standard general history. The first half of the book offers a brief history of the early movement. At mid-point, however, Murch begins to direct his account to the thinking of the "centrist" group which eventually became the Christian Churches and Churches of Christ. Toward the end of the book Murch's narrative becomes more and more personal, as he relates events leading to the break with the Disciples in which he was very much involved.

The perspective of the Churches of Christ is reflected by the exhaustive history by Earl Irvin West, *The Search for the Ancient Order*. The first volume (Nashville: Gospel Advocate Co., 1949) offers a brief history of the early movement and then brings the story up to the Civil War. The second and third volumes (Indianapolis: Religious Book Service, 1950; 1979) cover the years between the Civil War and the final division of 1906; and from the turn of the century until 1918, respectively. A fourth and final volume was published in 1988 (Religious Book Service). West writes extensively about individual preachers. The first volume has a brief bibliography and the others have none, but West's footnotes are a valuable reflection of the sources he used.

The Great Awakenings and the Restoration Movement by Max Ward Randall (Joplin, Missouri: College Press, 1983) is the result of more recent research.

Randall's theme is the close connection between the Restoration Movement and the series of "Great Awakenings" which marked American religious history, but in the process he writes a general account of the movement from its origin to 1860. There is an excellent bibliography.

Another important way to study Restoration history is through biography of the founders of the movement. There has been surprisingly little written on Thomas Campbell. One modern work is William H. Hanna, *Thomas Campbell, Seceder and Christian Union Advocate* (Cincinnati: Standard Publishing Co., 1935, reprinted by College Press, Joplin, Missouri, no date). Hanna uncovered the minutes of the Chartiers Presbytery which detail the trial of Thomas Campbell and he reproduces much of this material in his biography. Also worth consulting is Lester G. McAllister, *Thomas Campbell: Man of the Book* (St. Louis: Bethany Press, 1954).

The oldest source on Barton Warren Stone is *The Biography of Elder Barton Warren Stone, Written by Himself with Additions and Reflections* by Elder John Rogers (Cincinnati: J.A. and U.P. James, 1847, reprinted by College Press, Joplin, MO, 1986). I found most useful William G. West's *Barton Warren Stone: Early American Advocate of Christian Unity* (Nashville: Disciples of Christ Historical Society, 1954). West is especially good in discussing the intellectual, i.e., theological issues that concerned Stone.

On Walter Scott, the *Life of Elder Walter Scott* by William Baxter (Cincinnati: Bosworth, Chase and Hall, 1874) is old but standard. I used the edition published in Nashville by the Gospel Advocate Co., n.d.

The literature on Alexander Campbell is very extensive. Essential is the *Memoirs of Alexander Campbell, Embracing a View of the Origin, Progress and Principles of the Religious Reformation which He Advocated* 2 vols. (Philadelphia: J. Lippincott, 1868, 1870, reprinted by Religious Book Service, Indianapolis, n.d.) As indicated, Winfred E. Garrison's *Alexander Campbell's Theology: Its Sources and Historical Setting* (St. Louis: Christian Publishing, 1900) is vital to the understanding of Campbell's thought. A list of other pertinent sources on Campbell and his thought will be found in the bibliography found in McAllister's and Tucker's volume.

Of course, the reader will find much information on all of these four "founders" of the Restoration Movement, and on others as well, in the general histories cited above.

Much source material is readily available through reprints. Most of the writing of Alexander Campbell took the form of articles written for the two journals he edited and published. He published the *Christian Baptist* from 1823 until 1830 and the *Millennial Harbinger* from 1830 until 1864, when old age forced him to hand over operation of the journal to others. These volumes have been reprinted, but because of their sheer size and cost they are undoubtedly difficult to locate. Campbell produced a more comprehensive version of his theology in *A Connected View of the Principles and Rules by Which the Living Oracles May Be*

Intelligently and Certainly Interpreted... (Bethany, Virginia: M'Vay and Ewing, 1835). This was revised and published as *The Christian System, in Reference to the Union of Christians and a Restoration of Primitive Christianity, as Plead in the Current Reformation* (Bethany, Virginia: Printed by A. Campbell, 1839). Very useful is *A Compend of Alexander Campbell's Theology* edited by Royal Humbert (St. Louis: Bethany Press, 1961). Humbert takes excerpts from the *Millennial Harbinger,* the *Christian Baptist,* the *Christian System* and many other sources and arranges them by topic, with critical and historical footnotes.

Alexander Campbell debated with many opponents over several decades. Most of these debates were published, but often run hundreds of pages. Bill J. Humble, *Campbell and Controversy, The Story of Alexander Campbell's Great Debates with Skepticism, Catholicism, and Presbyterianism* (first published in 1952 and reprinted by College Press, Joplin, Missouri, in 1986) offers a summary, with quotations, from Campbell's major debates. Finally, there is Charles A. Young, *Historical Documents Advocating Christian Union* (Chicago: Christian Century Co., 1904, reprinted by College Press, Joplin, Missouri, 1985). This is a very useful compilation because it contains documents fundamental to the understanding of the Restoration Movement, including "The Last Will and Testament," the "Declaration and Address," and the "Sermon on the Law."

Some specialized studies deserve mention. John B. Boles, *The Great Revival, 1787-1805: The Origins of the Southern Evangelical Mind* (Lexington: The University Press of Kentucky, 1972) is insightful. Boles examines the Southern religious mentality which spawned the Great Revival and specifically discusses Kentucky and Stone at some length. David E. Harrell, Jr. has written the definitive social history of the Restoration Movement called *A Social History of the Disciples of Christ* 2 vols. Volume One is entitled *Quest for Christian America: The Disciples of Christ and American Society to 1866* (Nashville: Disciples of Christ Historical Society, 1966). Volume Two is entitled *The Social Sources of Division in the Disciples of Christ 1865-1900* (Atlanta: Publishing Systems, 1973). Both volumes have a generous number of footnotes and exhaustive bibliographies.

Although this study focused on the intellectual origins of the Restoration Movement and did not really go beyond the nineteenth century, I found it useful to see what contemporary leaders within the Churches of Christ were writing. Three are recommended: Rubel Shelly, *I Just Want to Be a Christian* (Nashville: 20th Century Christian, 1984); Batsell Barrett Baxter, *Family of God: A Study of the New Testament Church* (Nashville: Gospel Advocate Company, 1980); Monroe E. Hawley, Redigging the Wells: Seeking *Undenominational Christianity* (Abilene: Quality Publications, 1976).

If I may allow myself one brief digression from the Restoration Movement proper, it seems to me that the movement effectively calls into question the notion of denominationalism. Those interested in the topic of denominationalism may consult the pertinent section in Winthrop Hudson, *American Protestantism*

(Chicago: The University of Chicago Press, 1961) and H. Richard Niebuhr, *The Social Sources of Denominationalism* (Cleveland: World Publishing, 1957, first pub. 1929).

Finally, I have made no effort to list the literature in article form. I would like to make two exceptions to this practice. The first is David Harrell's "The Sectional Origins of the Churches of Christ," *Journal of Southern History* 30 (1964): 261-77. Although Harrell summarizes his conclusions in his *Social History,* the reader interested in Southern religion is advised to consult this important article in its original form. The second article I cite for very different reasons. It is Edwin S. Gaustad, "Churches of Christ in America," *The Religious Situation: 1969* Donald Cutler ed. (Boston: Beacon Press, 1969): 1013-1033. The eminent Gaustad is poorly represented here. His is precisely the wrong approach for an outsider. Gaustad is condescending and insulting when he uses terms such as "cliches," "hackneyed," "minutiae," and "Pharisaism" to discuss some of the most central tenets of belief associated with the Churches of Christ. This is not to suggest that the Churches of Christ, or any other religious group, is above criticism. But to so obviously impose one's own beliefs and judgments on others is at the very least not to take those you study seriously. In turn, how seriously can anyone take such research? This is a plea for understanding, respect, and seriousness in the writing of religious history, especially when the researcher is an outsider.

C. Leonard Allen and Richard T. Hughes, *Discovering Our Roots: The Ancestry of Churches of Christ* (Abilene, Texas: Abilene Christian University Press, 1988) was published after the completion of this manuscript. This book takes an unusually broad view of the roots of the Restoration Movement. It is highly recommended.